Alfred P[axton] Brotherhead

Himself His Worst Enemy

Alfred P[axton] Brotherhead

Himself His Worst Enemy

ISBN/EAN: 9783744666213

Printed in Europe, USA, Canada, Australia, Japan

Cover: Foto ©ninafisch / pixelio.de

More available books at **www.hansebooks.com**

HIMSELF HIS WORST ENEMY:

OR,

PHILIP DUKE OF WHARTON'S CAREER.

"The scorn and wonder of our days."—POPE.

BY
ALFRED P. BROTHERHEAD,
LIBRARIAN.

PHILADELPHIA:
J. B. LIPPINCOTT & CO
1871.

Entered according to the Act of Congress, in the year 1871, by
WILLIAM BROTHERHEAD,
in the Office of the Librarian of Congress, at Washington.

PHILADELPHIA:
COLLINS, PRINTER.

PREFACE.

THIS, my first book, is presented to the public with the usual forebodings of all authors. All I claim for it is a fair and candid perusal, and an impartial criticism. For the historical data I must thank various and many historians; for all else I am responsible.

A. P. B.

BROTHERHEAD'S LIBRARY:
    205 SOUTH THIRTEENTH STREET.
        PHILADELPHIA, January 1, 1871.

CHAPTER I.

THE STORM—LONDON, 1703.

> 'I have seen tempests, when the scolding winds
> Have riv'd the knotty oaks; and I have seen
> The ambitious ocean swell, and rage, and foam,
> To be exalted with the threatening clouds:
> But never till to-night, never till now,
> Did I go through a tempest dropping fire.
> Either there is a civil strife in Heaven;
> Or else the world, too saucy with the gods,
> Incenses them to send destruction.'
> JULIUS CÆSAR, I. III.

> "So when an angel, by Divine command,
> With rising tempests shakes a guilty land
> (Such as of late o'er pale Britannia passed)."
> THE CAMPAIGN.

A DEEP silence reigns over London, and although it wants but an hour of midnight, the quietness feels too intense even for so late an hour. The moon hangs in the centre of the ragged clouds, lurid and red, totally unlike its usual radiant light and mellow color; thin leaden clouds scud swiftly before it, and, for a time, dim its glow, making it dull and copperish until they pass. The heavens in every part present an unusual appearance; an opaque, light-colored mist floats between the sky and the earth, and dims the brilliancy of the few stars that cluster around the sun of night. It is, however, beginning to break; wide crevices already yawning and cracks opening, the huge clouds show their threatening ranks, piled mountain high, and filled with the thunderbolts of Jove's great armorer, Vulcan. People afterwards said that this mist formed itself into the semblance of an immense angel, whose wings covered the half of the city, and whose face was lowering and angry. Be that as it may, they had scant time to notice it before the lightning began; its quick, sharp, blinding flashes push out in bold relief the torn clouds and vaporous banks whence it comes; the low rumbling thunder moans its solemn accompaniment, and the air grows more stifling, sticking in the throat, as do the sulphurous blasts from the depths of Ætna, or the mouth of Apollyon. At the corners of the streets, on the old-time roomy porches, and on the sheltered stoops of the coffee-houses and taverns, stand or sit groups of anxious people conversing in subdued, awe-stricken tones on the unusual signs in the firmament; they look constrained and uneasy, as though they feel the awful shadow of this coming event.

Now, there being a momentary cessation of both thunder and lightning, they breathe more freely and begin to hope that after all the storm may blow over; scarcely, however, have they time to exchange their whispered thoughts ere a quicker, but more sustained, more blinding flash deprives them almost of sight, making them see things "as through a glass darkly," and the thunder meanwhile crashing out a sublimely grand symphony. Globes of pink fire coruscate simultaneously in all parts of the heavens, whirling around for a few seconds with inconceivable velocity, bursting with a sharp report, and filling the air with millions of fiery fragments which saturate the atmosphere with an unnatural, suffocating smell. Meteoric flashes scintillate around, mother Nature appearing to be working herself up to an angry, revengeful mood.

Great, heavy drops patter sullenly on the dry pavement, and leave clots of mud where they fall in slow succession. Again for a few minutes there is a cessation.

Once more they hope that the storm will blow over and break elsewhere; but, with a wilder, heavier crash than its predecessors, the thunder roars aloud and the tempest begins in real earnest. The Storm-God shrieks with fierce, savage joy as he bursts in all his might upon the devoted city—palace and cottage, church and gaming hell alike he shatters in his mad career.

Bolts upon bolts leap from cloud to cloud, and hiss in very terror at their own appalling deadliness, as they rive and rend in their swift passage to the earth.

The Thames, now a seething mass of muddy billows, rushes and boils over its banks with strange violence, dashes its waves even into Westminster Hall, and floods the city with its cold, slimy torrent; London Bridge meanwhile threatening momentarily to fall asunder, and precipitate itself from its piers into the angry flood which swirls and eddies beneath it like an immense maelström.

In Saint James' Park whole avenues of noble elms are uprooted, and lie prostrate far away from their former positions, a part of the palace has been struck by lightning, and hurled to the ground with an all-destroying force and impetuosity, while the same power has killed its human victims by the score—a happier fate, to be sure, than that of those who were maimed and wounded by flying signs, falling walls, and the large hailstones which now begin to add their terrors to the dreadful scene; down they come! rattling on the many roofs like volleys of musketry; the wind whirls them in all directions; glass is flying about, and hundreds of persons are knocked senseless by these frozen bullets hurled from on high.

The leaden coverings of the church and houseroofs are

rolled up like ribbons and as quickly unrolled by the howling wind, as it shifts and careens to all quarters in the same instant.

The terror-stricken people close their eyes in fear and trembling, and cover their pale faces with shaking hands to screen the dread sights from their view. They cower in groups, scarcely knowing which to fear the most, the enormous hailstones, the forked lightning ricochetting and hurtling about their ears, or the thunder-claps which set their heads whirling and their ears humming.

The tumult is beyond all conception; it is as though all hell had again rebelled against the Divinity, and were trying to scale the summit of the heaven which they had forever lost.

Houses and churches are falling in all directions, adding to the din and confusion and sending up clouds of dust, and in many cases myriads of sparks, which the pouring rain soon quenches.

Amidst this mad struggle of the elements can be seen a group of terrified men, crying babes, and sobbing women, who cling together in the middle of the street waiting in terror for the storm to cease, so that they can return in safety to homes which they have forsaken for fear of the lightning which strikes and levels so many of the taller houses; the while a courtly gallant surveying the huddling crowd with a look of supercilious pity and proud disdain. He is dressed in a cloak and doublet of gray velvet, lined with pale blue, the outside is covered with deep bars of black lace, silken hose cover his well-shaped legs, and his shoes are made in the latest mode and fastened with small diamond buckles. His body is erect and soldierly, and his haughty bearing betrays his patrician origin. His hat, very wide in the brim, is looped up on one side with an aigrette of brilliants, the other drooping over the right cheek and leaving it in deep shadow; it is rakishly cocked and hides half of a handsome, wicked face, adorned with the peaked beard in the style of Vandyck. He looks, as a girl close by him says, " Every inch of a rakehelly ruffler."

Hearing the remark, he turns to her with a smile, and says, reprovingly, " How now, Mistress Impertinence! art frightened at old Tom Wharton? S'bodkins! Once was a time when a pretty girl would have given him a better reception than cold words and sour looks!" And he extends his hand in order to raise her face to the light and scan her features more plainly.

Thomas Wharton was born in the times of the Covenanters, his father being a sour, rigid old Calvinist, and a firm believer in Cromwell and his Ironsides. His boyhood was passed amid a dismal set of sombre, psalm-singing roundheads, half preachers, half soldiers, firm believers in the church-militant and the sanctity of their own persons.

Growing older and gradually breaking loose from such associations, of course a decided reaction took place, and in the London of the Restoration he became such a libertine, scapegrace, and blasphemous wit that he shocked even the wildest of such a dissolute crew of Cavaliers as never England boasted before, nor wishes to boast again. Ribald and profanely witty in his conversation, impious and insolent, he fought so often, coming unscathed out of so many duels that he attained the reputation of bearing a charmed life. Utterly shameless, the barbed arrows of his assailants' tongues he shot back, with a jeer at their impotence. Being a Whig of the most virulent type, he is as true as steel to the party he supports with his talents and his genius. He even carries his proclivities into his sports, and often at a race-meeting, when a well-known Tory had put his horse in to win, down would come Wharton's " Careless" or his bay gelding, for which the *Grand Monarch* had in vain offered a fabulous price.

As an electioneer he is invincible; Buckinghamshire is all his own, besides various other counties, which he always canvasses in person, and by his good humor, unmatchable impudence, and affability, he always leaves his opponents far in the lurch.

At this time he is well advanced in years, but is still possessed of all the buoyancy of youth, a dangerous quality to those about him, when you add to that the thorough knowledge of state affairs and party secrets he has gained during his long experience in the political arena. His intrigues were formerly the dread of every honest citizen or jealous Cavalier in London, and even now an uxorious husband would rather see Moloch in his house than old Tom Wharton with his flattering speeches and expressive glances. His temper is imperturbable to the last degree, and he can pink his opponent with the same grace and coolness as he eats buttered whiting at the tavern in Clare Market. "He had never given a challenge, had never refused one; had never taken a life, and yet he had never fought without having his antagonist's life at his mercy."

He is a steady frequenter of the Saint James Coffee House, where his opinion is always listened to with great attention, and where his eagle eye is always on the young patricians, and if he notes one who he thinks might be useful to his party, he is sure to secure him by his adroit flattery and his consummate diplomacy. Honest Tom, as he is familiarly called by his associates, is a strong Whig pillar; and this is the man who has favored the world with a son worthy of himself, the famous Philip, Duke of Wharton, of whom more hereafter.

At the instant Lord Wharton caught hold of the shrinking girl there was a loud crash, and a large gabled mansion, which stood a few yards below them, was levelled to the ground by a stroke of lightning; the crowd swayed to and fro in alarm, and amid the incidental confusion she elbowed her way into it, and escaped from his pleasantries.

He laughs aloud at their terror, occasionally screaming out, so as to be heard above the roar of the wild tempest, a blasphemous remark or an impious jest, until they begin to stare at him with a mixture of awe and fear, and shrink from him as though he were peststricken; and now he stands alone and prominent amid a circle of blanched, gaping faces.

Here a 'prentice lad, in dirty woollen cap and smirched ruff, dries his tears with his greasy fustian sleeve or his greasier hand. There an artificer's pretty wife 'draggles her skirts in the dirty pools, and glances occasionally at the " wicked lord" who is so bold amid all this crash and ruin; her fine cambric ruff, lace cuffs, and the pretty velvet cap perched on her brown hair are limp and disordered with the combined effects of rain and sundry hailstones which struck her when they first began to rattle down. Now my lord turns quickly on his heel, and cautiously picks his way through the falling debris towards Whitehall. The street he passes through is a fair sample of all London at this moment; narrow, crooked, and ill-paved. Shattered signs, broken coaches and carts lumber the way; fallen houses cover the pavement and kennel with their ruins; the water runs almost knee deep, and is as cold as ice, from the hailstones. Lord Wharton looks for a chair to carry him to his destination, but even the carriers have gone home to see to the safety of their wives and children. He twirls his beard and strides resolutely on, with the muddy water wetting his silken hose, ruining his rapier and velvet small-clothes; but he is a philosopher in these little things, and pleasantly hums "Lillibullero bullan a la," the famous doggerel generally accredited to him.

He has proceeded but a short distance when a girl's form becomes dimly perceptible through the gray curtain of rain; he quickens his step and exclaims, "Egad! the hussy hath a good shape; I'll e'en speak with her!" She is evidently aware that he is pursuing her, and she considerately slackens her pace until he reaches her side, then she turns to him and says in a sweet, though rather bold voice, "Good-night to ye, my lord, rabbit me if ———." She happens to see his face while the lightning plays with unusual brilliancy; she stops suddenly as if spellbound, and then cries in a bitter anguish-stricken tone, "Oh God! Tom — You?" Then her utterance became choked, she ran away from him with great precipitancy, and drew her hood low over her face. He made an effort to stop her, but she eluded his grasp; and now she is lost to view.

"S'blood! This is strange! A pest on the jade to run away ere I saw her face. 'Tis a pretty one, I'll be bound, or she would not have been so chary of showing it; and to call me Tom, plain Tom! Egad, she must have known me before; her voice hath a familiar ring now I think on't, but I cannot for the life of me recall where I have heard it. Jupiter Pluvius! how it pours."

Let us follow the object of his thoughts. She does not run far before she bounds up the steps of a gaudily painted house and raps quickly with her knuckles; the door is at once half opened, and a husky voice exclaims, "Who's there?"

"Nellie," she answers, impatiently; the door-chain clangs heavily on the floor, and she totters in, wet and dirty. Her face, though pale and not over clean, is pretty and expressive; but in her bright eyes there is a wild, hunted look which ill-accords with their azure hue.

She goes up stairs, entering a close dark room in the back part of the house, and lights a dirty tallow candle, which she places on the table; now she goes towards a small trundle-bed where lies a pink, flaxen-haired boy, whose pure breath comes softly through his little open lips, on which she imprints a passionate kiss; the wild look leaves her eyes, and in its place a glorious radiance—a mother's love conquers all other feelings. She gathers him up very closely, and strains him to her bosom. "My poor babe, I must deny myself even the consolation of your innocence and your darling prattle; father will keep you for my sake, for the little Nellie's sake who was once his only joy." Her tears fall thick and fast, while outside the storm still continues with scarcely any apparent diminution. The room is bare and gloomy; it has but one ornament in it—a withered bunch of wild violets under a dusty glass case.

CHAPTER II.

"He 's a downright pest in all sorts of ways."
MELEAGER.

THE Wharton estate is situated in the loveliest part of picturesque Buckingham. The castle is venerable and romantic. A spacious terrace surrounds it on every side, luxuriantly beautified with the wanton musk rose, myriads of lime-blossoms, the sweet-smelling hawthorn; and interspersed in artistic profusion are cupids, fauns, dryads, and floras, most of which are draped with the delicate tendrils of the sweetbrier which cling lovingly to their gleaming limbs. The rusty creaking vane, the fluted chimneys of moulded bricks are quaint and bygone, smacking of the Elizabethan period and its customs. Inside are long broad rooms; winding passages, dim hallways hung with stamped leather, or panelled in black oak which is decorated with heraldic devices. The low ceilings are interlaced with heavy rafters of some dark wood, whose gothic corbels are shaped into fantastic grinning faces.

In the hallways, on the head of the stairs and between the mullioned windows, stands stiff and stern the armor of the Wharton warriors, which adds to the air of antiquity which surrounds the castle and its adjuncts; truly meriting its venerable air, for it was built by the second Baron Wharton about the middle of the sixteenth century. The round, castellated towers which adorn either end were added later to give greater defensive and offensive powers in times of forays and maraudings, of which the whole front shows many traces in broken buttresses, undermined walls, and splintered gateways. A moat, once filled with stagnant water, which was formerly crossed by a drawbridge, is now filled up and transformed into an odorous garden; this adds a glowing loveliness to a picture which might otherwise have been too sombre. In the middle of the hall is a massive stairway wide enough for a dozen bowmen to walk abreast without jostling one another. It is highly polished, and elaborately carved like its surroundings.

Down it are descending two persons; one of them is the Lady Wharton, who is tall and handsome; her carriage is very stately; she bears herself haughtily, as becomes the female representative of a high and noble family; like her husband she is a Whig, and, to show her politics to all the world, she has stuck two conspicuous patches on her right cheek. Her eyes rest on her companion, who walks by her side with all the dignity and grace of a courtier of twenty years' standing. He has scarcely seen fourteen summers, but he might easily pass for much older. He is tall, well-shaped; his hair is parted in the middle, falling on his shoulders in thick natural curls; in front it is cut low on his forehead, and brushed smooth; his eyes beam with liveliness, wit, and good humor, with just a perceptible trace of arrogance in them, bred doubtless by the servile attendants who are ever ready to obey every nod and beck of young master Philip. His mouth is the most attractive feature about him; it can bestow the most persuasive and endearing smile; it can curl itself into a spiteful bow, and bandy caustic wit and biting repartees with any dame or cavalier who chooses to play with such keen weapons. His nose is a trifle sharp at the extremity, but large at the base; and his complexion surpasses in brilliancy the vaunted skin of any court belle in London. His chin rather detracts from his manliness; it would be perfect in a girl, but for a man it is too feminine, and shows a lack of stability or principle, or both.

Young as he is he can boast unusual parts; in classics and belles-lettres he is better posted than is many a pedantic professor in a provincial college; in politics, diplomacy, and the use of the rapier he has been instructed by my lord, who saw his aptitude for learning, appreciated his talents and ambition, feeling proud of him, with his handsome face, his reckless courage, and his various accomplishments; among these he is remarkable as a linguist, for he has already thoroughly mastered the chief European language, as also Latin and Greek.

He looks up at his mother with a caressing smile, and says, "My lady mother, why do you always get so mightily angered if I but look kindly on sweet mistress Margery? Sure she is as proper a girl as your ladyship did ever see."

Her lips curl contemptuously as she replies, "Why, my little Whig, do'st imagine that I could stoop so low as to fret myself because my son deigns to smile on an awkward country girl?"

"Nay," he replies in some heat, "you are misled in thinking her an awkward rustic; she is the daughter of General Holmes, whose family vaunts good blood and a score of quarterings, though their revenue is small; and, I pray you, call me not Whig; I hate its very sound; Tory and high church sound more pleasantly in my ears, Wharton though I am!"

He stops in some confusion, for spite of his bold words he stands in awe of his stately mother; she looks at him in surprise and mortification for a moment, then says in cold, measured tones, "My son, I can dispense with your company; leave me!" He makes a deep obeisance and attempts to kiss her hand, but she waves him away, exclaiming, "No, Philip, not from a Tory!" He blushes scarlet, turns quickly on his heel, and walks proudly along the hall towards the gamekeeper's lodge.

Her eyes follow him with a troubled, wistful expression in them. "I fear he will be as his father was before him, and as they say he is yet, wild and reckless. I would rather see him in his grave than see him a profligate and a bully, or, worse than all, a traitor to our party. He is so headstrong, so extravagant, and contrary, that if my lord is one thing, Philip is sure to be the other."

She sits wearily down in the large, high-backed oaken chair, near to the painted window which represents a thrilling incident in the life of one of her husband's ancestors, Baron Godfroi Wharton. It is in reference to a duel he once fought. He had entered the lists against an unknown knight who had grossly insulted him, and then challenged him to the combat *à l'outrance*, on foot or on horse, with spear or with sword; they fought, and the Baron was the victor; he was just about to dispatch his adversary with a thrust of his misericordia through the bars of his helmet, when his hand was tightly griped, and a voice whispered in his ear, "Desist! most puissant of chevaliers; he is thy son, whom thou didst discard so cruelly some year or so agone!" So his life was spared; when he recovered, they lived on terms of amity until death parted them.

She is looking at the scene depicted on the glass in all the hues of the rainbow. "I wonder whether *they* will ever fight against each other? Philip is excitable, and my lord is not slow to anger. But I must go and steep Granny Leedsie's feverwort; she will need it to-night."

She rises gracefully, walking slowly to the refectory or herb-room to discharge her charitable duties, and also to have an eye to the servants.

Philip stalked into the lodge with a sullen air, quivering lips, and eyes bright with suppressed tears, and demanded peremptorily of the stripling who was engaged in polishing a long yew bow which looked as if it might take a Goliath to handle, "Where is Shem?" He did not give him time to answer, but again ejaculated, "Quick! Begone! send him here." And he waved his small white hand with a gesture worthy of Louis or my Lord Chesterfield. The boy darted out of the door like a deer "uncovered," startled by master Philip's rough manner, generally so gracious to all the dependents.

"Mornin', Master Philip," says Shem Throck the gamekeeper, as he darkens the door with his broad shoulders, and touches his cap respectfully. He is a good type of the bluff, courageous Englishman of the lower class; his quick brown eyes are full of conviviality and fun.

He throws a keen glance at Philip, and continues, "Art sick, sir? Thou dost not look ower weel this mornin'."

Without noticing his interrogatory, Philip says, "Shem, my crossbow! and select me a few good shafts, well feathered and true."

Shem executed his commands, and asks, "Shalt want we along?"

"No, I would rather go alone: if my lord inquires anent me, tell him I have gone a shooting, and will not return till late. Hast seen Mistress Margery in the Chase or the dingle, Shem?"

"Nay! Master Philip, I did na see her at either of they two places; m'appen I mought have, if I had looked hard eno' down by Rooksnest; she is often thereabouts," and a twinkle shot out of his eye as he turned to the window and hung his crossbow on its accustomed peg.

Philip steps out and walks swiftly towards the forest, and he is soon lost to sight among the thick hedges and bushes.

Shem has his eyes on him, and chuckles knowingly, "Little game he wants, I trow, or his memory would no' be so bad as to forget his gamebag forbye; I think mysel' that Mistress Margery has mair to do wi' his hunting the day than e'er the pretty pheasant or the swift red deer, though he has shafts for both. Weel, weel, his young blood is hot and springsome, but an' I were he, I suld think twice ere I braved my lord's scowl once; I ken his lordship is sorely against him meeting her as he does. Philip was aye wilfu', and some day there will be sair greeting and wet een for his sake, for all his winnin' tongue and his bonnie face." He ceases his soliloquy, and proceeds to affix to his door two otter heads and a long-toothed, foam-flecked head of a veteran fox, the spoils of the morning. The stout oaken planks are almost covered with similar trophies, some fresh and moist, others dry and hard; most of them have been caught or shot by Shem; but still there are many of Brad's trophies there also, his father having made him a skilful woodsman and a cunning hunter.

He stops his work for a moment, and abstractedly lets his arm drop to his side; a perplexed expression ruffles his usually placid countenance; suddenly he roars out in stentorian tones, and with his hand to his cheek as if about to give the view-halloo, "Brad away! Brad away!" "Away—away" echoes in every direction, and repeats itself in varied tones in wood and marsh, mere and loch.

He appears in obedience to the paternal call—a healthy, rosy-cheeked, sinewy lad, who springs rather than walks into the lodge, flushed and panting. He stands motionless and quiet, awaiting the commands of his father, whose voice had penetrated far into the woods where he had been tracking for otters on the edge of the lake.

"Brad," he growls in a gruff voice which his genial

face belied, for it is one of his notions that if his son found out how tenderly he loved him he might become unruly and fractious, and take advantage of it, so that he always shows him a stern front and no favor; but unfortunately Brad had long ago discovered this trait, and humored his father accordingly.

"Go down to Rooksnest, just this side o' t' Weird's cave; thou 'lt find the young master—mark whether Mistress Margery be wi' him. If she is, come back at once, an' mind! no bow-twangin'; thou mightst be heard. Go!" As Brad set off at a long, swinging pace, he continues, "and bless you, my boy"

"Ay, Shem, ye may well say bless him, for he is the core o' my heart, the varra apple o' my e'e," burst in his good wife as she shuffles in at the doorway, her hands grasping the corners of her apron, while on her broad shoulders hangs a confused mass of wet fishing-tackle, cords, hooks, and the rest of the paraphernalia with which his lordship had been thinning the scaly denizens of the mere over the low hills.

"It's thee, is it?" Shem stolidly replies; for, like most of his class, he considers "womenfolk" good for nothing but to obey their husbands, particularly if said husbands happen to be gamekeepers.

"Ay, it's me. His lordship wants you to clean an' mend the tackle weel, an' put it away carefu' like, so that it will not rust."

Debbie Throck is the cook at the castle, and she seems well fitted for her office and its onerous duties. She is robust and comely, albeit red and a trifle sooty, for she has been busily engaged all the morning in cooking a dinner to please the palates of the gentlefolk who are to dine with his lordship to-day. She still grasps the corners of her apron, and a vast sigh heaves the expanse of her bosom as she says: "Ah! Shem, to think o 't, all the gude things that mun be sarved at table the day—"

"Umph!" interpolates Shem.

"Stewed broth, wheaten flummery, an' hotchpot to begin on."

He licks his lips and frowns slightly.

"Then marrer puddings and quakin' puddings; then collops, veal toasts, and roasted partridges."

Shem is plainly becoming angry, but still she pursues her tantalizing catalogue.

"To finish up wi' custards, caraway cakes, an' pear puddings, besides the syllabubs, suckets, and—"

"Stop thy rantin' noise, fule! What need to tell me o' all these when I can touch naught but a bit o' dry ven'son, or happen a roasted partridge?"

A demure look twinkles in her eyes, which he seems familiar with, for he encircles her stout waist with his arm, and growls quite amiably, "Come, dame, I know thou hast summut for me: come—what is it?"

"Go away, Shem; dost see how ta rumples my pinner and a' that's in it?"

He at once transfers his arm from her waist to the apron, which, he observes, contains something bulky.

"Ha' done, now; thou 'lt spoil all 't syllabub if thou 'rt not more carefu'."

So saying she gives him a peep at the contents of it.

He lifts them out carefully one by one—samples of the dishes for the company—and arranges them neatly on his ash sideboard. His eyes sparkle as he discovers fresh tidbits at every incursion, and as he lifts out the last, an orange sucket, he gives her a sounding kiss in sheer gratitude, and then says, in a shamefaced sort of a manner, "Now, dame, they may want thee up at the kitchen." She seems to think so too, and sallies towards her own quarter; but, before she left, she said coaxingly, "Shem, be kind to the lad; don't be over cross wi' him, will ye?" "All right, Debbie; I can manage," he replied in a confident tone; but whether he referred to Brad or the delicacies on the sideboard she was doubtful.

We will leave Shem arranging the fishing tackle, and watch his son's conduct in his new position—a spy—an office he hates and despises. He had said to himself, as he left his father, that if he did happen to see those for whom he searched, he would not let a soul know aught about it but himself; in fact, he had inwardly determined not to find them if he could help it.

CHAPTER III.

"She rose, she sprung, she clung to his embrace,
Till his heart heaved beneath her hidden face.
He dared not raise to his that deep-blue eye,
Which downcast droop'd in tearless agony;
Her long fair hair lay flashing o'er his arms,
In all the wildness of dishevell'd charms."

MEDORA.

"Thine eyes' blue tenderness, thy long fair hair."

GENEVRA.

A FEW yards beyond the cultivated portion of the Wharton estate is a clump of trees, which has borne from time immemorial the name of Rooksnest, on account of the myriads of noisy rooks that have built their nests amid the leafy boughs, and cawed and bred in bold security since the birth of the first Baron of the Wharton line. To the right is a dripping, unwholesome den, which penetrates nearly fifty feet into the solid rock; it is known all the country around as the "Weird's Cave." The tradition in regard to it runs that, over one hundred and twenty-five years ago a wizard, or one who passed for such, lived here, who never left his lair unless misfortune or death threatened the Wharton family. On such occasions he would totter out and bring with him some rude symbol to typify the kind of misfortune that was boding.

The old Baron had held him in great respect, and in a degree even stood in awe of him, until one day when his eldest born was leaving the castle with an armed retinue to go to the crusades, the wizard prophesied his sudden death, which so enraged him that he at once hung him from the battlements with the sneering remark that "as he was so ready to foretell others' deaths, i was a pity he did not know the time and place of his own and thus escape." The weird had replied solemnly, " My death will not prevent his; he will follow me ere the sun grows yellow in the west." And, sure enough, they brought his son back with his feet to the door and a Lochaber axe-cut across his young head; he had been killed in a brawl with a hostile retinue scarcely a mile from the castle.

There is not a man in the county who cares to pass by the cave at night, or even to wander too near it in daytime, there are so many treacherous holes and slippery places around and about it. Philip alone had once examined its interior, and brought out as a trophy a flint hatchet of uncouth make, deeply cut in quaint characters; it now hangs on the wall in the banquet-room, where it is regarded with awe by the wondering tenantry and the servants.

Close by the cave begins a narrow, sequestered alleyway, reaching far away into the forest; along its sides grow in profusion many varieties of vine-flowers, the modest lavender and the delicious sweetbrier, which shed their refreshing perfume on the air; above, the patriarchal trees keep silent watch and ward, lest too much sun dispel the soothing, transparent darkness which they throw over the scene; they form an intricate roof of glorious fretwork through which blue patches of sky are now and then perceptible when the south wind rolls through the long green aisle and tosses the limbs to and fro, making the cheery sunlight dance in quick measure on the ground and flash between the rustling leaves which sigh at the gentle tumult.

The yielding turf, here green, there dun or black, forms a fitting carpet for the dainty feet of the lovely girl, who stands so quiet; her high-heeled brode-

quins are of pale amber silk, with coquettish bows
trimmed with white and gold lace; in the centre of each
is set a small stone, which glows and sparkles very
prettily; and, truly, she seems to admire them herself,
for her eyes are fixed intently on them, as she stands with
one charming little hand resting against the low, drooping boughs of an old oak. But why she should tremble,
as she certainly does, and breathe so quickly as to cause
her young bosom to rise and fall so tremulously, demands
a stronger reason than the idle inspection of the most
elaborate slippers, or the prettiest French bow, affords.
She looks like a picture from Lely, with its languor
and wantonness transformed into purity and innocence.

Her hair diffuses a subtle perfume while the wind
blows it to and fro and toys caressingly with the golden
tresses; a trustful, devoted expression dwells in every
feature of her face, and fills her eyes, which are as
blue as the sapphire and as bright as a fresh dew-
drop. Her brows are light brown and delicately curved,
her complexion as fresh as the flowers in May. Her
figure is very girlish, and shrinks sensitively from the
hand which rests on her waist, a piece of officiousness
she hardly knows whether to pout at or to reward with
a glance; but the struggle is not long, love conquers, and
she lays her blushing face on her lover's shoulder, whilst
he, with face suffused with happiness unspeakable, gently
strokes her soft hair, kissing it with a vehemence that
tells its own tale.

"Look up, sweetheart," he says, in low murmuring
tones. "Look up, that I may read in your eyes whether
your love can fathom mine."

She bends her head back, looking him fairly in the
eyes with such a look of passionate devotion that his
head turns around with the sight, and a giddiness for
the moment overpowers him; he lowers his face nearer

and nearer to hers, and drinks in her every beauty in an intoxicating draught, until her eyes close in ecstatic joy.

Here in the dim light, and amid the sweet perfumes of the wild flowers, their breaths mingle and send Cupid's arrows stinging through all their veins.

"Margery, love, my own, why do you tremble? If there did happen to be anybody espying us——." She started, but Philip soon reassures her by a never-failing method in such cases.

"They might compare me to a gerfalcon flown at a dove; one would not think you were a soldier's daughter."

"Philip," she replies in a hurt manner, and with a little quiver of her red lips, "you call me a coward; I am when our love is concerned; in aught else, try me, and you will find I am still a Holmes."

"Tut, darling, I was but joking."

She looks at him long and earnestly, as if a new thought had struck her. "Philip, will you always love me as now? I know that if you should ever grow to hate me, or even if you should ever fail to love me above all others, it would break my heart."

He looks tenderly at her, and replies, "Margery, if all England's beauties—but I'll recite you a few lines of a great dean's poem which will tell you in better words than mine what you already know."

A half thought forms in her mind to deny the possibility of the dean speaking better or even as well as her Philip, but she fears to offend him, and he recites in a low voice Swift's "Receipt to Form a Beauty," a sonnet on Mrs. Biddy Floyd, which is ingenious and witty. In the last line he said "Holmes" instead of "Floyd," a change which destroyed the rhyme, but added to its truthfulness, in Philip's opinion at all events.

As he finishes, she enunciates demurely, yet with an

anxious expression, "Lord Wharton!" His face grows pale and angry, and he makes no answer except to strain her more tightly in his arms. Apparently he hears somebody in the bushes, and he steps hurriedly to the place whence the noise comes. He looks carefully around; there is no one in sight, and he can hear nothing except a mellow whistling in the distance which he recognizes as Brad Throck's; he returns to his frightened sweetheart and says regretfully, " 'Tis time for us to part, and Margery, if by any chance your father does find out our meetings, you will always find a trusty fellow in Maldran Gudru the gypsy."

"Oh! Philip, I always feel afraid when he is about, his eyes are so black and treacherous; he never looks me in the face, I would be afraid to trust him."

"You are childish, little one. Why should he betray us?" he replies, in a chiding tone.

She answers, rather timidly, and with a downward look, "I fear me he is more faithful to your father than to you."

He laughs incredulously, as he well knows the power of his fascinating qualities over most people, and keeps them bright by constant use.

To explain the secrecy of their meetings, it is necessary to recount circumstances which happened some time before.

Margery and Philip from their infancy had been playmates and inseparable companions; as a natural consequence a mutual love had taken possession of them, which grew stronger and deeper as they grew older; this Lord Wharton with his usual penetration had noticed, and noticed with some uneasiness; accordingly, he determined to put an end to their further companionship, fearful lest Philip might balk his future intentions by declining to espouse the noble dame he had secretly selected for him—an alliance with whom would strengthen his political influence, and also still further enrich his overflowing coffers. His first measure was to forbid Philip ever to see her again in private; his second was to converse with her ladyship in a loud tone about the insolence of a Holmes wishing to ally herself with his family. The servants as a matter of course heard the remarks, which in a short time reached the ears of the irate General, who was so incensed at the arrogance of his neighbor that he peremptorily forbade Margery ever to speak or correspond with Philip again. So matters stand—diplomacy and experience against love and innocence; the old, old tale on which so many changes have been rung, and will be rung until the sun ceases to rise and the world to revolve.

To resume, Philip replies excitedly, "Let them find us together; let them send their spies to watch our slightest movements; if the worst comes to the worst, there are other places in the world besides Buck's!"

She looks pained at his words, and replies in a pleading, soothing manner: "Please don't, dear—I could never consent to leave my poor old father alone and desolate; mother is in the kirkyard, now, and I am the only one he has to love or be loved by now."

"Then leave *me*," he says abruptly; nevertheless, he continues to hold her closely to him; she is pained and perplexed; her blue eyes grow brighter as she nervously twitches the long points of her laced sleeves.

"We will not talk about it, Philip dear, will we?" she says, after a short interval. "I will tell you about my visit to Queenie, and what she—"

"Wait a bit, Margery; now tell me what you went to see her for?"

She answers him with a sweet smile on her lips, and

without the slightest hesitation, "I thought you might be there."

"I thought so," he replies, rather egotistically.

"Well, she seemed very angry and excited when I entered, and she showed me the portrait of a very pretty girl, who she said had been a great friend to her when she was a little child; she said that a noble gentleman had done this girl a great harm, and that if he did not give her enough money to support herself on until she died, she, Queenie you know, would avenge her. I asked her his name, but she replied, with such a curious smile, Philip! that I might learn it soon enough, and she was silent for a long while; then said suddenly, 'Mistress Margery, Master Philip was here yest're'en, and I read him his fortune.'"

"Yes, I recollect she did tell me a heap of wonderful things—but proceed with your tale, sweetheart."

"'His life,' she said, and I almost hate her for it, 'will be an expiation of another's sin, his path will be crossed by one of his own race, and he will never know peace until the expiation is accomplished.'"

He laughs as he listens to the wild recital, and feels glad to think that Margery should become so excited at the gypsy queen's foolish words.

"Oh, I forgot," she resumed, "Queenie told me the girl's name; it was Nelly—Nelly—— I forget the last, but it is no matter, is it?" as if she dreads displeasing him.

"I' faith, no. What should I want to know about Nelly unknown or anybody else when I have you, sweetheart?" She looks happier, and a brighter light illumines her eyes at his fond words.

Brad returned to the lodge and dutifully told his father that he had been unable to see Mrs. Margery, but *had* seen Master Philip, who was tracking for deer in the forest and seemed rather unlucky. He was answered in this strain by the suspicious Shem: "I'll be bound, thou glamourin' skipjack, that thou looked not too hard for either; like enow thou 'st been trackin' thy own game—Meg Busbie, wi' her finicky gewgaws an' her flighty ribbons an' graces; I knaw weel what thou 'rt after, so don't stop glowerin' there like a deer in a covert, but set thee down an' eat th' dinner; for th' mun be rare an' hungry." He took his plate and helped him with a wooden spoon to an immense quantity of hot pease and pudding, and a glass of bubbling, humming mead.

Brad smiled covertly, and proceeded to refresh his inner man, an operation for which he was always ready. He had the reputation of being the strongest, healthiest lad on the estate, and of course it took a deal of food to keep his appetite down; in fact, when he was smaller, the chaplain, a learned man, had playfully christened him "Omnivorous Brad;" a cognomen which still sticks to him; but it has been corrupted by his comrades into "Nevereat," which rolls off the tongue more easily than its ponderous origin.

CHAPTER IV.

"*Don John.*—I heard him swear his affection.
Bora.—So did I too; and he swore he would marry her to-night.
Don John.—Come, let us to the banquet."
  MUCH ADO ABOUT NOTHING. II. I.

THE Wharton banqueting-hall is fully a hundred feet long and about half as wide; at both ends glow two delicately-stained, deeply-embrasured windows, which reach from the shining floor to the groined ceiling. On either side is a large fireplace set in with Dutch tiles, which are painted in stiff, quaint designs; each fender is guarded by stone dogs, one of which has had half its nose chipped off, probably in some bygone brawl of Cavaliers and Covenanters.

The ponderous sideboards are carved with bacchanalian subjects, satyrs, vine-leaves, and the jolly Bacchus, who disports himself in attitudes free and wanton, while the grinning satyrs and the dancing fauns keep time with pipe and feet.

The walls are panelled, and decorated in a fanciful manner with pictures that have reference to feasting and gayety—all except one, a portrait which hangs over the high mantel; it is the full-length figure of a stern, gloomy, straight-haired Cavalier; in his right hand he holds a Bible, the left grasps a long, bell-mouthed petronel; it is old Sir Philip, the father of the present Lord Wharton. One of his eyes is shot out, and in its place is a round, jagged bullet hole; it was his loving son who had maltreated it in this manner after he had received a lesson in obedience from him when he was young and insubordinate to the authorities that were.

Lord Wharton often tells the occurrence with many a laugh and jest, and avers that he keeps it there as a Roman of old did his skeleton, to remind him of the shortness of life, and the wisdom of enjoying the passing hour.

The table is set with all the ceremony and profusion usual on such occasions, and the serving-men and the carvers await the advent of the guests to begin proceedings. They have not long to wait; the doors fly open swiftly and noiselessly; Wharton and his guests stroll in, laughing noisily, and exchanging free jests and stinging repartees. Carelessly resting his hand on Wharton's shoulder, and, to judge by the twinkle in his eye, retailing a famous bit of court-scandal or town-talk, is the nobleman, whose arrogance, vanity, and venality have long since passed into a proverb. He has passed over fifty years of intrigue, politics, and turmoil, but, to judge by his smiling face and his jovial manner, one would never imagine that in that time he had been continually involved in the wildest schemes and the most daring villanies; he is of medium height, and dressed with scrupulous care in a costume of black velvet, with laced and slashed satin trunks. On his breast glitter and tinkle the many orders of which he is a member; most of these he has acquired by acts which any courtier might feel too modest to own; he is known as Charles Montague, Earl of Halifax, Dryden's parodist, and the author of a poem on the death of Charles II., which procured him the friendship of the powerful Earl of Dorset, as well as an introduction to Will's coffee-house, with its attendant profligacy and cold-hearted libertinism.

Here is the venerable Lord Somers, whose long-flowing wig, calm, sedate face, and magisterial air give him a look of quiet dignity which well befits the representative of so many high posts and honors, and one who single-handed coped with fourteen distinct charges, as false and as dangerously sophistical as Belial himself could possibly devise, brought against him by cunning and powerful enemies, and overthrew them all.

Close by him is a tall, large-chested, robust man, dressed in plain black; his features are strongly marked and manly; his keen blue eyes penetrate and scrutinize everything and everybody; a sarcastic smile hovers about the corners of his mouth; and as he converses with the gentlemen near him he speaks quickly, and snaps his thumbs energetically, as if the subject under discussion were of great interest. You possibly recognize him? Dean Swift! What sad memories of poor Stella and Vanessa does that name recall! Did he never think regretfully of the unhappiness he had caused? The first so trustful and devoted, who gave him the name by which he always wished her to call him; once he was happy only when she was by his side, commanding him in girlish pettishness, "Presto, come and tell me what this is," or "Darling Presto, you must take me to the fields to-morrow." The other so reserved and haughty to all others, yet so humble and loving when he was with her. The man who could thus fill the hearts of two such women with undivided love must have possessed a power of fascination which he did not always choose to exert, or else he certainly would not have had so many enemies as he did have, even with all his vile caustic lampoons, his party squibs and satires.

It may seem strange that Swift is here, whose Tory propensities and personal animosity towards his host are well known, but he is an erratic being, and this is possibly one of his freaks; or just as likely, his presence may be ascribed to the workings of his astute host, who has always regretted his attachment to the Tory interest; however, be it as it may, he is always welcome among those who appreciate wit and learning, even if the wit is directed against themselves, and the learning is of rather a truculent nature. The remainder of the guests are Whig notabilities, or those who their designing entertainer intends shall be, if it lies in his power so to make them.

The conversation at table is rather freer than I care to chronicle, so loose are the morals and so depraved the ideas of the gentlemen of this period.

After a reasonable time has been allowed for the discussion of the well-furnished table, Wharton rises and proposes the following toast: "Her sacred Majesty and the party which supports her!"

"Umph!" sneers the genial dean. "Pity she can't support the party; but——." His, the only voice that did not join in the cheer, is drowned in the din.

Montague, who has heard Swift's sneering remark, rises, and as soon as the noise abates, he says meaningly, "Gentlemen, I have a toast to propose which I am sure will mightily please *all* that are here." He holds his goblet poised in his jewelled hand. "To Cervantes and Rabelais as *original* writers, and to Lady Somerset as a true woman."

It is a common charge of the dean's enemies that he plagiarized from these two authors—a lie, for his was a genius that only borrowed from itself, but still any mention of the ridiculous charge sorely vexes him. Lady Somerset is his bitter enemy, so it is plainly to be seen that the Earl intended the toast for his especial benefit, especially as they are not on the best of terms.

The Dean drained his goblet in company with the others, and is now standing erect and looking straight at Montague, with his blue eyes scintillating ominously. Again he fills his goblet.

"My Lord Montague, it ill becomes you above all others to touch on so delicate a subject as stealing—you, who were once Chancellor of the Exchequer! As for the Duchess of Somerset, I respect her as an enemy, but would hate her as a friend." He raises his goblet. "To the memory of Cervantes, Rabelais, and the Duchess of Somerset" (he bows obsequiously), "and to yourself, and any other gentleman who wishes to take it to himself."

He drains his goblet, and turns it bottom upwards on the table. There is a hush of expectancy, and all eyes are turned on the Earl. He is as white as a sheet, and plays nervously with the scented curls of his French peruke.

Wharton, seeing a brawl impending, rises, and says calmly: "Gentlemen, I pray your attention for a few minutes, and I will recite to you what pleased me vastly when I read it; I think it will please you too. It is a selection from a poem by that marvellous clever fellow, Gay."

With graceful gestures, and in a loud, sonorous voice, he reads:—

> "Far in Cythera stands a spacious grove,
> Sacred to Venus and the god of love;
> Here the luxuriant myrtle rears her head,
> Like the tall oak the fragrant branches spread;
> Here Nature all her sweets profusely pours,
> And paints the enamell'd ground with various flowers;
> Deep in the gloomy glade a grotto bends,
> Wide through the craggy rock an arch extends.
> The rugged stone is cloth'd with mantling vines,
> And 'round the cave the creeping woodbine twines."

All listen attentively, thankful for their entertainer's kindly tact in preventing a quarrel at table.

Swift's countenance beamed with delight while it was being read, for Gay is one of his few favorites, and he is now loud in his praises of its excellences.

Comments on the poet's style and sentiments pass around the board; some favorable, others unfavorable; the latter unfortunates the Dean attacks with spirit, and vindicates every word or line carped at or ridiculed.

Lord Somers, who has for some time been the centre of an engrossed admiring group, is about to speak, and rises slowly to his feet; but, unfortunately, at this instant, a rich harmonious tenor trolls out the famous Jacobite song of " Charlie over the Water."

All listen in blank amazement, and several instinctively lay their hands on their rapiers; some turn to see whence comes the treasonous refrain. Still it rings high and clear above their astonished heads, until Wharton looks up, and starts with surprise and anger. All eyes follow the direction of his, and lo! high up in the embrasured window, with his head touching the groined arch, and his feet supported by the heavy moulding, stands, or rather clings, his son Philip, the destined prop of the Whigs.

He looks down on the astonished guests with a mocking smile on his lips, and finishes his song with a merry laugh, and a pert request to Swift to throw him an *orange*. He, fully alive to the humor and spiciness of the affair, tosses one up to the young scapegrace; he catches it deftly in his loose hand, and lays it on the ledge of a grotesque corbel, directly under his feet. This done, he places his heel on it, and crushes it with such hearty good-will that the juice and pips go flying about the room and on the table.

" Long live the Hanoverian rats," he cries satirically, and adds in earnest tones, " and God help poor King Jamie!"

He begins to descend from his perilous position, and finally bounds in safety to the floor. He bows gracefully, and stands erect and confident, as though he awaits the reward which surely must follow so good an action as he has just performed.

He knows well that his father's sentiments, and also the sentiments of his guests, with one or two exceptions, are eminently loyal, and obnoxious to the claims of the Pretender, or James III., as his adherents call him.

Wharton says, in a stern, suppressed voice: "Philip, seat yourself!" He does as he is commanded, and settles himself in a chair close to Swift, with the finical affections of a beau as to whether his rapier hangs correctly, or the skirts of his satin coat crease elegantly. He pulls his lace ruffles daintily over his hands. These slight details satisfactorily arranged, he looks at his father, and lifts his eyebrows interrogatively.

"Philip, you must either retract what you have said, and drink to the health and prosperity of her sacred Majesty, and to the eternal perdition of the Pretender and his cause, or, by God! I'll disown you. Make your choice quickly, and in the presence of these gentlemen whom you have insulted." He stops abruptly; his lips tightly compressed, and his hands twitching violently.

Philip is about to answer him with hot, angry words, but Swift breaks in: "My lord, mayhap Master Philip does not wish to drink; I, for one, would be satisfied if he but admitted that he was not in earnest."

The rest of the guests declare the same; and Wharton, who fears that he might refuse to drink the toast, wisely acquiesces, and chokes down his wrath.

Philip rises and says, with an affectation of perfect sincerity: "Gentlemen, I candidly acknowledge to you that I did not mean all I said." He adds in a low tone, which none hear but Swift: "And that part is 'Long live the Hanoverian.'"

He turns to his father and says respectfully: "Is it your wish that I retire?" He nods his head, and Philip saunters slowly out. As he passes the orange he grinds it again with his heel, and mutters "Nassau—seesaw; it may be my turn next."

Ere long the company disperse, and leave my lord to the companionship of his thoughts, which are apparently not of the most pleasant nature. His brow is knit and furrowed, and his face is troubled. His capacious mind is taxed to its utmost limit for schemes to ruin the ascendency of the Tories, who, with Harley at their head, give him great uneasiness by their bold movements and subtle machinations, which, together with the unfavorable popular opinion of the Whigs, in consequence of the trial of Dr. Sacheverell for his sermons concerning the doctrine of passive obedience, gave the Tories many advantages. The Whigs are under the direction of Godolphin, whose egregious blunder was so hurtful to his party. At the conclusion of the trial bonfires were lighted, and his name was shouted with cheers and acclamations; while Godolphin's met with groans and hisses. These same riotous proceedings were repeated on the expiration of his sentence, and it seems inevitable that Harley will now carry things with a high hand; while at the ear of majesty itself whispers the Tory tool—handsome, fascinating Mistress Abigail Masham, who has superseded the vixenish Sarah, Duchess of Marlborough, who had herself made Mistress Abbie lady of the bedchamber, whence she has worked herself into the love of her royal mistress. Wharton muses regretfully over his party's lost power, and the defeat of their pet measure—the continuance of the war with France, which, had it been carried on, would certainly have brought the Bourbon rule in Spain to a conclusion.

CHAPTER V.

Theseus.—"'Our proposed hunting shall be set aside."
                MIDSUMMER NIGHT'S DREAM. III. i.

Puck.—" Yet but three ? Come one more."
                MIDSUMMER NIGHT'S DREAM. III. ii.

PHILIP is going a deerstalking to-day with Shem and his son. He is a keen sportsman, and loves dearly to send a whizzing shaft clean home to the feather in the noble game as it in vain strives to outstrip the messenger of death which springs with a twang from the strong ashen bow.

It is early morn, and the sun is yet entangled in the branches and limbs of the forest, and has still the heavy dew to drink and the rolling mist to scatter.

All three are on horseback. Philip and Shem are conversing anent slots and scents, and counters, and suchlike jargon of the hunting field. Brad canters respectfully behind with the crossbows and ropes to pack the carcass with, and he also keeps the hounds in leash who are fresh and unruly.

The lair is empty, but the shape of the buck's body is plainly discernible in the flattened grass. Shem makes a motion to jump from his horse, but Philip anticipates him, and, laying his hand on the recent bed, exclaims in loud tones, " It is warm, Shem ;" and his eye betokens his satisfaction.

Shem scans it narrowly, and replies, " Ay, he is none far away." The hounds find the scent, and begin to whimper and strain in their leashes ; but a stern " Back !

back! Soft! soft!" from Brad quiets them at once, and they stand like statues—heads outstretched and nostrils distended.

Philip is just about to order Brad to unleash the hounds, when a black-eyed, weather-rusted gypsy thrusts aside the bushes near the lair, bows low to Philip, and places a note in his hands. He is one of a gang that Lord Wharton allows to live unmolested on his estate, and to whom he occasionally gives a feast in his kitchen —which kindnesses have so endeared him to the impressionable Ishmaelites, that they would do anything to please him.

Philip offers to reward him, but he, shaking his head, retires as silently as he came.

Philip recognizes the superscription on the letter as Margery's writing. Bidding Shem to wait a moment, he breaks the seal with glad eagerness. He is half afraid to learn the contents for fear something evil has happened to her. He spreads the little, scented sheet, and reads in a low tone.

"My own darling PHILIP: Love, my own, I will be at Rooksnest at midday. I have no time to write any more, so good-bye. Your true MARGERY.
HOLME GRANGE."

He calculates what time he has left for the chase, and finds that he will have to start for the trysting-place before they could hope to run the buck down, for Shem's experience declares it to be full-grown, and one which would lead them a long chase ere he would consent to stand at bay to receive a huntsman's keen, glittering knife deep in his panting side. So bidding them good-speed, he turns back to Rooksnest, his heart bounding in anticipation of the meeting with his bonnie Margery. He tries to sing, but for very joy he cannot, and the words are choked and indistinct. Taking the missive from his pocket, he re-reads it, to be sure that his eyes had not deceived him. He has not seen her for a whole week, nor has even had a line from her until to-day. He has not even been able to write to her, so closely has she been watched by her offended father. How she can get out to meet him he cannot surmise; nor does he care; if only she is there, he will be content.

He is now within a few yards of the Holmes' Estate, which is contiguous to his father's. Thinking he hears, above the rustle of the trees and the purling of the brook which runs close by, voices in angry discussion, one of which resembles his father's, he presses forward to see who they are that converse in so high a tone. A thought decides him to peer through the trees hiding the disputants from his view.

A sickening sensation chills his blood as he perceives his father and General Holmes standing face to face, their eyes flashing, and speaking in angry tones. Little Margery leans trembling against a neighboring tree; her hands are clasped on her throat, and her face pales and flushes alternately. Her eyes are fixed on the angry men with a pleading, pitiful expression that goes straight to Philip's heart.

As he gazes fascinated on a scene which fills him with the liveliest apprehension, the General says, in an excited manner, " My lord, your charges are false, and at some other time"—he glances at his daughter, who turns her eyes on the ground—" I will prove my words, either at the sword's point, or in any way most agreeable to your lordship!"

" General," Wharton replies, in icy, cutting tones, and with punctilious gestures, " whenever and wherever you please." He raises his hat to Mistress Margery and bows lowly to her father.

Philip determines at all hazards to interfere, and if possible prevent the duel which he sees must take place if they part in this manner. He is aware of his father's aversion to both the General and to Margery—to him for his politics, and to her for Philip's love towards her; and he dreads his father's masterly use of the rapier, feeling sure that he would not lose such an opportunity as the duel presented, to place an impassable barrier between their union. Throwing himself at his father's feet, he cries, "Spare him for her sake! I could not live without her!"

Wharton looks down on his son with surprise and vexation depicted on his countenance.

"Philip, rise at once! cease this masquerading! How came you here? Methinks your chase of the wild deer has not been a long one, since you have had time to quarry other game so successfully." He twitches his thumb in the direction of Margery, who has fallen senseless.

"Father, spare me! If you but knew how madly I love her, you—"

"Tut, tut; let her be your light-o-love; but never let it be said that a Wharton stooped to a Holmes. Why, man, an eagle never mates with a crow"—he answers in a low tone.

Philip springs to his feet, and looks him boldly in the face as he replies, "My lord, Mistress Holmes is as proper a woman as was ever begot in our house—and more—"

He is interrupted by Margery, who has recovered from her swoon. She stands between them, with her back to her lover, and says to Wharton, with a sob that shakes her from head to foot, "My lord, I give him up forever. I'll try to hate him for his own sake.—You will be a friend to my father?"

My lord stares in astonishment, and allows her to

lead him to the General. Beginning to see how matters stand, and convinced, in spite of himself, that the girl is in earnest, he extends his hand to the General, and says persuasively, "General, allow me to apologize for the hasty expressions I made use of in our conversation. It is folly for us to quarrel like raw school-boys."

Holmes' face brightens as he grasps the hand of the wily diplomat, and he energetically protests that it was all his fault in being so hasty.

As soon as Margery sees they are friends again, she endeavors to dart down the path leading to Holme Grange, but Philip intercepts her, and clasps her securely around the waist, demanding, in excited accents, to know the meaning of the previous scene.

"Unhand me, Philip, for Heaven's sake!" Her further utterance is checked by a torrent of tears, which threaten to end in hysterics.

Philip is amazed at her language, and silently mourns over the fickleness of woman; but soon all his sympathy is aroused by the evident pain she is in. Leading her to a broken rustic seat, made of a huge tree which had been cut down and sawed into many portions, he sits down beside her, while his eyes show his perplexity and vexation.

"Philip, my own, I cannot give you up."

"Give me up? What mean you, Margery?" he replies in wondering tones.

Her conversation with his father had been carried on in so low a tone that he had not heard her words.

"It means, dearest, that you can do with me whatever you will, forever and ever!" Her soft white arms wind about his neck, and her lips meet his with a passionate kiss.

"Only a love quarrel after all, Margery, eh?"

"No," she replied in serious tones, "it was no quarrel

at all. I'll tell you all about it.—I was at Rooksnest before the time, and was waiting for you at the very spot where you saw me, when I met father, who asked me— oh, so crossly—where I was going, and what I did alone in the forest, for he had forbidden me to leave the house without an attendant, as you know. I could not answer him, I was so afraid. But Lord Wharton, who happened to be in the same part of the grounds, and must have heard him, said, ' Sir, if she is unable to tell you, I can doubtless do so;' and to my terror and surprise he read, in icy, cruel tones, that quite froze my blood, every word of the letter I had written you!"

Philip starts, and feels for her letter; it is safe in his pocket. "Maldran has betrayed us; a curse on the knave!" he mutters.

"Then angry words passed between them; and if I had not placed my hand on father's sword, I am sure there would have been bloodshed—and between them!" She shudders, and clings closer to Philip.

"Margery, sweetheart, I will find Maldran, and if he has done us this foul turn, I'll stab him in his camp, the black-hearted villain!"

"Please don't, Philip; those gypsies might do you some harm."

He laughs scornfully at her fears, and is about to scout such an idea; but she turns her head, and says quickly:—

"Hush! Yes, it is my father. Quick, Philip, hide yourself until he passes. If he sees you, it might anger him again. Quick! he is coming this way. Hide yourself, and I will be in my room before he overtakes me."

He draws her to him, and—well, she looks happier after the embrace.

Like the zephyr now she flies, swift and noiseless to

hide herself in her own little room, and think over the day's doings.

Philip has scarcely concealed himself when the General strides by with a firm, commanding step, the plumes on his hat, and his long hair dancing and tossing in the breeze which sighs gently through the tangled branches overhead, and swirls the dead leaves round and round in swift circles of brown and yellow, scarlet and green.

During the time that his lordship and the General had been left together, the former had employed his time in flattering and endeavoring to sound the latter, to see whether he was in possession of any secrets of the Harley administration; but the General either knew nothing or else was too old a soldier to be caught even with the well-baited hooks which his lordship sent out for him to seize. So drawing his gray velvet cloak about his shoulders, Lord Wharton called to Philip to follow him. He was surprised to find that his son had disappeared. He scowled, and said, " I was a dolt to trust the pretty wench, for all her pleading eyes and innocent ways. Why I should have done so surprises me. To trust a girl's word, after my experience of them!" And he smiled scornfully. "A good impulse probably. Mighty few have found their way to me lately, and I shall take care it is the last. Curse me! She give up Philip? Possible. Philip give her up? Never! He is too much like myself in such things." And the courtly sinner chuckled knowingly. "If he had more sense, and a trifle less of what he calls 'honor,' she might have been his own long ago, sans Hymen. S'blood! if I was not his respected father, I would certainly advise him on that point myself." A malicious smile curls his lips as he says: "Shem will do; I'll to him." And he proceeded in the direction of the keeper's lodge.

CHAPTER VI.

"*York.*—God for his mercy! What treachery is here?"
KING RICHARD II.

"*Ursula.*—The pleasantest angling is to see the fish
Cut with her golden oars the silver stream,
And greedily devour the treacherous bait;
So angle we for Beatrice;"——
MUCH ADO ABOUT NOTHING. III. I.

SHEM had scarcely finished his luncheon and begun to talk with his son on the glorious run they had, of the feints and doublings of the old buck, of the high wall on the moor which they had taken flying, and to approve the gallant manner in which Brad had sheathed his knife clean to the haft as the desperate beast stood at bay with horns lowered, feet pawing, and back bristling, ere a quick, sharp rap sounds at the door, and footsteps grate on the ground in front of the lodge.

"Don't be asleep, lad! open the door!" Shem cries; but, before Brad can get there, the latch is lifted and Lord Wharton enters and nods pleasantly to Shem; he tells him that he would like a short conversation with him at once; turning to Brad, he says shortly, "My lad, you may amuse yourself in the chase for a half hour;" and he points to the door.

Brad, only too willing to leave so high and mighty a presence as soon as possible, walks shamefacedly to the door.

Shem scratches his curly head, and wonders what his lordship wants to see him for, "rebeck him! may be to arrange a good hunt, or to chide him for some fault."

His lordship takes the old arm-chair, close by the lattice window, through which a wide sweep of beautiful and romantic landscape can be seen, and tells Shem to seat himself also. He knows the sturdy upright nature of his gamekeeper, and knows that, in order to have his cordial co-operation in the vile job he is about to broach to him, he will have to glaze it over with sophistry and dazzle his understanding by varnishing it with words beyond his comprehension. He begins in a careless, matter-of-course manner. "Shem, it lies in your power to do me a service, which I know you will do, not only to please me, but to have a hand in so good a joke yourself."

Wharton looks at him as if he expects him to say something; Shem, however, bewildered by his master's condescension, answers not a word, but appears grave and embarrassed, and shifts his legs and arms about uneasily, looking the very embodiment of awkwardness. He did not dare to refuse my lord's command to seat himself, although at the same time he thought it a sad breach of good manners to do so.

Wharton continues: "This is what I mean. You are aware that Master Philip has a liking for pretty Mistress Holmes, and he thinks that I know vastly less about it than I do; so, in order to enjoy a mighty good joke at his expense—ah! ha!—I want you, when next you see him, to mention her name, and cautiously insinuate that you think him fondly foolish for not running away with her to London, where she can be all his own!"

Here Shem is about to ejaculate something, but he restrains himself, and reddens to the roots of his beard.

"I will pretend to know nothing about it until the last moment; then, to prevent any scandal attaching to her—" He narrowly watches Shem's face, and smiles inwardly as he notes his relieved look, and surmises that the first part of his plan alarmed him for Margery's sake, whom he loves next to Brad and his falcons. "I say, to prevent any scandal attaching to her, I will stop the proceeding, and none will be the wiser but ourselves. If you would not like Master Philip to know that you have a hand in the affair, of course I will never tell him. I will not insult you by offering you a reward, for I know there is not a Throck living who would not feel happy to fulfil my wishes; but if you should like 'Queen Anne,' who is, as you know, by 'Careless' out of 'Lightning,' you are welcome to her, and she is as fine a colt as there is in all Buck's."

Shem can scarcely sit still, so elated is he at his master's present, for it is one of the best horses in the stable, and one for which he has sighed time and again.

"My lord, I thank ye kindly. Ye could ha' given me nowt I wad prize so highly as 'Queen Anne.' As for the favor, it was your lordship's mind to jest wi' me a bit, for well ye knaw whether or no I wad' or wad' not do such an a thing, if only out on' love for a bit o' jollity." He reddens again as he proceeds: "Excuse me, your lordship, but ye are sure that no harm can come out on it to either o' the young folks?"

"No, no, Shem; you are getting nervous, timid."

My lord rises, walks to the door, and bids him "good-bye" in a suave, conciliating manner, his scabbard point scattering the white sand which the care of the gudewife had swept into squares on the red tiled floor.

"Nervous! that's what the gentle folks, more so, the women part be. It's French, I knaw, and modish, so I'm no' nervous; but I wad sair blame mysen if aught I did suld bring sorrow to wee, gowden-haired Margery, for she is mair an angel than a child o' earth. It was once before that my lord wanted to knaw whether master Philip was wi' her down by Rooksnest!—Queen

Anne! rebeck me! My heart jumps wi' joy. Sure my lord must mean well? Of coorse, of coorse."

If Shem had had his eyes at the door, he might have seen Brad standing there in a listening attitude, but his ideas were so taken up with the colt that he had thoughts for nothing but its glossy coat, its great speed, and its docility.

CHAPTER VII.

"*King.*—We'll put the matter to the present hush,
Good Gertrude; set some watch over your son."
                                    HAMLET THE DANE.

THE day is drawing to its close. The sun is falling through a sea of fire, glowing in wondrous hues and mazy colors unspeakably lovely and sublime. Vast masses of white clouds float and billow in detached fragments—snow-banks in the blue ether—through which long quivering rays dart fiery streaks that are mellowed to a pearly-pink in their struggle to pierce them through.

The spot we are on commands an extensive view of the wildest and most glorious part of the country. Here we can revel in all the varieties of an English landscape, and feast on such views as Claude or Hobbema would have thoroughly enjoyed. The moors and the fells; the valleys and the hills; the bounding mountain torrent, tumbling and rumbling over its rocky bed; and the more placid stream winding through forest and meadow—all have a beauty that can only be appreciated by the keen observer and the lover of the beautiful in nature.

Far off, beyond the reach of bow-shot, can be traced the graceful outlines of a noble buck, his antlered head tossed proudly back; the hawk's shrill cry grates above, as it circles with quickening rapidity over the nest of its frightened prey, and from the meadows beyond comes a faint, nutty smell as of dying flowers and ripening fruit.

As the vivid tints of the expiring day grow dimmer, lurid lights as of bonfires flicker and gleam in the depths of the woodland. There let us go, being careful to avoid the deep, silent tarns whose waters are icy cold and clear, and the deep gulches whose treacherous sides are covered with luxuriant foliage and thick vines with many-hued berries.

We reach an open space where a curious scene presents itself, whose rich tones, deep shadows, and picturesque accompaniments would require a Poussin's color to depict. The great, majestic trees raise their heads to the sky, and throw glancingly off the silvery beams of the rising moon which essay to break through their interweaving branches. In the centre of two or three dingy, tattered tents, and as many rickety hovels, stands the gypsy queen's abode, rather larger, and outwardly cleaner than its companions. On the summit waves a small yellow flag adorned with Oriental characters and symbols; it is weather-stained and ragged, looking a fit standard for the motley group who flourish under its shadow, and at present sprawl in ungainly attitude around the fire. At the largest of these the evening meal is cooking in a large iron kettle, which hangs between two green boughs, simmering and bubbling noisily, while its aromatic smell of herbs, meats, and condiments diffuses itself about.

At the smaller fires are stalwart men, big-limbed and ruffianly; women with long, black hair falling in tangled masses on their bare shoulders; and half-naked babes and children, who warm their feet in the welcome heat, and crow jubilantly at the rising sparks.

At the entrance to the camp is a tall, muscular vagabond, who stands stolidly at his post, surveying the hotch-potch kettle with listless eyes. It is Nanar, the most cunning tinkler—the best wrestler in the county, and his queen's favorite besides. See! he raises his head and cranes his neck as if to catch a far-off sound. Suddenly throwing himself full length on the ground, he places his ear to it. Listening attentively for a few minutes, he springs lightly to his feet, and cries in a low, but penetrating whisper, "Wha's there?" Almost immediately he receives the answer, "You have a quick ear, Nanar." The voice appears to reassure him, for he assumes his former position with scarcely a look at the intruder, merely pulling his forelock as a sign of respect to a superior.

The flames of the fires show us Lord Wharton!—an odd, unlikely place for him to visit at this time of the evening. Stamping the thick dew off his shoes, he brushes the wet leaves and twigs from his cloak, draws it tightly around his shoulders again, and steps quickly to the queen's tent, where a password admits him at once. The little room is feebly lighted by a short, clumsy candle which sputters and gutters complainingly in its rude holder—two nails hammered slantwise into the table, and pushed tightly against the soft tallow.

The queen is a tall, handsome woman. Her face is peculiar and strongly marked; her eyes are blue-black; her brows are well curved, but thick and heavy; eyelashes very long; her skin is as dark as the darkest of her tribe; and her lips are full, and rather sensual. Greeting her visitor with a respectful smile, she points to a stool close beside her, on which she requests him to be seated. She reclines on a pile of soft deer-skins, looking careless and languid; indeed, her attitude showing a spirit of coquetry and wantonness, exhibits scarce enough dignity for the ruler of such a turbulent, unruly set as are outside. But, under this apparent "easifulness," she has an iron will that can awe the roughest, the most mutinous of her followers, if it is necessary for the sake of law and order, and she can scourge them with words as keen as their own knives, and be as imperious as ever was Cleopatra or good Queen Bess.

Wharton lays his hat and cloak on the table, and replies, in answer to her inquiries anent his health. "How is it with thee, my bonnie queen?" "As well as ever, my lord, thanks to the good man." He adds—"And just as bewitching." Laughing at his compliment, she says: "My Lord, ye will drink wi' me ere I ask you anent the business that brings you here—though welcome ye be, whether ye come on business or pleasure." "Sooth," he answers, "the pleasure is for myself alone; the business for myself and others." A meaning smile crosses his face as he says this. She notices the expression on his lips; but her eyes give no indication that she is attending to anything but the filling of a pewter pot with an aromatic wine, yellow as amber, and as clear as crystal. This operation finished, she hands him the pot with a hand which, though brown and dusky, is as perfect in contour as ever painter dreamed of or poet imagined. On its index finger sparkles the signet ring used by the tribe as a means of message carrying which insures the identity of the wearer.

"Queenie," says Wharton, as he raises the wine to his lips, "to yourself, a true descendant of Jockie Faa and the dark-eyed beauties of the East." Tossing it off, he returns her the empty pot. Replacing it and the liquor bottle in the closet behind her couch, she turns to him, and says gravely: "Now, my lord, what can the gypsy queen do for ye or yours? Speak, and let the moon be my witness, I will do it willingly, be your wishes good or bad, true or fause!"

Crossing her hands on her bosom she awaits his reply.

"Well, to begin with, I wish to leave this purse with you, half of its contents for yourself, and half for Maldran." So saying, he tosses a well-filled purse on her lap. She does not even glance at it, but remains as motionless as a statue, keeping her eyes steadily on his face. He resumes: "And I would see Maldran ere I go, to give him further instructions how to act during my stay in London." She lifts a small silver whistle from her neck, and blows a piercing call on it. The summons is answered like magic; the door opens, and the gypsy enters, greasy with his unfinished supper; saluting his queen, he looks towards Wharton with an inquiring look.

Says the queen in the Rommany dialect: "Maldran, my praw, his lordship wishes to patter wi' ye anent his going awa'; chee, chee, and you will know." "Baurie Raunie, I listen," he replies sullenly. But the money she hands him creates a palpable difference in his feelings, as his brightening countenance evinces.

Wharton, who seems desirous of leaving, says hurriedly, "Maldran, I am going to London, and I want you to watch Master Philip and Mistress Holmes while I am away. Take note of all their actions, so that I may know how they behave when I am not near. If anything important happens, send a messenger with the news at once to Christopher Catt's, Fountain Tavern, in the Strand." Drawing a seal-ring from his finger, he proceeds: "This will be his token."

Maldran nods his approval, takes the ring, and secretes it in a pocket of his dirty leather breeches, which he has worn until they are as black and as shiny as satin, and takes his departure.

Wharton is about to follow him, but the queen exclaims quickly, "Wait, my lord! I have a word to say to you ere you go!" He drums impatiently on the table, and looks surprised at her request. "'Tis a story I can tell in a few minutes, for all a life's wrong is contained in it: I was a little girl once, and I committed a great sin against our laws—I need not tell you what it was. I was sentenced to banishment frae our tribe; but a sweet lady interceded for me wi' her tongue and her gowd, and—"

"What is all this to me? I have no time to waste on childish fooleries," he cries angrily, laying his hand on the latch.

Springing from her couch like a fawn, she places her back against the door, and replies: "More than you think, my lord. Hear me out! I say she interceded for me, and procured my pardon. From that moment I became her debtor for life. Now listen! Her name was Nelly Valentin! *You* ruined her. She is now in London, a starving, shame-stricken outcast. You must send her enough money to keep her from want until she dies; or—I am your enemy for life."

Her eyes are glittering and angry now, while her teeth show white through her half open lips. Wharton reddening with anger at her audacity, and, unable to control himself, strikes her on the face with the back of his hand, cutting a little gash in her cheek with his diamond ring. She involuntarily puts her hand on the cut, but takes it away instantly, opens the door, and says calmly, "Go, my lord; you and the gypsy queen are enemies." He laughs scornfully, and steps out, past the fires, through the swarthy groups, and into the darkness of the forest.

"'A God's blood," he mutters, "what a tigress! It is strange how she could have discovered my frolic with Nelly! But I must hie me home, or her ladyship will wonder at my absence on the eve of my departure." * *

It is now time to explain how it was that Lord Wharton, General Holmes and poor Margery should have both happened to be in an unfrequented part of the grounds at the same time. It was in this manner: as soon as Margery had given Maldran the message to Philip he took it to Wharton, by whom he was employed as a spy on the lovers. Wharton read it, copied the contents, and then instructed the faithless rascal to take it to its proper destination. He then sat down and wrote in a feigned hand to General Holmes, telling him that his daughter was to meet Philip in the woods at noon; he signed the letter "A Friend." He waited until nearly the time she had appointed for the rendezvous, and sent the letter to him by a disguised servant. He then took his way to Rooksnest and awaited with malignant pleasure the fiasco which he knew must ensue, and which he hoped would at one blow break up the relations between the lovers. How it turned out we know.

CHAPTER VIII.

"There's some exception, man an' woman;
But this is gentry's life in common."
THE TWA DOGS.

"My heart is sair, I dare na tell,
My heart is sair for somebody;
I could wake a winter night
For the sake of somebody."
"MY HEART IS SAIR, I DARE NA TELL."

HOLME GRANGE fronts on a clear, swift stream, which is lined on the other side with drooping water grasses and showy river-weed—Philip's Stream, Margery calls it, as with heart and eyes engrossed by the one object she sees her ideal in all things around or about her. The house is surrounded by a large garden laid out in the Elizabethan style, with sprucely cut hedges and intricate pathways whose sides are clustered with all the flowers that are in season. The "drive" from the gate to the stables is adorned with marble fountains, whose Rubenesque nymphs and Cupids pour streams of water on the gold and silver fish disporting themselves in the basin.

The old hall was built in the Tudor days, and the effect produced on the educated mind while surveying it is a feeling of true admiration and delight. The roof is of a high pitch, and it is chastely beautified with delicate tracery. Arched beams protect a row of small stone figures, which stand over the main entrance and seem the guardian angels of the house and its pertainings. The square mouldings over all the windows and doorways have the family quarterings cut on them—an arm erect, and clutching in its hand a dagger, on a field *gules*, and surrounded by the legend "Soyez Tranquylle" in old Norman letters. The long Gothic windows are minutely panelled, and reflect in parti-colors the cloud-flecked sky and the waving, rustling trees.

The General's stalwart figure can be seen, and the jingle of his spurs heard, as he walks by the side of his daughter, talking to her in a tone of parental reproof, to which she listens with downcast countenance and eyes suffused with tears that momentarily threaten to fall on the dainty pink hood which she twitches so pettishly. He speaks to her in a kindly manner: "Margery, hinny, I desire above all things your happiness, and for yours I would willingly sacrifice my own; but in this case I am determined. His lordship does not wish the match, nor do I think that, with all Philip's talents and his unusual forwardness, he would make you a true, faithful husband. I distrust your geniuses!"

Margery does not answer him, but her lip quivers, and her hands tightly clutch her trailing dress. He looks at her with pitying sympathy, and heartily regrets that Master Philip is forbidden by his father to betroth himself to his bonnie daughter, both for her sake and his own, for the alliance would be honorable and politic—especially in these times, when it is now Tory, now Whig, who make the laws and break them at their pleasure, and it is well to have a friend on both sides if possible.

While the father is occupied with his thoughts, Margery lifts her eyes to his face to see whether he really is as firm in the cruel resolve as his speech betokened; and now, as he turns to her to renew the conversation, he finds her sweet face upturned and close to his, with lips half parted, and such a pleading expression in her azure eyes that he impulsively ejaculates:

" Bless you, little one! If I could help you in this, God knows I would, natheless his lordship's insolence to me; but I am as helpless as yourself!"

Margery clasps her hands excitedly, and cries in a joyful voice, " Then you *will* let me meet him at Rooksnest sometimes?"—and stops abruptly, with a vague idea that she has said something bold and unmaidenly.

The father looks perplexed again, and answers firmly: "No, Margery. If he cannot take you for weal or woe, he shall not have you at all. Besides, darling, you are too young yet. Save us! scarcely fourteen, and wants to marry? What is the world coming to, now-a-days? It would be very wrong in you to see him alone under these circumstances; and all that I can allow you at present, is to close my eyes while forbidden letters are flying to and fro."

After this unexpected outburst, Margery is thankful for even so small a privilege; for is not a letter from him the next best thing to his own dear self?

The General, almost regretting his permission to allow her to correspond with Philip, mutters: "Even that is more than the jade ought to do under such circumstances." Margery, hearing him, her cheeks pale with apprehension, and anxious to avoid discussion on so dangerous a topic, kisses him good-bye, and runs in to be suitably attired for the rustic wedding which is to take place to-day in the village—Will Happun and Nanny Prevent being the happy couple who are to be united in the "holy bands of matrimony;" and as they are dependants of General Holmes, he and Margery have graciously promised to superintend the ceremony, and also to give the bride a handsome "tocher." She skims along the odorous path, up the high marble steps, across the veranda, through the low window opening on it, and finally bursts almost breathless into her own pretty room, her cheeks flushed and her hair dishevelled with the air and the exercise. "Nanny! Nanny! where are you?" Margery calls, and at the summons the future bride enters to dress her young mistress for the last time. She is a comely, rosy-cheeked, small-waisted lass, whose well-turned ankle and neat foot are cased in clocked silk stockings and bright red brodequins, whose heels are skilfully shod with brass so that they will click-clack properly when she walks up and down the chapel aisle, the first as a maid, the second as a wife.

" 'Sooth, Nannie, you look mighty pretty to-day," says Margery with a smile.

Nannie turns as red as her shoes, and replies with a demure air, "Please ye, Mistress Margery, that's how I want to look, for Will's sake."

Margery thinks how curious it is that she has always that thought in her own head whenever she is going to see Philip, and a confused idea of the universality of love crosses her mind.

" That is right, Nannie," Margery utters with a grave, motherly air; and the next minute she laughs outright at the wonderfully solemn accents in which she had spoken. She resumes: " Quick! or Will may have to wait for you at the chapel door, and that is unlucky, you know."

At once the girl sets deftly to work, and removes the light coif holding Margery's hair in its place. Whilst she is gently passing her hands through the silky mass, a tap is heard at the door, and she ceases her pleasant duty to inspect the intruder. It is one of the bridesmaids—soon to be a bride herself, by the way—curly-headed, merry, frolicsome Meg Busbie, the possessor of a dangerous pair of hazel eyes, dancing with fun and mischief, and of a trim little waist and swelling bosom. There are a charming demureness and an air of restrained vivacity about her at the present moment which are foreign to her; she curtsies low to Margery, and remains quiet until my lady of thirteen—say fourteen—is ready to speak to her, which will be as soon as she lets fall the golden coil she holds between her red lips.

Dear reader, as all weddings resemble one another in important particulars, and as the above differs in no wise from the general rules, with your permission I will allow your imagination to finish this otherwise abrupt chapter, and turn to Philip and his doings.

CHAPTER IX.

"*King.*—If it should prove
That thou art so inhuman—'twill not prove so—
And yet I know not—thou didst hate her deadly—"
. ALL'S WELL THAT ENDS WELL.

WHEN Philip returned to the castle, after the occurrence at Rooksnest, he had felt greatly disinclined to face his father's penetrating eye or hear his sarcastic remarks; but when they sat down at table, my lord never even mentioned the subject—ignored it entirely. He was too politic and far-seeing to hazard any more "scenes" until he saw how the project which was now in hand turned out. If it failed, then he had determined he would send Philip abroad for a year or two, to complete his education under the guidance of some Protestant Whig who could control his actions and put a check on his turbulent spirits.

My lady and Philip are at present in the blue room, so called on account of the color of its tapestry and its hangings. She sits in a high, straight-backed chair of ebony, inlaid, and fancifully worked in mosaic around the sides and on the arms. Her dark velvet dress is profusely trimmed with black lace, and her glossy hair is dressed in the foot-high mode peculiar to the time. On her right cheek are the inevitable two patches—one a crescent, the other a star.

She looks admiringly on her beautiful son, who is seated at her feet on a low foot-rest, studying over a speech which he has just finished declaiming before a large company of people who are guests of my lord's, and for which he was loudly applauded. He is boldly giving his opinion of it, and criticizes it with a rare judgment in one so young. He sneers at the falsity of this expression, the bad rhetoric of that, and condemns its style in unmeasured terms of contempt and scorn—the while his mother wonders what he will be in future when he is so talented now?

She says, in a deprecating manner, but withal a gleam of maternal pride in her eyes: "Phil, dear, you must be wrong! Why, faith! it was written and spoken by as clever a speaker as ever thrilled the Commons, and it is considered mighty fine by all who have either read it or heard it delivered except yourself!"

"Mother," he answers with kindling eyes, "under favor, I care not who liked it, or who disliked it, I still have my own opinion, and I will keep it, despite them all."

She sighs as she thinks of the dangers his quick, volatile temperament will surely lead him into if it is not governed more strictly, and she has a faint idea that she ought to reprove him; however, not caring to irritate him further, quietly says: "My son, it is now time for you to practise with Monsieur Vitesjambe; so I will bid you good-day."

Philip kisses her respectfully, and turns to leave the room, when a better impulse induces him to turn and pick up the speech which he had thrown on the floor in his previous anger. Placing it on the table beside her, he leaves the room without a word, and proceeds to the *maitre-de-danse* to be perfected in the various dances in vogue.

The courtly minuet, the lively coranto, and the javotte, as well as the proper way to enter and leave a room, the bow and the congee, Philip practises under the diligent attention of Monsieur Vitesjambe, a dried-up dapper

Frenchman, whose affected strut brings forcibly to the mind ludicrous visions of pin-wire and strained catgut. In truth even his ordinary steps are regulated with the nicety and precision of one whose whole soul is in his art—or his heels. Monsieur Vitesjambe was forced to fly from France—that is, Paris—on account of his pecuniary affairs, in which he had been swindled by treacherous friends; and he is never tired of talking and gesticulating about *La belle France et le Grand Monarque.* And his voice! Voltaire, give me a name for it! Our English "crackling" might do; but the French *pétillant* is better, and expresses better what I mean. Although openly professing Whig sentiments, he is at heart a Tory, as far at least as he is interested in English politics; and Philip owes it partly to him and partly to his own reckless spirit of opposition, that he is adverse to his father's principles, for his vivid imagination and his chivalrous sympathies were awakened by the Frenchman's tales of the royal exile, who was thrust from his throne by an ugly, phlegmatic Dutchman, who could not speak the language of the people he governed, and whose sad-colored raiment had been the ridicule of his court. Philip even carries his resentment to Anne for her continued usurpation of her brother's throne, and often says that if he ever has the power, he will once more restore their inheritance to the Stuarts.

After an hour's practising, Monsieur Vitesjambe declares the lesson to be over, and Philip pays a visit to Shem Throck to converse with him about hunting, hawking, and other outdoor sports. When he enters the lodge Shem is busily engaged in feeding a pair of gerfalcons perched on the frame beside him, for he is a master-falconer as well as gamekeeper; although the position is a comparative sinecure, for hawking is not now so fashionable as it was in the days of Queen Bess, when, if an imputation was cast on the courage of one's falcon-gentle or Barbary, it was as necessary to draw Bilboa and fight to the death for its honor as for one's own.

Shem has just come in from the stream, where he has been flying his pet falcon-gentle at the wild fowl, and in excited accents details to the admiring Philip his courageous deeds. "Kestrils and Sacers! When I cast her off aloft she reet deftly plumed her bird, an' twice remewed it from the river! Then she took her at the souse an' struck her down wi' a rousin' prod! 'Fackins! Master Philip, it were a goodly sight!" He ceases, to look admiringly at the falcon, while with half-closed eyes he points out its various beauties to his attentive listener. "Look ye, Master Philip," he exclaims; "see her wide nostrils, an' her big black e'en an' e'elids! What a roun' head an' a thick blue beak she has! An' did ye ever afore see such broad shoulders an' long wings?"

"Never," replies Philip heartily.

Shem continues: "An' the other is a beauty too, I warrant ye! She is as sma' as the tiniest o' them a'."

"She is, indeed," says Philip. "And her red plumes betray her species; she is a fine Barbary."

"She is that, Master Philip; she comes from a far-awa country, hundreds of miles away, they tell me."

"Yes, Shem, from the Levant, where I will go some day to see the long-bearded Turk mumble over his Koran, which he considers quite as good as our Bible."

"God help us!" cries Shem, with uplifted hands. "Not that I am ower righteous mysen, but it's fearful!"

Smiling at his horror, Philip begins to tease the falcons, which snap playfully at his fingers. While thus engaged, Shem casts a quick glance at him, and says carelessly: "If I be no too free, Master Philip, it seems queer to me that wi' a' your love for Mistress Margery, you don't run awa' wi' her; then ye see ye could ha' her a' to yoursen, for—"

Philip's face is ashen pale as he interrupts Shem, and says in quick, angry accents: "Stop, Shem, I know what you are going to say; but that you are too innocent to comprehend the black-hearted villainy there is in my lord's scheme, 'fore God! I would sheathe my dagger in your throat!"

Shem, speechless with surprise, stares like one bereft of his senses, as well he may. At the first outburst he instinctively placed his hand on the haft of his hunting-knife.

Philip looks at him closely for a few seconds, and proceeds in a gentler manner than before: "Good, faithful Shem, let me tell you the whole of this vile project. I'll lay bare my father's treacherous meaning. You think it is a mere joke to amuse my lord—a harmless jest. His real design is that I shall run away with Margery to London. Once there, he thinks I will certainly ruin her, and keep her as my dishonored mistress. But I tell you, Shem, that when Margery goes to London with Philip Wharton, she goes as his intended wife."

Shem shudders as he hears the details, and sees how near he has been towards compassing the destruction of his "wee Margery." "Eh! my soul! if I *had* done it!" he exclaims in thankful tones; and he watches his young master, who paces the room in a frenzy of rage. Well is it that my lord is not at home, or there would be such commotion at the old house as had not been seen since the days of the olden moss-troopers.

Philip's blood boils as he goes over in his mind the well-planned details of the cunning scheme. Shem breaks the silence by saying, "Ye are sure, Master Philip, that ye are no' wrang i' your thoughts?"

"Shem," he replies angrily, "I was told of it by an

honest, true-hearted lad who overheard every word of the conference. I will tell you his name, but you must keep it a secret; it is Brad Throck!"

"Bless the beggar!" Shem exclaims. "If I had known that the young loon was so close till us, I'd ha' put his ear out o' kelter, I warrant ye. But it's a' for the best I trow!"

"Yes, Shem, it is all for the best," Philip replies; and he looks abstractedly out of the window, while the keeper plays with his hoods and jesses.

"Good e'en to ye, Shem," Philip says so abruptly as to cause Shem to start from his seat, and he walks out and strides swiftly towards Rooksnest, with bitter, unfilial thoughts in his heart, and with a firm determination ever after to run counter to his father's wishes, and to thwart his purposes whenever he can.

6*

CHAPTER X.

"*Pierre.*—A council's held hard by,——
——There I'll lead thee.
But be a man! for thou 'rt to mix with men
Fit to disturb the peace of all the world,
And rule it when it's wildest.——"
VENICE PRESERVED.

WE are now in the room sacred to Whigs and Whiggery, mutton-pies and politics. The atmosphere is redolent of the fumes of wine and the fragrant Orinoco, whose smoke fills the lungs and calls up visions of Turkey and the colonies. The walls are almost covered with portraits of celebrated belles and toasts, nearly all of them the work of Godfrey Kneller. Around one side runs a row of walnut shelves whereon are the glasses of the previous year, on which, according to custom, the name of the lady who was the toast of that year is engraved. In the centre of the room is a large, circular table covered with wines and edibles, at which are seated a goodly company of noisy, laughing cavaliers, whose gay costumes, slashed doublets, and scented cloaks, curled wigs, and knightly orders make a brave display as they lounge about in careless, graceful attitudes.

Here an irritated politician exposes to his attentive listener the crafty schemes of the arch Tory Harley, and expatiates at length on Mistress Masham's alarming ascendency at court.

There is a group of dissolute, reckless gallants. Among them the licentious Congreve; his mouth wide open in boisterous merriment, uncovering a set of teeth which many a beau envies him; he exclaims, in a ringing, manly voice: "Egad! gentlemen, I tell you that Mistress Middleton must be our next toast, or revie me, I'll——"

"Congreve, man! stop your unearthly clatter," cries the proud Duke of Somerset. "You once said, 'Music hath charms to soothe the savage *beast;*' so I prithee, quiet, or I'll give you an air on my viol;" and making a motion as though he intended to play. Congreve exclaims, in assumed terror: "Hold! My lord, I am dumb; for truly I would rather keep my tongue between my teeth for a whole year than hear yon thing screeching its direful lays."

Opposite to Congreve are three keen-eyed, watchful cavaliers, engaged in deep discussion; they whisper in low, guarded tones, and frequently cast stealthy glances about them as if they are fearful of being overheard. And well they may be, for they debate on no less a question than the feasibility of totally overthrowing and destroying the party now governing England.

The group consists of My Lord Wharton, whose face, usually placid, is gloomy and anxious; Charles Montague, Earl of Halifax, who blows balls and rings of pungent smoke from his Indian bowl, with a grace peculiar to himself—in fact, at Will's, and among the men about town, he is considered a mighty fine smoker; lastly, and least in point of rank, is the architect and dramatist Sir John Vanbrugh, whose indecent writings and immoral doings once aroused the ire of the righteous Collier, who scourged him in such a scathing style that directly after he wrote a moral epic comedy entitled "Æsop," which, as might have been expected, was hissed off the boards of Drury Lane; he is an eccentric genius, and has passed his life, as he once averred, "in sinning and repenting." The reader will recall the couplet written on him by Dr. Evans in allusion to his heavy, solid style of architecture:—

> "Lie heavy on him, Earth, for he
> Laid many a heavy load on thee."

His face is handsome, but haggard and pallid, the consequence of his riotous, exciting life.

In answer to a question put by Vanbrugh, Wharton replies angrily: "Yes, John, it was Sarah Marlborough's waspish tongue which stung Harley and Abbie in, and ourselves out."

The country is at present in a state of great political agitation. Rancorous violence and malignant speeches are the order of the day. In no previous times did pamphlets and "broadsides" exercise such an influence as they do now. Formerly a man's sayings were confined to the few who heard him, and their influence went but a little way beyond his own immediate circle; but now, where Earl Somers, or Cowper, or Wharton, or any other able speaker enunciates a telling speech, it goes from London to Liverpool, and to all the country around, in the form of a pamphlet, which is widely distributed by zealous partisans and would-be officials, who know the effect that might be produced by a single good speech if read and appreciated.

Far back in 1707, Sarah, Duchess of Marlborough, had—unlucky woman—brought to court a poor relative, Mistress Abigail Hill, and procured for her the post of bedchamber-woman to the queen, who was so greatly pleased by her good nature and unassuming love, that she began to contrast the poor relative's engaging disposition with the vixenish, arrogant temper of her patroness—a temper the queen knew and greatly feared. In consequence, the influence of Sarah declined considerably, and despite her strenuous exertions to retain her old ascendency over "Mistress Morley," as her majesty permitted herself to be called by her, "Mistress Freeman" slid slowly but surely down the royal scale. Once rid of her, the queen determined never to give her a chance to resume her old despotism; so, from that time, Mistress Abbie Hill, or, as she soon afterwards became, Mistress Masham, gradually gained more and more power over her royal mistress, until she now stands the acknowledged favorite. Harley, who is her kinsman, influenced her mind very much, and consequently the Whigs were ousted from power, and himself and his party installed in their place.

But enough of these dry details. We will return to the worthy members of the kit-cat whom we left so unceremoniously.

Montague, who listened attentively to Wharton's remark, replies, "My lord, I agree with you. Pity 'tis; but Mistress Abbie governs her majesty, and Harley governs Mistress Abbie—a bad state of affairs for us, eh? Curse me!"

"The Laärd presarve us from the wicked Moabitess!" whines Montague, clasping his hands on his breast, and turning up the whites of his eyes.

At this, Vanbrugh laughs aloud; but Wharton exclaims impatiently: "'S 'blood, my Earl of Halifax, be serious! We discuss affairs of moment, and can spare little time for jack-pudding pranks!"

Montague's face sobers instantly, for he respects and indeed almost fears his crafty, unscrupulous friend.

Wharton mutters: "If we could but reinstate Sarah! But 'tis impossible; the shrew has ruined us for a time, at least, with her haughty airs and her arrogant capriciousness."

Vanbrugh interpolates meaningly, "Bribery!"

"Ay," adds Montague; "a few golden plaisters would better us, I warrant."

Wharton elevates his eyebrows contemptuously as he replies, "Begin with Harley!"

These three words settle all discussion on that point, and it is not mentioned again.

A loud clapping and pounding on the table draw their attention to Congreve and the gentlemen opposite. Congreve is strutting with mincing steps and affected gestures across the lower end of the room; speaking with such a laughter-provoking drawl that even Wharton smiles as he looks at him, and says aside: "The light-hearted knave!" He is ridiculing the gait and manners of the most insufferable coxcomb in London—Sir Evelyn Pierpoint—and he hits off his girlish voice and his strained gestures in a really clever manner.

"Gad!" he cries, "'Fore Gad! I was most mightily astounded that my Lady Betty did not succumb on sight; for 'pon my soul, I had exercised almost half my attractions! And stars and garters! Where I, Sir Evelyn Pierpoint, fail, let no man try—or, trying, fail ignobly, Gad!"

This wind-up sets the whole company in a roar of uncontrollable laughter—the words dropped so trippingly from his lips, and his eyes ogled them so conceitedly. The spice of truth in the caricature renders it doubly amusing, so much do we all enjoy the sight of a ridiculed neighbor, especially if the ridicule falls on those points on which we are untouchable, or so consider ourselves.

Wharton, turning to his companions, says in amused despair: "Gentlemen, it is worse than useless for us to converse on serious topics at present. Let us leave them for another time, and help to laugh at or with roistering, careless Congreve!"

Vanbrugh, nothing loath, joyfully assents; of course Montague follows his leader.

"A toast! A toast! hurrah!" Glasses clink noisily, and every hand pounds loudly on the table. Wharton rises and says: "Gentlemen, let us all drink 'Long life and prosperity to her majesty, and perdition to the warming-pan prince!'"

The toast is received with acclamations, upturned glasses, and elevated noses. Now there are sundry calls for "more lights and the card-tables," and the attentive host enters with a bow and a smirk. Christopher is short, stout, and servile; his eyes are like twin specks in a good potato—small and reddish; but there is a twinkle of humor and good-fellowship in them notwithstanding. His nose is a Liliputian carrot, with an upward tendency.

"Yes, my noble gentlemen—in a minute. Diggory! Sam! You dogs! Quick! the tables for my lords; more lights and—*did* you say more wine and punch, my lords?" He is answered affirmatively and backs out again with more bows and smirks; reappearing in a few minutes with a bowl of foaming, lemon-scented punch, followed by Sam and Diggory with sundry cases of wine and bunches of candles in their arms.

In a very short time the noise and confusion subside, and nearly all present are absorbed in the chances of the games they are playing—ombre, basset, whist, or gleek.

At one table are Halifax, Wharton, and Vanbrugh pitted against one another at gleek; and when Wharton or Halifax plays there are always interested lookers-on. Says Halifax to Wharton: "My lord, I'll vie the ruff."

Vanbrugh rejoins, "Faith, I'll see it!"

Wharton adds, "I'll see it and revie it!"

Wharton, who is a skilful, practised gamester, raises

the stakes so high that Vanbrugh says with a curse, "I'll not meddle with it longer. Poor devils like myself must not risk over three figures," and he ceases to play. Accordingly, the contest now lies between the other two.

It must be known that Halifax is a player of no mean calibre, and is not to be despised by any player, however skilful. He asks, " Two thousand—did you say my Lord ?"

Wharton replies carelessly, "Four would be more interesting."

Halifax nods his head, and they play on.

The words two thousand and four thousand at once draw the other players from their tables to watch the contest between the two whose stakes have so quickly reached such formidable proportions ; all cluster around and intently survey these veteran gamesters.

Wharton deals, and turns up the ace. "Tib!" he calls : "fifteen to my score."

Halifax smiles, and congratulates him on his good fortune.

After this, the stakes grow gradually higher until Wharton says, "My lord, if you do not object, we will raise it to fifteen thousand—sans revenge; one game either way it turns ?"

A murmur of astonishment runs around the table. The offer is a bold one, for at present Halifax stands the higher. He looks doubtful for a moment, but finally says, in an indifferent, half-attentive manner, " An' you wish it, my lord ?" His eyes, however, betray the tumult in his heart ; and when his cards are given him, the intensity of his gaze is almost frightful.

Vanbrugh says with a laugh to Congreve: " It was well I retreated. Faith ! Where would I have been now ? eh ?"

His words are interrupted by Halifax, who slowly rises, and asks him in a tranquil manner for the pen which is on the escritoire: he gives it to Halifax, who scribbles an order in favor of Lord Wharton for fifteen thousand guineas!

CHAPTER XI.

> "I think on thee in the night
>   When all beside is still
> And the moon comes out, with her pale, sad light,
>   To sit on the lonely hill!
> When the stars are all like dreams,
>   And the breezes all like sighs,
> And there comes a voice from the far-off streams,
>   Like thy spirit's low replies!"
>
> T. K. HERVEY.

THE two large rooms in the Wharton mansion that are kept for special or state occasions are now filled with a large number of patrician dames and cavaliers, all apparelled in their brightest. White and pink tapers, perfumed with delicate scents, dispense a mellow, moonlike lustre, which adds greatly to the beauty of the guests; while low strains of music float about and die away through the open windows.

Many couples stroll slowly from end to end and back again—flirting, laughing, or feigning love for amusement. Others, older or more sedate, sit about in groups and talk of her majesty's illness, the last pattern in bonelace, the state of politics in France, the best cure for the vapors, or Mademoiselle Scudery's last divine romance, which fills only two folio volumes!

Fans are in great request—less, we opine, on account of the heat, than for the purpose of tapping attendant beaux coldly, lovingly, or reprovingly; a science cultivated with great assiduity by all who set themselves up for belles.

Let us listen to the conversation carried on by the couple who walk by us. To judge by their serious countenances and grave demeanor, it is of great import.

"Most true, Mistress Robsarte; the corranto is in the main superior to the Javotte; in that I agree with you entirely; but as to the minor question of the three tips and a half turn with the left foot, in preference to the four glissades, I would disagree with you had I but the boldness."

Whereupon they are more solemn than ever, and walk consequentially past, out of earshot.

Again, a couple of cavaliers come toward us, quietly laughing and twirling the waxed ends of their moustaches, which, by the way, are cut in the Italian fashion. Says the older of them: "Tut! my lord, it had been better if I had touched his heart at the first passado, instead of shilly-shallying with him for fifteen minutes, and then sending him to a parson and six feet of earth, with the conceit in his mind that he was a good swordsman."

So goes the world. Subjects that are not worth the breath we spend on them, or the ink that we waste in writing about them, are talked of and written about with a solemnity and seeming profundity worthy of the solution of the Sphynx; while such light trifles as life and death are laughed at, and handled with a smile and a jest.

Philip, standing by the lattice window which looks out on the garden, gazes abstractedly on the assemblage, while his thoughts are far away, as his motionless countenance and his vacant eyes evince. He ponders drearily over his love, and wonders whether he will ever be permitted to enjoy it without a drawback. Anon thoughts of *her* devotion surge up in his heart, and he grows angry with himself for allowing ideas so saddening to take possession of his mind.

Lady Wharton, who is performing her hospitable duties, and receiving the guests with her usual high-bred courtesy, now and then casts a glance at Philip and seems irritated at his taciturnity and retirement, for she has prepared this party especially for his enjoyment, and to show to the guests how well her Philip can dance, sing, and speak. In these accomplishments he is far beyond his years, and is a match in the lists of love for any London courtier, much more for the beaux of Buck's, who, though refined and well-bred, lack Philip's power of phrase turning and his audacity; they do not possess his quickness of repartee and his comprehensive observation which tell him at a glance how to comport himself in matters that require delicacy or boldness, denial, equivocation, or agreement. In such arts he can be perfect when he chooses; but his innate recklessness, his love of praise, and his rollicking dare deviltry often lead him and others into situations embarrassing to the last degree. Fortunately for himself, however, in such cases, he generally manages to come off scot-free—leaving his companions to flounder about in the slough of mistakes, exposed to the scornful glance of an offended beauty, whilst he basks in her kindest smiles.

The last guest has received my lady's congratulations, and she crosses over to Philip, who starts impatiently and ejaculates in a decidedly unpleasant manner, "Well?"

To this monosyllabic interrogation she replies: "Philip dear, do get rid of your gloominess; it only keeps you from enjoying yourself; while your mother cannot be happy while her son mopes in a corner like an owl in a barn; it is not like his usual behavior."

"Mother," he replies, "I am sick of this riotous gayety and confusion. I would rather be alone. I do not feel fit for company to-night;" half turning his back to her he looks moodily out of the window, as though to put an end to the conversation.

"Lovesick!" she murmurs with a knowing smile, and bethinks her of a plan to rouse him a little—a plan which, with her knowledge of his weak point, is sure to succeed. She says, as if speaking to herself, "Aha! I see my lord of Dale monopolizes the fair glances of Mistress Hawthorndon, and, faith, she seems greatly taken with him!"

Philip turns his head towards the couple apostrophized: my lady notices the movement, and returns satisfied to her seat, confident that her words have piqued his vanity, for it is well known that he once laid a wager that he could rival this same Lord Dale in Mistress Hawthorndon's affections whenever he chose, and, although she knows of this same insolent wager as well as any one else, his speech is so insinuating and honeyed that she is powerless to repulse him, and sometimes hopes the wager may result in his really loving her, and terminate in an alliance into which she would be only too happy to enter, although he is two years younger than herself.

Philip arranges his curls and settles his cuffs; smooths his cravat, pushes his rapier into a more elegant position, and walks slowly towards Lord Dale and his partner. He addresses her in an euphuistic strain, and bestows a cold nod on her cavalier: "Fair Mistress Alice," he says, with a truly refreshing impudence, "I now claim the promise you gave me a se'nnight ago!" Extending his arm, which she takes with a slight hesitation, and at the same time bowing to Lord Dale, he coolly remarks, "My lord, Mistress Hawthorndon can now dispense with your company, as I claim an engagement with her which is doubtless prior to any that you may have!" The deserted beau leaves her with ill-concealed chagrin, and casts a spiteful look at his rival. Philip is not in the least discomposed, but gracefully leads Mistress Alice to the upper end of the room, where he strengthens the influence which he boasts that he is able to exercise over any woman with a heart capable of the tender passion.

My lady observes the success of her ruse, and after a time calls Philip to her, and gives him some directions in regard to the music. Returning to Mistress Alice, he excuses himself on the score of business, and leaves the room to attend to his mother's commands.

Mistress Alice is very pretty, vivacious, and sprightly. Her hair is cut short in front, and dances in tiny ringlets almost to her eyes, which fashion, together with her uncovered bosom and arms, gives her the appearance of one of those beauties of Lely, who might have exchanged small talk and scandal with his majesty of blessed memory.

* * * * * * * * *

Philip walks slowly along by the spiny, scarlet-flowered hawthorn hedges, and lets thoughts of Margery wander through his brain, dreaming of happiness as he swears to himself that she shall yet be his wife, spite of all obstacles; but his "chateaux en Espagne" are suddenly shivered to fragments by a stealthy noise as of some one treading softly behind him. Drawing his rapier, he turns quickly on his heel, and lo! the figure of a tall brawny man confronts him!

"In Satan's name! who are you, that you follow me so closely? Answer me at once, fellow! or I'll give you a taste of cold steel in your stomach!" cries Philip, angrily.

"Master Philip," replies the rough, harsh voice of the gypsy Maldran, "I was but goin' to the camp."

"Oh! it's you, Maldran, is it? I have wanted to see

you for some time! I have a question or two for you to answer ere we part;" he still keeps his rapier drawn and pointed threateningly at Maldran's neck, while his brow lowers and his voice is ominous.

"Yes, Master Philip," he replies.

"Fellow! Mistress Holmes some time ago gave you a letter to carry to me! This letter you first carried to my father! Answer me at once, and truly—did you not?"

He answers sullenly: "I did, for his gowd were too strong for a poor gypsy to resist, and—"

"Enough!" interrupts Philip; "get out of my sight while you are alive, and never again cross my path, or you and your whole treacherous tribe shall be cudgelled off the grounds;" and he stamps his foot in suppressed rage.

Maldran, muttering something between his teeth, strikes off at a quick pace in the direction of his camp.

Philip continues his walk, and, consciously or otherwise, he approaches Holme Grange. Where the heart lieth, do the feet turn. "Why should Maldran happen to be so close to the mansion at this hour of the night? and why should he have been so close to me?"—are questions that arise as he treads on the soft gorse and kicks the fallen leaves and boughs about with vicious energy. Vague suspicions that the gypsy is employed by his father to watch his actions flit through his mind; but he can scarcely think such baseness possible. Anon thoughts of London, and its sights and fascinations enwrap him, and his heart beats high as he foresees how he will some day astonish even London's *blasé* cavaliers with the beauty of his Margery, and force the sickly court beauties to envy her for her rosy cheeks and her pure complexion! Anon the bare possibility of some one taking her away from him chills his blood and makes him uneasy and restless. But in a short time he smiles confidently as he recalls her undisguised love for him, and exclaims, "Bah! Philip Wharton can hold his own in anything; from a stramazorm or a stoccata—" and he fingers his rapier significantly—"to a fight for a woman's love!"

He has gradually approached so close to the Grange that he can see into the large hall where the General often sits in the evenings; and a hungry, wistful look lights his eyes as he perceives Margery sitting alone in the low balcony scarce a score feet away from him! A single taper lights up the hall, for it is late, and everybody has retired save Margery. Her face is turned away from the light, and she seems to scrutinize the very spot where her lover lies concealed. She looks aweary and troubled, and her chin rests in her little hand, while her lips are pressed closely together. Once in a while a smile flickers on her lips and dies away in the sad depths of her eyes. Philip can no longer restrain himself, he advances boldly towards her; but she does not see him until he is almost close enough to touch her; when, with a low cry, telling of her intense relief and enjoyment, she flies into his arms and has to indulge in a few womanly sobs before she can control herself enough to say, "Philip, darling! I wanted to see you so much to-night; it seems as if God has heard my prayer, and you have come;" and she lifts her lips to him with a wild look in her eyes. He caresses her tenderly, and eagerly, asks, "Why, Margery, sweet! why are you so agitated?"

She does not answer him, but her renewed sobs almost madden him. Again he demands, "Tell me quickly, sweetheart; what ails you that you are so sad this evening? There is some trouble, I fear!"

Scarcely able to articulate, she cries: "Philip, they are going to send me away from you!"

"Who are going to send you away from me?" he cries in thick, hoarse accents, and holds her closer the while.

"Father!" is all she can answer.

"Furies!" he mutters; "what shall we do?"

She replies, in a broken voice: "Let us fly together, Philip; let us leave this place! I will give up all for you! Do with me as you will!"

He is perplexed and troubled beyond measure until a ray of hope breaks in on him, and he says, "Tell me, darling, when is the time fixed for your departure.".

"I know not; my father but told me that ere long he would send me to Italy; but whether he means to-morrow or a year hence, I know not; for my heart nigh burst at the news; and I could not trust myself to question him!"

Her words reassure him, and he replies cheerily: "Let your tears wait awhile, then, lassie; we must not meet trouble half-way; and, darling, cease your violent grief; you will certainly do yourself some harm! 'All's well that ends well,' and the end may yet be as we wish."

She smiles at him through her tears, and feels, now that he is with her, that all *must* be right; and she sits chatting in his arms a long, long while before they can leave each other to get the night's rest which is necessary even for lovers.

CHAPTER XII.

> "A wanton chaos in my breast raged high,
> A wanton transport darted in mine eye;
> False pleasure urged, and every eager care,
> That swell the soul to guilt and to despair."
> CRABBE'S "MIRA."

WE turn to events a year later than those recorded in our last chapter, merely intimating that Margery's fears of a separation from her lover were justified only too soon, for the day after her meeting with him her father sent her post to London, thence to set out for Italy. Leaving Philip in great dismay and grief, she, poor girl! felt bad enough; but she had no other resource than to obey, as she was closely watched by her father, who feared that she might do something foolish and ill-advised if she was not looked after with a careful eye.

Everything after that went on as usual at the castle. Philip employed his time as best he could in hard study, in hunting, hawking, flirting with Mistress Hawthorndon, and in other amusements, but longed continually for the return of his lost love.

Margery has returned from her travels as beautiful as ever, and just a trifle more womanly and polished by her sojourn in the sunny south.

Suppose we go to the old trysting-place and see whether we can find any traces of her or her gladdened lover. Listen! We can hear a manly voice exclaiming, in low, murmuring tones, "Margery, sweet! long, weary, weary months have dragged along since you and I last met here—! Has time altered you from my true heart of olden times? If it has—never mind telling me so—but a curse on time and on him who took you from me!"

As he finishes, his voice is irregular and broken. Her answer is surely enough to reassure the most uxorious lover.

"Philip, my own, time and life are nothing to me, save when you are with me!"

There is a long silence after this, until he says, in a serious, determined manner: "Margery, we must part no more! Come with me to London, where we will be united beyond fear of separation except by death."

She grows pale as she listens to a proposal of so decided a nature, and whispers, "Your father—and mine."

"A god's will!" he exclaims, fiercely. "Let them do as they wist, if you come. But I see; you are like all the rest—a short absence, and all is forgotten! Once you would have gone with me to the end of the world; now, London is too far!" He speaks in a bitter, reproachful manner, which cuts her like a knife.

She answers him in two words only: "Oh, Philip!" but in them he reads her consent, and proceeds in excited, happy eagerness: "To-morrow then, darling, we will go! Meet me here at nightfall; we can reach London in a few hours, and—leave the rest to me; I will manage everything rightly!"

Tears fill her eyes as she kisses him good-night with a fervor telling him how truly she is all his own to do with as he wishes.

After a night of feverish spells of broken sleep, Philip wanders uneasily about the house and through the garden and stable, and finally saddling "Careless," rides swiftly through the avenue of old Elms, passes Rooks-nest, and surveys with a fond regret all the many spots endeared to his memory. However, a few hours' hard riding soon restores his spirits, and makes him feel that he is ready to do and dare all to call Margery his wife.

He has packed up over night all that he will need in the shape of clothing, arms, money, and a hundred other little things of more or less importance; and he has also written an explanation of his conduct to his father, in which he tells him that General Holmes is entirely ignorant of the whole proceeding.

To Philip's great joy, the day begins to draw to its close; never has day seemed so long to him as this; it wants now but an hour of the time appointed for the meeting. He can wait no longer; striding to the stable, where he has the two swiftest horses in the stud, ready saddled and bridled, he quietly leads them to the door. Here he hesitates a minute ere he springs into the saddle, and looks towards his mother's room. "God bless you, mother!" he mutters, in a trembling voice, and he is off like a shot down towards Rooksnest.

Margery awaits him, with hood and wimple on, tearful but hopeful; and he kisses her with many and many a passionate embrace ere she is mounted on her pillion.

Away they fly through the forest gloaming, swiftly and noiselessly, for their horses' hoofs fall so soft on the springy sod, that naught is heard but the jingle of Philip's spurs and his rapier clinking against the stirrup. They arrive safely in London without let or hindrance, and a new world is open to their young minds.

Philip is cognizant of the fact that they are both too young to hope to be married in the orthodox manner; he knows, however, that there are clerical prisoners living within the Rules of the Fleet who are poor, unscrupulous, and characterless, whose marriages are nevertheless held true and valid in the eye of the law. There he determines to go with a pocketful of guineas to stop inconvenient mouths which might impertinently question them relative to their ages or their names.

They take lodgings at the Blue Bell, where the bustling landlady soon has a warm supper ready for them, which neither feels overmuch inclined to eat; they are both nervous and excited, and Margery is so dazed and bewildered that she can scarcely speak.

As soon as the meal is finished, Philip says to the landlady, in an assumed careless manner, "I pray you, Dame! how may we get to the Fleet without much loss of time. They say it is very amusing to strangers to see the sights about there." He is too new to London life to know that such a question is enough to turn all eyes on him and his companion; fortunately, however, there is no one near enough to hear him, beside the landlady, except, indeed, the bar-maid, who, quickly looking up, grins significantly at the unsuspecting couple.

"Truss me! I were sure ye were baith frae the coöntry," cries the landlady in a loud voice.

Philip replies, with a haughty stare which causes her broad face to flush, "S'blood, jade! attend to your kitchening, and meddle not with the affairs of your betters! Either answer my question, or begone and send some one who can!"

The landlady curtsies deprecatingly, and answers humbly, "My lord, ya mun tak a chair to get there; I'll ca' Pat and Dermont, who can carry ye there, as quick as e'er a horse that rins." And she leaves the room to execute her mission, while Philip, though anxious and troubled himself, consoles his future wife with endearing and hopeful conversation.

When the chair comes, Philip calls the carriers aside, and tells them of his design, whereat they wink, stick their tongues in their cheeks, and generally show him that they know all about such delicate matters; and they shoulder their burdens, and trot at a long, swinging pace towards their destination. Turning, as they near the confines of the Fleet, Dermont asks Philip whether he prefers any particular parson to splice them. Philip replying in the negative, leaves the choice with the carrier, wherefore he replies, " 'Troth! thin we'll take ye till the Horseshoe and Magpie! Sam Turenall is as good a clark as any, and Dick Wildair is a roarin' parson." Philip agrees, and in a few minutes they come to a halt, the door is opened, and the carriers obsequiously help them out.

Philip and Margery hesitatingly enter the bar-room, the usual place for Fleet marriages, and are huskily welcomed by a fat, frowsy, blear-eyed imitation of Silenus, who, by instinct, knowing what they want, wheezes out, "Wildair! ye're wanted here." The door of the public bar opens, and the parson enters. He is a good specimen of a licentious dissipated clergyman of this quarter; he holds a greasy, dog's-eared prayer-book in his hands, and affects a devout look, but the effort is a sad failure.

Philip smiles as he compares him with the venerable pastor at home; and Margery, in spite of her fears, is amused at his appearance.

Without entering into minute particulars of the marriage formula, which was mumbled and slurred over as soon as possible, let it suffice to say they are now man and wife.

A rather laughable incident occurred at the close of the ceremony, which is worth mentioning. The parson, in accordance with his custom, was about to imprint a chaste kiss on Margery's blushing cheek, when Philip interposed his hand to shield her from the profanation, and received the smack of a pair of swollen, unctuous lips on it—a diversion which caused the holy man to redden a trifle, while the host and the carriers roared delightedly at his discomfiture. Philip said nothing, however, but gave him a liberal douceur, out of which the carriers received a shilling; he then led his wife to the chair, and directed the carriers to return to the Blue Bell.

CHAPTER XIII.

> "Jubilate! I am loved;
> Now am I like a little queen,
> And very pleasant 'tis, I ween;
> Whatsoe'er I do or say
> Seemeth right and good alway."
> ELIZ. YOWATT.

> "O Nature! we a' maun yield to thee."
> JAMES HOGG.

ONCE more they are alone in the cheery little room allotted to them. Margery is full of vague terrors and doubts which she scarcely knows how to define, and says distractedly, "Philip, do you—oh! what will father think of me? What will he do? It will break his heart! I have been so cruel to him!"

Philip consoles her, and replies manfully, "Cheer up, wifie! All will be well in time, be sure; and ere long our fathers will be better friends than ever. There is no real cause for trouble. We will remain here awhile, and then return home. I know that all will be right, and then we will all live together and be as happy as the day is long!"

Margery smiles at the happy picture he has drawn, while her woman's prescience tells her that the odds are against them, and she shudders as Lord Wharton's cruel face passes before her mind's eye, and she involuntarily recalls dark stories of his crafty determination, and his utter lack of principle, which had reached her even in the seclusion of Holme Grange; and she fears that his power may wrest Philip from her again. Her own father, she knows, will gladly welcome her home even after such a flagrant disobedience of his orders as she has been guilty of in running away with Philip. The artful beauty, conscious of her power over him, knows that the old warrior cannot withstand the tears and entreaties of his only daughter.

Philip's thoughts are of the most mixed and startling character; will his father pursue him? or mayhap disown him? But that, he proudly thinks, cannot harm him: for are there not in this great city fifty things at which he can make, at least enough to keep them both from starving? "Separate us!" he cries; "Pah! I feel myself a giant when Margery is the stake to be fought for! God forfend I should ever draw steel on my father; but—" And he coughs ominously, and says, in a bold, confident tone, "Well, Margery, we will not fret about it. If needs must, we can live by our own exertions!"

"What can we do?" she asks, with a demure glance at him, as if she knows that the question will pose him. He looks perplexed, for a moment, and laughs good-humoredly as he declines to answer the question; and he closes her mouth by a process commendable in such cases, in which process, by the way, she assists him right deftly.

The next day Philip proposes a walk to view the wonders of the metropolis, to which she of course assents, and they are now gazing with eager eyes at the strange sights presented to their view. Immersed as he has been in the seclusion of the country, Philip has never thought that he should see so vast a number of houses, or mix in such a beehive of busy pedestrians, who jostle and swarm about in countless multitudes.

They peep into the china-stores and bric-a-brac shops, and mutually smile at the grotesque josses and uncouth images; and Philip, who has read about such things before, imparts information concerning them to his young wife. She listens admiringly to him, and wonders at his vast and varied knowledge. But I am sorry to state that, on several occasions, when she requests an explanation of something which he knows no more about than she, he draws largely on his imagination, his pride not allowing him to betray his ignorance.

He buys numerous trinkets for her; in most cases paying far more for them than they are worth, owing to his ignorance of their value, and the adroitness of the sellers, who notice his rusticity, and cheat him accordingly. Once or twice his natural shrewdness tells him that such is the case, but he disdains to bandy words with a tradesman, and so pays all demands with the air of a czar with all the Indies at his nod and beck.

Now they come to Temple Bar, with its sooty, blackened gateway of Portland stone. Margery shivers in affright as Philip calls her attention to the traitors' skulls whitening on the poles above the arch; and he tells her about the vast processions which have passed through these muddy gates, and how the doors have been barred against the King until the herald sounded a parley, to all of which she listens with intense interest, meanwhile counting the many lumbering carriages that rumble noisily by; she had never before seen so many together.

Whilst they have been admiring Temple Bar and its adjuncts, they have not noticed the gradual approach of a swaggering cut-purse, dressed in a suit of faded tawdriness who now suddenly clutches at the little package which Margery holds, and makes off with it at great speed. Philip starts to pursue him, but Margery prevents him, and beseeches him not to leave her alone. "She can better spare the trinkets than lose him." A few who have seen the occurrence, gather about them, and officiously advise Philip to go to the nearest magistrate, describe the rascal and offer a reward for his detection; declining their advice, however, he tries to walk away unperceived, as he is not desirous of attracting too much attention, for Margery's sake, who begins to be frightened at the crowd which is gathering and thickening. Various remarks pass around, and a few persons begin to praise Margery's beauty and her freshness, for a face so pure and innocent as hers is seldom seen in jaded London. A gang of mischievous Arabs and pseudo-beggars begin scrambling and pushing about in all directions, in order to excite the testy, and thereby create a fight, which is always looked upon by them as a treat of the highest order.

Two gallants, ruffled and dressed to the tip of the mode, and scented with pulvilio and honey-sweet, brush rather nearer to Margery than Philip thinks consistent with good manners, particularly as they severally favor her with a long stare, that makes her shrink closer to him; so, placing himself quickly in front of her, he catches the foremost dandy by the nose, tweaking him so fiercely as to cause him to scream with pain, at which the crowd roar and yell with a deafening noise, and cries of, "A fight! a fight! form a ring—fair play!" are heard on all sides.

Margery swoons in affright, and Philip supports her, while he cries, in a voice trembling with rage: "What now, Sir Malapert? Out of my road, or I'll run you through, and spoil a hangman's carcass!" He draws his rapier as quickly as he can under the circumstances; the tweaked cavalier does the same, and their blades meet with a harsh, rasping sound. Philip is so excited and desperate that he does not care for consequences, and determines to essay his father's famous passado in carte, a sure and fatal lunge; when cries of "The watch! the watch!!" burst from several bystanders; his opponent, sheathing his rapier at once, mingles with the crowd, and is soon safe from detection. Philip, however, less conversant with city life and its stratagems and usages, still holds his blade on the offensive. In a minute a hand is roughly laid on his arm, and he is told in a gruff voice to "sheathe his slit-bully, and take up his march to the round-house!" Seeing the futility of resistance, he puts up his rapier, and points to Margery, who lies senseless in his arms. The watchman looks at her a moment, and mutters, in a low voice, "A pest on the trull! We mun carry her, I doubt na!" Philip, who has heard part of his speech, replies sternly, "What say you, fellow, touching my wife?" The man's manner changes as he replies, "Ah! my lord, that alters matters. Zounds! I don't know what to do wi' her;" and he pulls his chin in perplexity. "I think I can help you to a solution of the difficulty," Philip says significantly, and he wisely drops a sovereign into the custodian's dirty, knotty hand. The effect is instantaneous, and the former grim official is now a truckling servant, who, at Philip's suggestion, yells vociferously for a chair, into which he helps him to seat Margery, who is scarcely restored from her swoon; Philip springs in after her, and once more they return to the Blue Bell without any serious mishap, Philip fuming at his ill-luck in getting into a brawl so early in his London life, and Margery still hysterical, and requiring a deal of consolation and many caresses before she fully recovers from her fright.

Philip, whose appetite is now sharpset, orders the landlady to prepare them a dinner, which in due time is set on the table, with all the ceremony of which the one waitress is mistress, for it is not every day that the Blue

Bell has customers who pay so liberally and profusely as does Philip. Veal pies, baked larks, and mutton pottage fill the little table, and send an appetizing odor about the room, and even Margery, who cannot live on cupid's fare altogether, deigns to test the delicacy of a lark's breast, and "just a wee crumb of veal-pie," at Philip's urgent solicitation.

9

CHAPTER XIV.

> So judged the acrid and the austere,
>   And they whose evil heart
> Incline them in whate'er betides,
>   To take the evil part.
>
> But others, whom a kindlier frame,
>   To better thoughts inclined,
> Preserved, amid their wonderment,
>   An equitable mind.
>
> ALL FOR LOVE.

THE flight has been discovered at both Castle Wharton and Holme Grange, and all is confusion and dismay Lady Wharton has despatched a messenger with an explanatory note to Lord Wharton, in which she beseeches him to come home immediately; while she scarcely knows what she intends to say or do when he shall arrive, knowing how fearful will be his passion at the turn affairs have taken.

General Holmes is wonderstruck at his daughter's wilfulness, and vows that she must have acquired a pretty spirit of independence during her tour abroad, to prompt her to leave him and fly to London with her lover. He regrets the step she has taken, but is somewhat comforted by a confident feeling that when she does return it will be as Philip Wharton's wife. Nevertheless, he has written to his lawyer in London, directing him to search for the runaways, and send him intelligence of their doings.

When her ladyship fully realized the news, a chill struck to her heart; and she was put to bed, burning in a high fever, produced by thoughts of the meeting which she knew must come, ere long, between father and son, and which she intensely dreaded. Then recollections of her husband's baffled schemes, and her son's fiery, reckless temper, boiled through her throbbing head, and she groaned at the future trouble whose dark wings even now cast a shadow over the house.

The servants and dependants, congregating in knots in the chambers, the scullery, and the stables, whisper of my lady's illness and Master Philip's behavior, and all concur in the opinion that there never was a better matched couple in the world than Master Philip and Mistress Margery. Shem, who abstractedly plumes the ger-falcon on his wrist, says to Peggy, the housemaid: "Aweel! I allus thought it 'ud end i' this way; forbye they were never easy like except in ane anither's company; an love laughs at bolts or bars, ye ken. I remember when I was younger by twenty years than I am now—afore Debbie war my wife—that old grandame Nestbin said to me wi' a shake o' her skinny finger, 'No! Shem Throck, ye canna hae her; sho'os a deal too good for ye or the likes of ye!' Ah! ha! the varra next neet Debbie an' me were spliced by t' ould parson, an' I gave him a shillin' for his trouble. Ay! ay! Love laughs at bolts!" And Shem shakes his head sagely as he delivers himself of this profound and original thought.

"Body's alive!" replies Peggy, "thou'rt no' comparin' thy sen wi' the young master?"

He answers her with a withering look, and words that must cut her, to judge from her expression, as he retorts, "Mistress Peggy, it 'ud beseem ye better to bide a wee bit an' get the experience o' one older—but mebbe *not so much* as yersen," which diplomatic allusion to her advanced age for single-blessedness, effectually silences her, and she walks sulkily back to her task of scouring stew-pans and kettles.

"Hood me, wench," laughs Shem, as he notices her discomfiture, "I but fooled wi' ye! Sure ye'll no' get mad wi' me for a bit o' nonsense?" This apology appears to mollify her, for she mixes again in the general talk of the kitchen.

Brad, who stands near the crockery-laden sideboard, close to Mistress Debbie, boldly volunteers, "I think Master Philip did no mair than reet in rinning awa', an' well I like his darin'!"

"Hold thy tongue, saucebox," roars Shem, astounded at his son being so audacious as to give such a free vent to his opinions, even when he agreed with him; he proceeds, "Hae mair respect for the hand that feeds us a', an' keep yersel to yersel! Mayhap ye'll try the same thing yersel, some day?"

This produces a titter through the kitchen, which causes Brad's red cheeks to assume a decidedly scarlet color, as he replies, rather doggedly, "I might do worse nor rin awa' wi' pretty Meg Busbie! I think so, at any rate," and with this parting shot the incensed Brad leaves the room in disgust.

The stable boy, a bow-legged, pimply-faced, red-haired lad, standing outside on the lawn, stares with lacklustre eyes on the "company" within, and drawls out in puling, heavy accents the news that "My löard's two best horses be gone, Careless an' Queeän Anne! wi' their bridles, saddles, and a'. What's more, my la'as best pillion be gone, an' I'm afeared to tell her la'aship o' it!"

"Out on ye," cries Debbie; "what cares my lady about a pillion or sac? Master Philip is mair i' her mind now than a' the dirty pillions i' the stables!"

This scornful rejoinder raises his wrath, and he replies, with an injured stutter, "Mistress Debbie, oi can tell ye that a guid horse an' pillion is often better nor the woman that rides her, wha's naught to recommend her but a red face an' a clackin' tongue! Now, then!"

Her reply is imperious: "Hold thy tongue, gallows-bird! An' recollect ye are near the kitchen, now, an' not in filthy stables an' among muck an' straw! So hold thy tongue!" And she turns her back to him to end the discussion.

Shem, walking to the door, starts towards the Lodge. Let us precede him, and once more peep into its mysteries of hunting gear and sportsman's implements. Brad is sitting on the floor; his head rests against the wall, and he is absorbed in a brown study, which is interrupted by the entrance of his father, who, slowly walking to his accustomed seat, says to Brad, who is now looking out of the window: "Brad, did ye knaw aught about the rinning awa' afore it happened?" And he looks searchingly at him as he asks the question. His reply is clear and distinct, and has truth's clear ring sounding in its every syllable, "No, father! I did not, on my honor!"

Shem is satisfied, and he resumes, "Rebeck me! but I never thought Master Philip was in earnest when he tould me ance in this varra room that if Mistress Margery did go to Lunnon wi' him, she suld go as his woife! He has kept his word, an' the worst I fear now is that my lord may find him out and stop him ere he can be married there. It 'ud be a sair thing for wee Mistress Margery to go to Lunnon a maid, an' come back wi'out bein' a wife! Master Philip is reckless, an' he is a Wharton!"

Brad says nothing, but whistles "Lillibullero" at the window, and inhales deep, strong breaths of the breeze which has to pass over Meg Busbie's house before it reaches the Lodge, by which time it gains a certain fragrance perceptible only to himself. Suddenly he starts and strides out of the door in such a hurry that wary Shem determines to have a look at his proceedings. He peeps out of the window, and, as he expected, sees Meg's pretty face over the hawthorn hedges, and catches a glimpse of her neat cap and fluttering ribbons as they dance and wave in the breeze.

Brad walks quickly towards her and exclaims: "Oho! Meg, I was sure you were coming this way, for as I looked out of the window scarce a minute ago, I saw two butterflies sailin' companywise, an' I knew it was a lucky sign!"

She replies, in a coquettish manner, "Brad, you told me that once afore! Are ye sure that ye are not telling a wee bit o' a lee? for I never see two pretty-wings a mating when ye come to see me!"

He replies, "Well, Meg, we'll no' discuss the question, as my lord says; but what errand have ye to the castle?"

"None for ye, be sure," she replies; "I have some lace ruffles for Master Philip."

"Master Philip?" he cries. "Don't ye knaw that he has rin awa' to Lunnon wi' Mistress Holmes?"

Meg is so taken aback that, as she afterwards declared, "she was that startled that if Brad had nae pit his arm aroun' her waist, she must hae fallen!" Brad is fully equal to the emergency, in fact seems to enjoy the whole proceeding. Now Meg is in her glory— "such a bold thing to do! So romantic," and plies him with question after question until she knows as much as himself, and with woman's shrewdness, surmises more.

Thus stand affairs in Bucks.

CHAPTER XV.

"Just when we think we've found the golden mean—
The diamond point, on which to balance fair
Life and life's lofty issues—weighing there,
With fractional precision, close and keen,
Thought, motive, word and deed—there comes between
Some temper's fret, some mood's unwise despair,
To mar the equilibrium, unforeseen,
And spoil our nice adjustment!"
M. J. PRESTON, "EQUIPOISE."

ENGLAND'S last Stuart is no more—hurried to her grave by the cabals and intrigues of two virulent, selfish, parties, each struggling for the supremacy. She died at a most auspicious time for the partisans of the Hanoverian dynasty and the Protestant succession, for, during the last year of her life, her feelings had become strongly enlisted in favor of her brother, the Chevalier, which sympathy had been taken advantage of by the intriguing Jacobites in order to secure to him the accession when she was dead. But, as I said before, her decease at a time when Bolingbroke's plans were immature, frustrated all attempts in that direction, and at once transferred the balance to the Whigs; and Harley, Bolingbroke, and Mistress Abbie were forced into semi-obscurity, with the odium of the termination of the French war and the treaty of Utrecht hanging over them like a pall, while the dominant party were praised to the skies for their diplomacy in accomplishing a work which had baffled and worried the ablest statesmen of the three preceding reigns—namely, the union of England and Scotland.

The Augustan Age, with its hosts of able writers, its pure, humorous "Spectator," and its many literary luminaries, is no more. The first Hanoverian has brought his gross tastes, his dull brutality, and his fat, ugly, mistresses to Saint James, besides having an eye to his boon companions and advisers, who look on England as a land to be despoiled for their especial benefit. I almost forgot to mention that he has a wife, who came with the rest of the court—the unfortunate Sophia Dorothea. The family quarrels and dissensions of the royal family are too notorious to deserve more than a passing notice. The ministry is composed of Halifax, Cowper, Stanhope, Sunderland, and other eminent Whigs, Robert Walpole, who primarily filled a low position, is now more fully appreciated, and has attained the high eminence of First Lord of the Treasury. Such are the men who hold office under the degraded Othello who imprisoned Philip von Königsmark in the Castle of Ahlden for thirty-two years, for a suspected intrigue with his truly beloved Sophia.

Lord Wharton, jubilant at the unexpected good fortune that has befallen his party, can scarcely contain himself for joy. He is now Marquis of Wharton and Lord Privy Seal in the ministry, where his unequalled parliamentary tactics secure him respect and admiration. One blight, however, sobers his happiness—the thorn of the rose; it is the news of Philip's elopement with Margery, who, he fears, is by this time his daughter-in-law, for the news has only reached him to-day—the second after the occurrence. Philip's action is a great blow to him, and his heart aches and his head grows hot, as he reviews the advantages that might have been secured to his family through Philip's alliance with the powerful house which he had selected for that honor. Alas, it is now too late!

He knows that Philip will reveal himself ere long, either in London or in Buck's, and then he determines to send him out of his sight, on the continent, where, with a due consideration of his volatile, capricious temperament, he can be made as polished a scholar and as staunch a Whig as circumstances will permit.

It is in the Kitcat room that Lord Wharton muses thus over the unfilial conduct of his recreant son, and thoughts of him fill his mind with chagrin and sorrow. His dreams of Philip's future greatness and his hopes that he would one day be the respected head of *the* party of which he is a mainstay, are now vanishing. The door opens and Vanbrugh strolls in, humming "Marlborough s 'en va en Guerre" with a jaunty air. Noticing his despondent attitude, and his obliviousness of the presence of his friend, Vanbrugh taps him on the shoulder. Wharton raises his head with a displeased expression on his face, but Vanbrugh's laughing, brown eyes force him to be good-humored against his will, and he exclaims, "Peace, you Goth! I am cynical, misanthropical!"

"Goth yourself, Sir Timon," replies Vanburgh; "we'll have a bowl of Kit's best punch. It will aroint the vapors. As for being cynical, I trow that I have as much right to that disposition as yourself, for the huzzy Malborough swears that she will never pay me my claims on her for the house. Faith, if she does not, my creditors will tremble, and all Jewdom will be in an uproar. Ugh!" he ejaculates with an expression of loathing, "how abhorrent to my feelings it is to have the dirty paw and black-rimmed nails of a bum-bailiff Shylock tap me on the shoulder. Have you ever felt the sensation, my lord?" he queries, laughingly.

"No," replies Wharton, adding, in a bitter tone, "but I have felt a worse sensation within a mighty short time."

"Possible! What may that be, if the question is not impertinent?"

Wharton replies briefly, "A wilful son!"

"S'blood! yes, I did hear something about Philip's escapade. Tell me all about the affair, I beg, if it is not private!"

"If it was, Vanbrugh, faith! I doubt your power of unquestioning. However, as it will soon be food for London scandal, I'll even tell you; it will take but a dozen words. The lad ran off with a Mistress Holmes, a country squireen's daughter, of course against my wishes—*c'est tout!*" His face grows gloomy and stern again as he finishes.

"A trifle like your own freaks when younger, my lord! except that with you, it never ended in hymen, as they say Philip's has—ta-ta," he exclaims; leaving my lord to honor Kit with a visit and so test the purity of his Nantz.

As soon as Wharton received the intelligence of the elopement, he sent a lawyer to inspect the registers of the Fleet-parsons, to see whether they were married there. The search was disappointingly successful, and for a small fee, the lawyer received a copy of the document, which Wharton stuffed into his pocket with a fierce oath.

His heart is savage as he muses over Philip's mean alliance, and he is so absorbed in his thoughts that he does not notice the approach of a servant until he is respectfully addressed, "My lord, a letter for your lordship!" He lifts it off the salver, and starts violently as he recognizes Philip's handwriting. Breaking the seal, he smooths the crisp paper on the table, and reads it with close attention: Philip tells him that Margery is now his wife, and the object of his deepest love—at which part my lord mutters, "Cursed idiot!"—and it now depends on his father whether he shall return to Buck's or remain in London; and he hints that it matters little whether or not his father disowns him altogether. The tone of the letter is cool and haughty, and is written in a spirit of careless indifference which cuts to its reader's heart. He considers long and seriously over Philip's communication, and notes his defiant attitude in every word. He knows that, if he disowns him, Philip will necessarily go to ruin in a very short time, and he has no wish to create further topics of scandal and incur the odium that will surely attach to him if he pursues harsh measures.

Lord Wharton resolves to go and see Philip at the address which he has given in the letter. Rising, he leaves the room, and sets out at a rapid pace toward the Blue Bell, which is about a half mile from the club-house.

In reply to his inquiry of the bar-maid, he is told that "Mister Wharton and his lady are both up stairs." He asks to be shown up, and says, "My name is Mr. Johnson!" Leading the way up, she announces, "Mr. Johnson, sir;" and Wharton enters. It is dusk, and the father enters unrecognized. Philip begs him to be seated, and asks his acceptance of a glass of canary, which he silently refuses. In spite of his chagrin, the father is amused at the part which he is performing in so laughable a play. Before him is his son, not yet sixteen, and married to a girl—a year younger than himself—against his express orders; while he, the father of the first, sits unknown to them in the same room. The situation touches his sense of the ridiculous so keenly that while he can scarcely keep from laughing outright, he is at the same time bitterly angry and sore at their doings.

"Your business with me, sir? My time is rather occupied, at present, with matters of pressing importance!"

"Oh, well! if it is of *very* pressing importance, Master Philip, I will call at your convenience!" cries my lord, in loud, mocking tones, that make Margery ejaculate a little shriek of terror and even force his son to turn pale. Although Philip had in a manner prepared himself for a meeting, still his father's sudden appearance takes him aback, for he had not the slightest suspicion of the identity of his guest when he entered, and he is struck dumb.

"So! Philip! you are married, eh? It was unkind of you not to let me know about your intentions. I would have taken great delight in giving away the bride! I—" Feeling that his anger is fast gaining the mastery, he stops for a moment, and resumes in graver, sterner tones: "Master Philip, for the present you had better remain in London, and I think—as no doubt you will agree with me on consideration—that 'your wife' had better return to Buck's for a short time. Think on what I have said. If you would like to hear my reasons for my wishes, come to that address!" giving him a card with the words, "Marquis of Wharton, Kitcat Club, Fountain Tavern, Strand," scrawled on it; he leaves the room without another word, and repairs to the club-room to spend the night in drinking and gaming.

CHAPTER XVI.

Omnia vincit amor; et nos cedamus amori—?
                                              VIRGIL.

As his father's footsteps die away up the street, Philip exclaims to Margery, "Did I not tell you that all would be right? See! my father is now appeased, and all that remains is for the General to follow in his steps; then we can return to Buck's and live in happiness!"

Margery replies, "My own Philip, I mistrust his lordship! Forgive me for the words! But he looked so stern and cold; and did you notice? He said never a word to me;" and her eyes fill with tears of wounded sensibility.

Her emotion affects him, and he replies warmly, "What need we care, Margery, if all the world forsake us? We have each other. Now listen to my programme. I will to my father, and hear what he advises. If his advice chimes with our wishes, we will obey him. If it does not, we can—"

He stops to consider on what they will do, but apparently comes to no definite conclusion, for he says no more on the subject, but proposes that they go to the theatre, a proposition to which she gladly assents; and so, instead of discussing a disagreeable subject, they go to Drury Lane to see the mimic heroes and heroines, kings and queens strut their hour on the Thespian boards.

Margery is both pleased and shocked at the play—pleased by the tender romance, the deep passion and gorgeous paraphernalia of the loving heroine and hero;

and shocked by the coarse language and free jests of some of the performers, part of which she cannot fail to understand; and not being accustomed to them, like the regular *habitués*, her scarlet cheeks attest her wounded modesty at each fresh allusion, until she begins to attract the attention of some of the *blasé* dames sitting near them, who are patched, powdered, and scented to the last degree. Philip enjoys it all with infinite gusto, and his appreciative laugh sounds again and again at the repetition of every spicy saying or highly-flavored allusion. He is charmed with this first glimpse of London life, and determines to see it more fully ere long. The play is Nick Rowe's "Fair Penitent," and the character of Lothario—Richardson's "Lovelace"—pleases him immensely, while Margery's sympathies are exclusively enlisted in favor of the ruined Calista.

After they have returned to their room at the Blue Bell, and as they are eating a light supper, Philip says, "Sweetheart, I will see my lordly father to-morrow and arrive at a full understanding as regards his position towards us."

Margery replies in an anxious manner, "Do not anger him, Philip dear, or speak too haughtily; for until we are all friends again, I shall feel unhappy, for I have been the cause of all this trouble."

He replies, "Tut-tut; if you value my love, dearie, never say another word about such absurdities! Why, what would have become of me if you had not been my own true love, when I begged you to fly with me and be my wife? And never was I so happy as when we were joined forever by that drunken, tattered Fleet parson. My benediction on him, if it will do him any good!

"And the best and the worst of this is
That neither is most to blame—"

* * * * * *

The next morning Philip attires himself in his azure velvet suit, and dons his drooping hat—the one whose long pearl plumes dangle on his shoulder—and buckles his jingling spurs on his square-toed shoes; then slinging his rapier on his thigh, he helps Margery into the chair which waits for them, and finally enters himself. In a short time they arrive at the Fountain Tavern, and are accosted by Kit, who looks admiringly at the handsome boy, and bows deeply as he enters the door.

Says Philip, "Is my Lord Wharton to be seen?"

Kit rejoins, "Yes, my lord; his lordship instructed me to send you up to him as soon as you came."

Philip is ushered up stairs, and directly finds himself in the room which he has so often heard about as the sanctum of wits, beaux, and statesmen. His father, who is writing at a low table in a corner by the fire, does not rise, but bids him "Good morning" in a curt tone, and waves him to a seat, but Philip's gorge rising at the authoritative gesture, he declines the silent command, and lounges carelessly around the room. He admires Kneller's beauties, looks at the engraved goblets, and inwardly sneers at the emblems of whiggery decorating the walls, ceiling, and the tables. On a small card table which stands beneath Anne's portrait, is a glass case, containing a lock of dark, wiry hair; below it is a placard on which is written

> "A lock of hair from the head of his most gracious majesty
> KING WILLIAM III."

A profane idea strikes him to raise the case, and make some ridiculous alteration in the lettering of the placard, or to filch the lock, or to do something irreverent to it, for he hates the memory of the taciturn, phlegmatic William; but a side glance at his father, who has been watching his movements, at once dispels all thoughts of his intentions; still, even with his keen eyes on him,

Philip curls his lips scornfully, and mutters, loud enough to be heard, "Pah! the big-breeched Dutchman." My lord's eyes blaze, and his brow contracts, as he catches this loyal exclamation; but he says nothing, and resumes his writing.

Philip waxes restless and impatient, and at last says testily, "My lord, *tempus fugit!* and, under favor, I would like to finish my business, if you are at liberty."

The cold, cynical tone in which Philip speaks, cuts Wharton to the quick, and he looks at him, and replies in an injured manner, "My son, I will not keep you very long with one you seem to hate so much!"

As Philip meets his gaze, he feels for the first time contrite and repentant, and suddenly determines to be in future a better son, and obey his father in all that he asks; he discovers also that he is loved with all a parent's love, more, far more than he deserves. He exclaims, in a thick voice, "Father, you can trust me in future! Be a friend to my Margery, and do with me as you will;" and extends his hand. His father presses it in his with a cordial grasp, and his eyes grow brighter as he exclaims: "Let bygones be bygones, Philip; and if you obey me in all things as you have promised you will, we can once more live happily together!"

After a short conversation, Philip asks, with some hesitation, "What do you advise us to do under these circumstances?"

He replies, "Philip, I still think it better that Margery should return home, and yourself also, in order to explain matters there. After that, return to me at once, and we will discuss your future travels, for you know as well as myself that it is necessary to the education of a gentleman that he should be thoroughly acquainted with foreign manners and usages, and also be somewhat familiar with their politics, all of which enable a man to bear himself properly in the eyes of the world."

Here Philip smiles, and thinks to himself that he is a master of that art, at any rate.

"And when you have been away a year or two, you will welcome Margery with the greater fervor for your long absence from her!"

Philip looks a little gloomy and doubtful at this, which his lordship noticing, adds, in a matter-of-course manner, "If you find that she is really essential to your happiness, after a trial of a month or so in Paris and the Low Countries, you can easily write home, and I will send her on to you!"

With his usual prescience, Lord Wharton sees that in time Philip's affection will cool, and he is sure that when his son is surrounded by the frail beauties of the continental cities, his fond recollections of Margery will be effaced by their allurements and their artful tongues, for he greatly fears that Margery will strengthen his Tory proclivities, in her romantic, womanish sympathy for the Pretender, and he determines to strain every nerve to make him a staunch Whig and a Protestant, and for that purpose he intends to look about him for some one who will be able to control him and instil into him the good seed that will ripen to the advantage of the Whig party.

Philip, finally overcome by his father's arguments, promises to do as he wishes in all things, with the proviso, that his travels shall not begin for a couple of months, and that Margery shall stay with him in London. Wharton gladly acquiesces in this plan, for the longer the young couple are together the more the defects they will find in each other—a knowledge which may produce a mutual satiety and dissatisfaction between them! Moreover, he can regulate their domestic life to a certain extent, and he sees a very easy way of creating a bad feeling between them, although at the same time his scheme will certainly do Philip a deal of harm. But he consoles himself with the jesuitical maxim, " The end justifies the means." A short outline of his plan may not be unacceptable.

There are in London two or three notorious societies of demoralized young scapegraces, who consider that ruining a woman and then running her husband or lover through the body for his insolence in interfering, is quite a laudable action; and boast of their shamelessness and profligacy as if they are cardinal virtues; and the way in which they make the night hideous with their ribaldry and obscenity is a disgrace to the city. No man is safe from their skilful rapiers; no woman safe from their wiles or violence. They designate themselves Mohocks or Spitfires, and are the scourge of London's honest cits, who curse and fear them. These patrician bravos stab a man to death in the most gentlemanly manner; and then, if the hue and cry become dangerous, they find a refuge in Thieves' Sanctuary, and laugh at the puny efforts of the law to apprehend them.

It is into this reckless society that Wharton determines to throw his son, in order that ill-feelings may arise between him and his wife, for Margery will naturally feel aggrieved at the amours, intrigues, and late hours which Philip will be, in a measure, forced into in such company, and will remonstrate with him. The result is plain to him. Philip's love will fade away and with it the influence of his wife. Thus, in a short month, he may gain more power over his son than he has ever had before. My lord, be it remembered, is no great enemy to the Mohocks, for among them are many men of high birth and great wealth.

So his father kindly agrees to all his son says; and it is arranged that in a month's time, Philip will leave

England with a tutor who is to be selected by his father. Wharton rises and embraces him, and bids him adieu with an apology for the state affairs that prevent him from indulging in a longer conversation.

Philip tells Margery of the result, while they are riding home, and she cries bitterly when she learns that their honeymoon is to be so short. He agrees with her that it will be "vastly unpleasant," and continues, "but you know I intend to send for you at the end of a month!" This communication comforts her a little, and she converses in more cheerful tones about the future, and is pleased beyond expression at his lordship's reconciliation.

As Philip draws her nearer to him and looks tenderly in her pure eyes, he says, " Wifie, he tells me that whilst I remain in London, he wishes me to associate for a time with a party of gentlemen who can enlighten me on many matters, which are essential for me to know regarding city life; for you know that I am a trifle ignorant on some points!" Here she looks at him with a smile, as though to deny such a disparaging statement; but he continues, "This may take me away from you a little; but for both our sakes I must learn the properest way of holding myself; manners here are so different from those of dear, quiet Bucks!"

She acquiesces with a troubled sigh, and they talk of Rooksnest, and Elm Avenue, and of her father, who, by the by, is to be in London to-morrow—a recollection that causes her to blush even to her shoulders, which glisten like veined Parian under the soft lace thrown modestly over her bosom.

CHAPTER XVII.

Othman.—There fled the guilty soul!
                              VIII. BARBAROSSA.
Zanga.—Is this Alonzo? Where's the haughty mien?
         Heavens, how pale!
         And art thou dead!—
                                VII. THE REVENGE.

ALL England is ablaze with the news of Earl Mar's "hunting match" in the Highlands, and the later tidings of the battle at Dunblane, where he met with a check by the Duke of Argyle. During the action, the right wing of the Highlanders had become so excited that they broke their ranks, and swooped on Argyle's left wing with irresistible impetuosity; and hewed them down with deadly two-handed sweeps of their broad claymores and their long Lochaber axes, the while screaming harsh, Gaelic war cries; but they receive a terrible retribution in the utter rout and destruction of the clans on the left of Mar, who, although Stewarts, Mackenzies, and Camerons, were tumbled over like sheep by Argyle's veterans and almost to a man destroyed.

Lord Lovat, who was in command of the castle of Inverness, and who has hitherto borne the reputation of being a staunch adherent of the Pretender, has surrendered it without a struggle, and in England Preston has followed suit. It is the same Lord Lovat who afterwards sneered, as he mounted the scaffold that expiated his villanies, "God save us! Why should there be such a bustle about taking off an old gray head from a man who cannot get up three steps without two assistants!" And now Mar's army begins to melt away very perceptibly, for the scum, which was ready enough to side with a rising cause, now, like rats, desert the sinking ship. The brave Earl sat in his camp-tent, and mused over the events of the last few days, and he began to grow disheartened by his misfortunes, when the news reached him that "King James III." had landed at Peterhead, and was on his way to visit him. His heart bounded within him as he exclaimed, "Thank God for this! I could wish no better news, short of hearing that he held his own again;" and the soldier bowed his head and wept.

Wharton, busier than ever with his political and domestic affairs, and absorbed in his many schemes and intrigues, gave never a thought to Him who nips all intrigues, ruins all schemes, and sends their fabricator to his last account. His benevolent design of placing Philip amid the select society which he had chosen for him, and also his scheme to estrange him from his child-wife, have failed, not because he lacked either the will or the power, but because death struck him with his chill arrow and sent him unassoilzied to the eternal shades. He died in great agony and remorse a few days after his conference with his son: with friends and servants about him, but neither his son nor his wife to wipe the death-dew from his face and lips, and kiss him good-bye forever. His last words were, " Philip—send him to me!—my boy is —" and the death rattle forced him to finish the sentence in heaven or ——.

Philip is promenading Vauxhall's shady avenues with Margery, or rather was, for they are now sitting at a little, bowlegged, rustic table in one of the alcoves, eating cheese-cake and syllabub—dishes that are quite *à la mode*. As Philip is about to call for another platter of cake and 'bub, a messenger brings the news of his father's death. Margery turns pale, and looks anxiously at Philip, who seems cool and collected, and puts some few questions to the bearer of the news, and rewards him for his trouble. Then turning to Margery, he says gravely, "This is a sad ending to our day's pleasuring, Margery! Let us go home;" and they return to their chair.

During the ride home, he scarcely speaks a word, and seems immersed in thought. Margery, who has hardly seen Lord Wharton a dozen times, grieves chiefly for Philip's sake, for she thinks that she appreciates his position by changing places with him and by thinking of her own father as dead instead of Philip's; and tears burst from her eyes at the thought.

Philip now hurries to the side of his dead father, and looks sadly on all that remains of the great Whig statesman. He drops a great tear on his brow, which courses slowly adown his cheek, enters his open lips, and rests between them on his white, clenched teeth, quivers there an instant, and disappears.

"Egad!" he exclaims, "it had pleased me better to see you once more ere you had left me forever; however, God or the Devil hath decreed otherwise, and faith I'll not repine at the decree, whoever put it forth. Now I am my own master, Philip, Earl of Rathfarnham and Marquis of Catherlough! but not as *yet* First Lord of the Treasury;" and an exultant smile crosses his boyish face. Anon thoughts of his dead father rise in his mind. Kneeling down by the bedside, he grasps his cold, right hand, and breathes a prayer to Heaven! after which he steps softly out and leads Margery in to look on the man who once conspired so cruelly against her happiness. But all is forgotten in the dread Presence; leaning over the corpse she kisses his cold forehead, and breathes a heartfelt prayer for the future salvation of her husband's father.

Philip leads Margery out again, and closes the door after her. He asks of the servants, whom he dismissed at his entrance, and whom he now recalls to renew their care of the body, whether his lordship left any orders for him; whereupon his former secretary replies, "No, my lord, his lordship died so suddenly that he had no time to say anything, except to call on your name!"

"Say you so?" he replies; "I did not think his death had been so sudden—that is all!" Leaving the death chamber, he goes to Margery, to whom he says, "I must send the sad intelligence to my mother at once, and she can be here by to-morrow evening."

So saying, he sits down and hastily scrawls a letter to her, signing it "Wharton, Earl of Rathfarnham and Marquis of Catherlough," but, on second thought, runs his quill through them and blots them out; and the death-summons goes post-haste to Bucks.

CHAPTER XVIII.

*"From the tower,
Heavy, slow,
Tolls the fun'ral
Note of wo.
Sad and solemn, with its knell attending
Some new wand'rer, on the last way wending."*
SONG OF THE BELL.

"REBECK me!" growls Shem, "I want ye to do as ye like, Brad, if ye will get wedded till her; I canna say but I think Meg's a good lass. Debbie can gie ye pots an' pans for your kitchen, an' ye can hae my place as head falconer!—a varra guid start for a young couple; but ye mind I think ye 're a fuil a' the same for bein' in such a hurry to leave home so airly; but o' coorse ye do as ye please. Ye hae my consent, an' your mither's, I knaw, wull not be denied. She war aye a fuil where you were concerned, an' in my mind, aye wull be!"

After this unusually lengthy peroration, Shem becomes flustered and slightly shame-faced, and thinks that he was rather maudlin and soft in talking so familiarly with his son about his approaching marriage with Meg Busbie; so, to take off any appearance of undue mildness that he may have been guilty of, he adds, grumly, "An' a pest on the fuilish pair o' ye!"—an observation which I firmly believe he repents of as soon as he makes, for he kicks the dog away from his seat, and recalls her with a low, coaxing "Down, my brach! down," and she crouches again and licks the boot that kicked her.

Brad, who looks cheerful and handsome in his best

suit, smiles as he watches his father's manœuvres, and finally cries, " Well, good-bye, dad! I will be in wi' Meggie. If you want me, sound the horn, and I will return at once;" and, with a step as light and springy as a panther, he steps out on the greensward in all the blithesomeness of a pure conscience and requited love. He has put the momentous question to Meggie, and after a dozen different refusals—according to the general custom of women in such cases, who half fret a man's life out in order to experience the keen, trembling delight of hearing and refusing an offer of marriage as many times as possible—has been accepted, all the preparations have been made, and the wedding is to take place this very day.

He strikes off in the direction of Dame Busbie's cottage, and is running like one of the wild red deer which he has so often shot, when the deep-voiced bell in the round-tower clangs an alarming summons far and near, and he stops and stands as still as a statue. Clang! Clang!! Clang!!! boom out the slow and measured strokes. Brad knows that the large bell is never rung except at a birth, death, or marriage of some of the family, and his heart is full of a vague, uneasy sensation, as of some impending danger.

Clang! Clang.!! Clang!!!

Quickly retracing his steps, he looks into the lodge; it is empty. Now he catches a faint, confused murmur like the sound of summer waves on the seashore, or of many people whispering or talking in a low voice! Then a long, woman's wail comes to his ears from the direction of the castle, thither he runs with all his speed, and there hears the story of my lord's death told in hurried, awe-stricken tones. The women folk are crying, and the men are grave and sorrowful, for despite his wickedness and his profligacy, Wharton was a kind, goodhumored master to them all; and if some of them could recollect a daughter or a sister who owed her shame to him, the recollection is drowned in pity for his fate: dying alone in London, neither his wife nor his son to close his eyes and pray with him for his future redemption.

When the news was conveyed to her ladyship, she had fallen into strong convulsions. and was carried stiff and senseless to her bed.

Most of those who are assembled before the castle are attired in their gayest dresses and their chapel-going clothes in honor of Brad's wedding, for he is a great favorite amongst them on account of his good nature and his generosity. But here a lad and there a lass can be seen unpinning a gay rosette or a fluttering ribbon and then hiding it from view in a pocket or a bosom, for they all know that the wedding will not take place this day. As for poor Brad! he is a double mourner, for at one blow he loses a good master and an expectant bride.

Mistress Meggie is here in all her wedding finery, her eyes are full of tears and her lip trembles pitifully—whether most at Lord Wharton's death, or the stoppage of her marriage, I know not. Brad glides to her side, and, unobserved by the crowd, puts his arm around her trim waist and presses her side sympathizingly. She seems to take little heed of his actions, and does not offer the slightest resistance to his caresses, but exclaims in a low, half-crying voice, " Oh, Brad, how unlucky! I am sure we will never be married now; it is so unlucky for a death to come betwixt a marriage!"

" Don't say so, Meg!" he exclaims. " It makes my heart ache."

Meg replies, affectionately, " Well, Brad, I winna say it, then, but I am afeared sometimes that I might lose you—dearie!"

His hands clasp more tightly around her waist, and

he feels his heart grow bigger and bigger in his throat, until it chokes his utterance so much that like a sensible lad he deems silence better than speech, but *looks* volumes out of his sunny, hazel eyes, and she seems satisfied.

"Well," he thinks to himself, "if our love is enough for man and wife, it will keep a fortnight."

Dame Throck, who is talking to Betty, says, "Yes, an' I recollect that yest're'en' a crow flew three times aroun' the tower, an' then pecked for nigh ten minutes agan the rim o' the bell. I knew summut evil would befa' the house afore the year war' out!" and the bystanders shiver as they listen to her doleful tale. "Ugh, I feel a grue," says one impressionable gossip. Another adds, "I knew his lordship war goin' to happen summut, for I dreamed o' a weddin' last neet, an' that is allus a sure sign o' evil." So they go on.

Shem, who is in a rather isolated position, calls Brad and Meg to him, and says, in a low voice, "Of coorse the weddin' will no come off the day; it is a sad thing that prevents it; but the Lord does it a' for the best;" and he turns away to hide his emotion by scowling fiercely at two little children who look up at him with streaming eyes, crying because others cry, and without the remotest idea of the reason of their grief.

Clang! clang! clang!

> "Heavy, slow
> Tolls the fun'ral
> Note of woe."

Lady Wharton has lain for two whole hours, scarcely breathing, and more dead than alive. When she does awake it is to realize to the fullest extent her misery and her loss, while her thoughts revert to Philip whom she has not seen since his mad escapade, and she trembles as she wonders whether she will be able to control him now that her husband is no more; she feels that she will not, and is sick at heart.

A servant enters, who exclaims, "My lady, General Holmes wishes to see you?"

She replies, "Admit him! this is no time for ceremony!" And she orders her maid to arrange the pillows behind her so that she can recline in a sitting position.

The General enters with a soft step, and a sorrowful expression smooths his worn face. He salutes her respectfully, and says, "My lady, words are useless. That I deplore his loss, you must know, particularly at this time, when we might have been drawn nearer together in friendship and interest."

She does not speak, for her heart is too full for speech, and she presses his hand thankfully. He gulps down an obstruction in his throat, and busies himself in arranging his waistcoat, whose creases seem to displease him, to judge by the pertinacity which he exhibits in smoothing it and pulling it awry. Now he plucks at his moustaches, bites them abstractedly, and at last he blurts out, with a reddening face, "My lady, you are not angry at Margery?"

"No, General," she replies, plaintively, "though I opposed the match, yet, as it is now accomplished, I say with all my heart, God bless them and keep them both happy, for Margery is a sweet, lovable girl, and was always vastly to my liking; I hope and trust that Philip will be steady and keep out of vicious company." And she sighs as she finishes.

"You are going to London, my lady?"

She replies, "Yes, General; and can I venture to ask you to accompany me? Will it put you to much inconvenience?"

He replies energetically, "My lady, there is nothing I

would prize more than to have the honor of attending your ladyship to London or anywhere else!"

He is delighted at the request she has preferred, and feels himself a greater man now that her ladyship reposes so much confidence in him as to desire him to accompany her on her journey.

She says, "We will set out to-morrow, then, if I can leave my room, and—Oh, Tom," she cries as her thoughts revert to her lonely position, "why did you die? I feel so desolate now that both my husband and my son have left me!"

Holmes, unused to such scenes, does his best to console her, but feels his utter inability to cope with a distressed woman. "My lady, moderate your grief; it is useless; you cannot bring him to life again! Egad, though, that is the very reason that you do grieve! But, egad, I'll stop talking, for I only make matters worse. It was ever a hopeless job to console a woman!"

She smiles faintly as she notices his evident embarrassment, and dismisses him by saying, "Well, General, I will not detain you any longer. If I am able to go to-morrow, I will send a messenger to the Grange to let you know."

Glad to escape, the General bows low, and leaves her apartment.

The next day she felt well enough to start, and in due time they arrived in London without any casualty.

CHAPTER XIX.

> But where began the change; and what's my crime?
> The wretch condemn'd, who has not been arraign'd,
> Chafes at his sentence. Shall I unsustain'd,
> Drag on love's nerveless body through all time?
> I must have slept, since now I wake. Prepare,
> You lovers, to know love a thing of moods;
> Not like hard life, of law.
> GEO. MEREDITH.

THEY are now on the threshold of his lordship's town-house, and Lady Wharton is so weak and agitated that the General is forced to put his arm around her to keep her from falling to the ground. They are quickly announced by the attentive hall-porter, and in a moment she is in Philip's arms, and is crying bitterly. She is too overcome to speak for a time, and can do nothing but hold Philip around the neck and sob and sigh piteously.

Margery's little hands are both clasped in her father's camp-hardened palm, while she looks shyly at my lady, who, noticing her hesitancy, exclaims with an emphasis which shows that she appreciates her feelings: "My daughter, come to a mother's arms!" and she turns to Margery with a loving light beaming in her saddened eyes. Margery, overjoyed at her words, embraces her fervidly, and the aged dame and the budding woman are friends through the medium of sorrow and joy—sorrow, keen and piercing for a husband's and a father's loss; joy for a disobedient son's return.

Her ladyship finally performs the sad, painful duty of

looking on the inanimate form of her departed husband, after which she retires to her room, heartsore and fatigued, to pray to the Almighty to give her strength enough to support her great affliction.

Philip, Margery and the General gather together to exchange news and to talk of home and its familiar objects; Holmes, in reply to an observation by Philip, says: "No, Philip; I fear that her ladyship will not long survive your father's death. When she received the sore tidings, she was attacked with strong convulsions, and for over two hours she was not expected to live!"

Philip whitens with fear at the prospect of such an event, and replies in a shaken voice, "God help me if she dies too! Sometimes I think that I have been the cause of his death, and the thought weighs heavy on me. My mother must not die yet; I cannot bear it until I have shown her how much I regret my wild conduct and reckless behavior while he was living!"

Margery, frightened at his appearance, moves closer to him, and lays her hand on his arm with a look of sympathy; but turning his face away from her, he gently removes her hand, and a curious expression of suppressed dislike momentarily disfigures his features. She notes the gesture with love's keen eyes, and a heart sickness comes over her as she tries to think that she must have been mistaken in imagining that he looked on her with aversion. Alas! the first cloud has come between them—a cloud from which peers a dead father's look of upbraiding and reproach. The General has watched Philip's behavior, and too truly reads its meaning; but keeping his thoughts to himself, he draws Margery to his side, and casts a searching side glance on her face, which is troubled and anxious; and they are all silent, and not a sound is heard but the slow, monotonous tick-tack of the old clock which stands on the landing outside.

Philip, anxious to break the dreary silence, which begins to harass him with its painful quietude, asks, in an uninterested voice, " General, has Brad Throck married Meg yet? They were to be united a week ago—so I understood."

Holmes answers in as vacuous a manner, " No, they were going to be married the day that we received the news of *his* death, which said event, of course, put an end to their festivities."

" Yes," he replies; and again there is dreary silence.

Margery once more shrinking close to Philip, impulsively throws her arms around his neck, and says, while the tears rain down her cheeks, " Philip, darling! do not look so strange at me. I know that your heart must ache. Philip, have I done aught to offend you? I—"

" Margery," he replies regretfully, " you are too good for me. I feel hard and cruel, now; yet withal I am sad and conscience-stricken."

Her quick perception solves his enigmatical words;" she turns from him with a heart too full for speech, and falls into her father's arms with a low, broken sob, and whispers, " Oh, father, he hates me for his father's sake! Hold me tightly. I cannot bear to look him in the face again—he hates me;" and her body shivers from head to foot.

" General!" Philip exclaims in a sharp, strained voice, " I pray you excuse my departure. I have business outside;" and with these words he leaves the room.

When his footsteps have died away in the distance, the General says to Margery, " My daughter, tell me truly. Do you love Philip as much now as you did before your marriage?"

She replies in a passionate voice, but without lifting

her head from his breast, "Father, why do you ask such a question? Such love as mine never diminishes, it grows greater by its food?"

The General seems as if he would have answered her, but thinks better of his purpose, and keeps his words between his teeth.

"He has grown tired of her—possession has sated him, and he now regrets his step—in time he may hate her! God help thee, Margery! It will kill thee. Thou wert never made for rough speech or cold looks!"

Drawing her on his knee as in olden times at the Grange, he strokes her hair and cheeks until she falls asleep with a long, deep sigh; while his own weariness produces the same effect on him. And he has a dream, and in his dream he thinks his child has died, and he awakes with a great start, causing his "little girl" to cling more tightly to him, and nestle her bonnie face closer to his shaggy beard, while her rosy lips half open as though she listens to a distant sound. The soul is freer when its case is inert and asleep, and can often foresee events which are unknown to the wakened mind. Does she foresee her future! Would it be better if she could?

When they meet at table in the morning, Philip is affable, but restrained, while the general conversation is naturally tinctured with a grave sadness. He seems regretful for his treatment of Margery the previous evening, and is now devoted and attentive to her, which Holmes perceives with glad feelings and a relieved mind. Her ladyship is pallid and tearful, the consequences of a night passed in sleepless sorrow and uneasy thought, and she seldom joins in conversation with the others.

During the day Philip gives orders regarding the funeral, which is to take place to-morrow with due pomp and splendor

*   *   *   *   *   *

The chamber is crowded with the dead man's friends, many of the mighty ones of London—chiefly members of the Whig party, who come to have a last look on the man who first in all England welcomed William the Third on his landing, and who had since led them to so many victories by the power of his able tongue, his subtle reasoning and his Ciceronian eloquence.

Charles Montague, who will also be laid in his grave ere the bones of his former friend are bared by the worms, stands by the side of the glittering coffin, and says gravely to Vanbrugh, as though he feels the nearness of his own dissolution, " I doubt that I'll long survive him; so, egad, Van! you may shortly have the pleasure of looking on me, as I at present look on dear, old, honest Tom."

" S'life," replies Vanbrugh; " we can ill afford to lose another good man and true; we are weak enough already. One such defection from our ranks is enough for one while, I trow!"

Philip entering at this moment, is warmly greeted by the visitors, who sympathize with him, and express their condolences with his loss in words and actions. He is dressed in sombre black, a long crape veil is attached to his right arm, and he has also a neckcloth of the same material, which gives a pallidity to his skin that is ghastly and startling. His mother, who walks beside him, is covered from head to foot in the trappings of death, and tears are bursting from her eyes. Her grief is not for comfort or sympathy, and so all feel with an intuitive knowledge.

Philip leads her to her room, and kisses her tenderly; when he has closed the door, she says, in an anxious manner, " Philip, dear, for your own sake as well as mine, avoid those men, Vanbrugh and Lord Halifax.

They are too dissolute and too old for one of your years."

He draws himself up haughtily, as he replies, "Philip Wharton, though young in years, needs not their adventitious aid to make him all men's equal, and the superior of most."

She does not reply to this outburst, but looks fixedly at him for a minute, and says sadly, " Good-night Philip, and God keep you from harm!"

Philip bows and returns at once to Vanbrugh, with whom and Halifax he converses of many things.

All day the room is crowded with visitors coming and going. All day long the rumbling coaches draw up before the door, and titled dames and famous men go and come.

Margery, who is with her father in a retired corner near the head of the coffin, surveys with curiosity or respect the owners of the famous or infamous names that are continually announced in measured accents by the pompous, powdered lackey who keeps out curious intruders.

The funeral next day was gorgeous and solemn; plumes waved, horses pranced, sable streamers fluttered in the air, and all the details and ceremonies that are essential to a noble's funeral were there. All that now remains of the great Whig is a fresh, earthy mound and an imposing tablet with its " Hic jacet Thomas Wharton", with a long array of virtues which he never possessed, and never a word of the vices which he did possess. Truly, sinners while we live, the world, thankful for our demise, almost canonizes us when we die.

A curious incident occurred just before the coffin lid was screwed down, which I hope it is not amiss to mention. Two burly carriers set their chair down in front of the door, and handed out of it a lady dressed in deep mourning. Her face must have once been very beautiful, but it had become wrinkled and disfigured by care or trouble. There were great hollows in her cheeks—caves wherein lurked despair and melancholy; and her large eyes were wild and haggard. Pushing the guardian lackey aside, and walking swiftly down to the corpse, she kissed its pale lips and laid a bunch of dusty, withered violets on its shroud, she then left as silently as she came, without vouchsafing a word to any one. Her face somewhat resembled that of the girl whom Wharton had once met many years ago—during the storm of 1703! The company stared at her abrupt entrance, and wondered at her singular action, but no one interfered with her by word or deed.

CHAPTER XX.

> "Now is the time that rakes their revels keep;
>   Kindlers of riot, enemies of sleep.
> His scattered pence the flying Vicker flings,
>   And with the copper shower the casement rings.
> Who has not heard the Scourer's midnight fame?
> Who has not trembled at the Mohock's name?
> Was there a watchman took his hourly rounds
>   Safe from their blows, or new invented wounds?"
>
> GAY'S TRIVIA.

> "Here is the devil and all to do with these Mohocks!"
>
> SWIFT.

ST. DUNSTAN's clock has just struck one. The moon diffuses a glorious light, and the many-storied houses throw deep shadows over the streets. All is quiet, and a solemn, thought-inspiring tranquillity broods over the city, disposing the mind to the consideration of high and important topics—when suddenly a loud shout, followed by noisy laughter and obscene curses, breaks in on the stillness of the night. A crowd of drunken, brawling rufflers sally out of a tavern, which is notorious as being one of the stopping places of the most ruffianly, drunken, and cruel of all associations, the Mohocks, many of whose members are of high birth and famous i' the state, but whose innate depravity has reduced them to the level of a Fijian.

These are the Mohocks who now desecrate the night's calm beauty with their infernal orgies. They take their name from a tribe of red men, who are natives of the colonies. Their leader is invariably the worst one of their worthy company; his title is Taw-Waw-Eben-Zan-

Kaladar, Emperor of the Mohocks, and he regulates their actions and proceedings with absolute powers and unquestioned authority. They are nearly all dressed in the extreme of the fashion. Velvet cloaks laced to a miracle, silken hose, ostentatious ruffles, long plumèd hats, and wide, lace collars are common to them all. Some hold a black satin mask or vizard in their hands, and a few have them on their faces. Two or three are flourishing their glittering rapiers above their heads, and occasionally pound on the shutters of the houses which they pass; and woe to the man, woman, or child who dares to remonstrate. They would be in imminent peril of their lives, for the crew are mad drunk and reckless.

The leader, whose forehead is adorned with a golden crescent, which is gummed to the skin, lifts his hand and at once there is comparative silence. " My lords and gentlemen—members of the Chosen Band! This night Philip Wharton, Earl of Rathfarnham and Marquis of Catherlough, a new member of our honorable company, must exhibit his valor and dexterity by either tipping the lion, or doing a sweater on such person or persons as we may meet to-night; or, as in case provided, pay a penalty of one hundred guineas. Have I said well?"

The noisy approval which greets his speech shows that all are satisfied, and content to abide by his words.

To those who do not understand the terms "sweater" and "tipping the lion," I will venture a short explanation. The "sweaters" operate in parties of four, five, or six. Surrounding their unfortunate victim, they form a circle with swords drawn and pointed toward him. They then begin to prick and prod him with the sharp points until they are tired of the sport, or until they think it is dangerous to continue the sport any longer. " Tipping the lion" means to slit the nose, or to bore out the eyes with the knuckles.

Such are the amusements of the society into which Philip has been introduced by Vanbrugh, who kindly volunteered to guarantee his character as a gentleman when he proposed him. In 1712, a royal proclamation was issued " to rout the association and arrest the members," but it was of no use; for the judges who should have enforced the law and brought the villains to justice, had in many cases, friends who were themselves Mohocks. Shadwell's observation is doubtless familiar to you; but I quote it because it gives a very accurate idea of the terror which this club inspired. "A man cannot go from the Rose Tavern to the Piazza once, but he must venture his life twice."

Philip, reeling and staggering in drunken uncertainty, replies to his chief's address with grandiloquent gestures and in a husky and indistinct voice : " Most mighty Emperor, I swear that the first human being who crosses our path, or violates the air of Drury Lane with his pestiferous carcass, shall suffer by my hands any penalty that you may adjudge—demme !" Whirling his rapier, with a rapid turn of his flexible wrist, he brings it gracefully to the salute. The consummate skill with which he performs this difficult movement would be creditable to a professed *maitre d'armes.*

" Bravo, egad, well done !" screams Lord Catachresis, delighted with his new confrère.

" Hist !" hiccups the Emperor, "I hear a step. Fall back, gentlemen ! Leave my lord to deal with this daring invader of our nocturnal rights !"

With these words and an injunction to Philip he retreats into the darkness of a shadowed doorway, the rest follow his example with more celerity, and noiselessness than one would think possible in such a rackety set; while Philip is left alone to accomplish his first duty in his character of a Mohock.

The unsuspecting pedestrian, who is coming rapidly toward him, is a man of medium size, and strong, heavy build. As the clear light of the full moon strikes on his features, Philip discovers, much to his surprise, that he is his father's former secretary, Geoffrey Scribset! "Curse the luck! The fellow will recognize me, to a surety!" Philip exclaims, as he pulls his hat down over his eyes to hide his face as much as possible.

He is now within a couple of yards of him, and Philip calls to him in a feigned voice, "Halt! knave! where goest thou at this—hic—hour of the night? St. Dunstan's has tolled this quarter or more. Speak!" and he draws his sword-arm back in a striking position.

Geoffrey is no coward, but the sudden challenge frightens him, and the sharp point against his throat makes him start back in dismay; unarmed as he is he sees no way to better his condition than calling for help, which he does, in stentorian tones, "Help! Watch!! Murder!!!"

In an instant he is griped from behind, and the doughty Catachresis gags him with his fist, whispering in his ear, "Silence, or you are a dead man. We are the Mohocks!" The poor secretary turns pale with fear as he hears the dreaded name, for he has once before been maltreated by this same crew of precious scoundrels. Lord Petronelle, a pallid but fine-looking man, now comes on the scene, and whispers to Catachresis, who releasing Geoffrey, nods significantly to Philip to put the usual questions to the prisoner before he is tortured. But Geoffrey, who has watched an opportunity, suddenly trips Petronelle—who falls with a thud of his head against the cobble-stone—and attempts to run. Philip, quick as thought, grasps him by the scuff of the neck, and endeavors to secure him. In the struggle his hat falls off, and Geoffrey recognizes him and exclaims: "Lord Wharton?" "Yes, hoddy-peck;" he replies, nettled at his discovery. "Is there aught remarkable—hic—in that?" and he shakes him fiercely, for he is both sinewy and muscular.

The advent of the rest of the crew interrupts any answer that he may have made, and in an instant he is the focus of a dozen bristling rapiers which goad him almost to madness. Geoffrey clenches his teeth, and looks his tormentors calmly in the face, until Philip, whom his cool endurance begins to shame, cries, "Come gentlemen, I think we may let him go now. He is well punished for his late hours and his insolence to my Lord Petronelle; and I'll warrant that he behaves himself better in future." Accordingly they each give him a final prick and sheathe their stained rapiers.

Poor Geoffrey is about to stagger home, when Philip stops him, and slipping a well-filled purse into his hand, says, "Master Scribset: prithee, what is the cause of your being abroad at so late an hour?"

"My lord," he answers, as he slyly pockets the peace-offering, "my lady sent me out to question of your lordship's whereabouts."

Philip's eyes sparkle as he asks, "Which 'my lady?'"

Geoffrey replies, "Please your lordship, her la'aship, your wife!"

"Umph! Go home again and give her my compliments. Tell her of everything that has happened—everything, mark you! or I'll thrash you to-morrow with my own hands. Tell her also that the next man who comes to seek me as if I were a truant school-boy, will not only be sweated, but will get a short shrift and a long sword!" and turning his back on the secretary his face becomes purple with passion and a sense of offended dignity.

His listening companions cheer him and pat him on the back for his independence. They now proceed to wrench the knockers off the doors, tear down signs amid storms of hurras and curses, and do all the mischief they can imagine, until the Emperor cries in a loud voice, "Away! Away! hide yourselves—the patrol!"

All disappear with wonderful rapidity down the dark alleys, which are plentiful in this neighborhood, all save Philip, who not as yet *au fait* in all of the stratagems of his confrères, stands irresolute, and bewildered at their sudden disappearance. The foremost of the patrol lays his hand on Philip's shoulder, and cries, "I arrest you, in the king's name!"

"Deil take you and the king," replies Philip, as he springs back, draws his rapier, and stands on the defensive; but second thoughts decide him to run ere they can close in on him, and at once he bolts down one of the alleys through which the others escaped.

He hears the hue and cry that is raised, but outdistancing all his pursuers, he arrives at the mansion flushed and bewildered. When he enters the drawing-room, he is dismayed at finding Margery there, who has waited for him until she has fallen asleep; she is curled in the large armchair formerly belonging to his dead father. Her hands are on one of the arms, forming a pillow for her head, and her breath is slow and regular, she looks so child-like, so innocent and pure that all of Philip's former affection for her—which I regret to say has been slowly but surely waning—comes back to him, and he presses his wine-heated lips on hers with a passionate kiss.

"Philip," she murmurs in her sleep, "My darling!"

A loud knocking at the outer door echoes through the

hall, and awakes her. When she sees Philip before her, she puts her hands over her eyes for a moment as though dazed at his appearance, and exclaims, "How you frightened me, Philip! I was dreaming of you. I thought that we were both back in dear Bucks and at Rooksnest! and I thought that you had the old look in your eyes which used to please me so and which I seldom see now: why—" she stops suddenly, for she sees the frown gathering on his face, and adds abruptly: "Oh, I know, dear. You have so much business to fret you, now that your father is dead, that you have no time for me; but I do not care so long as you really love me."

He nods his head in an intensely grave manner, but says nothing, for he feels the wine fumes rising in his head, and dares not risk an answer.

Margery, who has seen her father under the effects of wine at many a dinner and supper, at once divines that he has been drinking, and she asks him whether it would not be better for him to retire; and he assents with drunken gravity. As they are ascending the stairs, the butler, a crusty, purplish old man, bursts into the room, and exclaims in terrified accents, "Lord have mercy on us! My lord, Master Scribset has been waylaid and wellnigh killed by the Mohocks; he is all covered with blood;" and after this wonderful piece of intelligence he bows and leaves hurriedly.

"Poor man!" exclaims Margery, turning pale with terror. "Attacked by the Mohocks! Who are they, Philip?"

"What should I know about them?" he demands angrily; "there is a company of very proper—hic—gentlemen who call themselves by a somewhat similar name; but whether these are the same that attacked Scribset, I know not and care less." His testy tone brings tears to her eyes, and she asks no more questions.

Geoffrey Scribset has roused the whole house with his cries, and all the servants are sympathizing with him as he relates the tale of his troubles and shows, as proofs of his veracity, his many wounds and his torn clothes. He does not criminate Philip, but apostrophizes the whole of the lawless troop as a "cowardly, guzzling set of murdering swash-bucklers and bullies."

CHAPTER XXI.

"I aince fell in love wi' a sweet young thing,
A bonny bit flower o' the wilder'd dell;
Her heart was as light as a bird on the wing,
And her lip was as ripe as the moorland bell."
JAMES HOGG.

"*Zara.*—As I could wish; by Heaven, I'll be reveng'd."
CONGREVE'S MOURNING BRIDE.

THIS day Brad is determined that he will wed pretty Meg despite all obstacles and remonstrances; and told his father so the previous day. Shem wanted at least six months to elapse before the ceremony should take place, but the impetuous Brad has overruled all his objections on the score of ill-timed gayety and frolicking by promising to have the momentous affair conducted with quietness and very little merry-making.

Shem is in the lodge conferring with Debbie anent the wedding tocher which the young people are to have. Says Debbie: "I mun gie the lad what I can, for he'll have none too many o' this world's goods to begin life on! Let me see. Ye say, Shem, that he is to have thy post o' head falconer? That's summut, to be sure!"

"Ay, lass. It's more than I began the world on. D'ye recollect, Debbie, we wed on five shillin's, a bedstead wi' out coverings, an' a cradle, wi' m'appen a few pots an' pans, an' we have got along well enough. Brad is a defty, clever lad, an' he'll manage a' reet I doubt not."

Debbie replies, "Ay, ay; he'll do reet, never fret; he was allus a steady-like lad."

As Shem must have his little growl, he answers, "Little thanks to ye, Debbie, for keeping him steady. If I had not been about to keep him in bit order, I'd not like to think what might hae come of him wi' a' they easiful an' saft ways wi' him. It's a wonder that he has na come to harm afore this!"

She replies good-humoredly, but with a slight flush, "Out on ye, Shem! Ye knaw better than that."

"Weel, Debbie," he returns, "we'll not quarrel about him; get yersen ready, an' we'll trudge to t' chapel."

At this juncture Brad enters with a sorrowful mien, and eyes welling with restrained tears. Debbie looks keenly at him as she asks, "What now? Who's been crossin ye? Ye look like a draggled hen."

"Ay! speak out, Brad; what's the matter?" chimes in Shem, and taking a seat, he begins to nurse his leg while he waits for an explanation of Brad's sudden change from his previous blithesomeness to his present dispirited appearance.

"She says she winna be wedded!" bursts out from Brad with a noise of something between a sob and a sigh.

"Winna wed! What does the jade mean!" Shem echoes. "Winna wed! Ye willing! What tom-foolery is this?"

Thus gently questioned, Brad tells his piteous tale to his sympathizing hearers.

It seems that Dame Busbie, who was nurse to the old lord, had told Brad when he called on her to make the final preparations, that Meg should not be married to him until this day three months on account of my lord's recent death. In vain has he promised that the wedding should be conducted very quietly, and has even declared that he would allow no dancing or singing. All was useless. The old dame was obdurate, and Brad was forced to return home almost broken-hearted at this second cruel stroke of fate.

"Go ye to Dame Busbie, and try to persuade her, Dad," cries Debbie. "Ye can do more wi' her than anyone else hereabouts;" and she finishes in ireful accents: "Mak' t' ould fool do as Brad wishes!"

Shem grumbles, but acquiesces, and crushing his forest-cap hard down on his head, he starts for Meg's abode, which is about ten minutes' walk from the lodge.

Brad awaits his return with burning impatience, and yet dreads it, lest he too may be unsuccessful. This idea he endeavors to ignore altogether, but it will persist in cropping up again and again, turning him almost crazy, for he dearly loves the girl, and would give the whole world besides to call her his wife. Debbie fusses about arranging and disarranging Shem's hunting gear and his fishing tackle with a recklessness which is almost appalling, considering Shem's irascibility and his dread of any one meddling with his affairs.

At last Shem's tread is heard, Brad turns pale, and Debbie stands stock still with her lips firmly closed, and her eyes fixed on Brad. Shem enters slowly, seats himself in silence, removes his cap, lays one knee gravely over the other, and finally, with many prefatory admonitions to Brad anent the folly of being in a hurry, says: "I went there, and after a bit talk o' the weather wi' t' dame, I hinted what we wanted." At this important part of the recital, he gives a pitcher to Brad, and orders him to go down into the vault and to fill it with the best October. Brad obeys and returns with a marvellous quickness. Shem's eyes twinkle as he notices his impatience, and he resumes his story, "After I plagued her a bit aboot it, she said that ye might wed one anither if—" Here he stops to drink a draught of the bubbling ale. "If there is not too much merry-makin' or noise."

Brad, leaping to his feet, gives a view-halloo which makes the old rafters ring again, and he proceeds to hug first the stolid Shem, and then his more impressionable mother, who is so happy that she must needs cry to relieve her feelings.

I will not inflict a description of the wedding on you, but merely mention that everything passed off pleasantly, and that Brad received the post of head falconer from his father with proper thankfulness for the gift.

Brad and Meg are standing together to the right of the chapel and are conversing in the strain usual under such circumstances, when they are suddenly startled by the deep, harsh tones of Maldran Gudru, and find him close beside them.

"Mistress Meg," he says, "may the moon look down wi' a lucky light, on your pretty face to-night, an' on yours too, Master Brad. Could ye give the poor gypsy a few pennies to drink to the health o' the first born?"

Meg blushes, and is so indignant at the man's impudence that she scarcely knows whether she is standing on her head or her heels; pulling out her little silk-netted purse, however, she gives him a couple of pennies, which gratuity Brad generously doubles; whereupon he invokes the blessings of the moon and all the starry host upon them, and turns to go, but stops again and inquires: "Master Brad, did his lordship leave a message for the queen wi' any o' ye afore he died?"

Brad and Meg both answer negatively, and Maldran walks away in the direction of the camp.

As the happy couple no doubt prefer silence and their own company to ours, we will now turn our attention to Maldran and his proceedings. He taps at the queen's door, and enters with a lazy air. She is lying in her old place, and she looks at him inquiringly with her black, eloquent eyes. Maldran scowls as he replies, "He died wi'out sayin' a word about ye, either by word o' mouth or by way o' writin'."

A frown furrows her olive brow, and her full red lips press close together as she replies, "So be it. When he struck me for daring to shame him for her sake, I told him that it would take a thousand pounds of his gold to clear his mark from my cheek! gold for her who starves in London. Maldran, hear my oath;" rising from her lounge she stands erect, and utters in low, vindictive accents: "I swear, on my royal oath, that his son shall suffer for his father's sins—unless he pays me my demand!"

Maldran bows his head as she draws from her breast the symbol of the gypsies' religion, which she kisses, as does Maldran also.

"You can go," she says, and Maldran leaves the room.

"Poor Mistress Nelly little thought that her kindness to me when I was a wee bairn, who thought of nothing but the pretty flowers and the wild forest, would be recollected these many years; but my memory for a kind word and a cruel one has ever been good. A favor done me or an insult given me, I ne'er forget. When I think that he was her ruin, and think too of her being a starved, pointed-at outcast in London, my blood boils, and I feel wicked enough to kill him." She lifts her hand and passes it gently over a small cicatrice on her cheek which mars the beauty of its smoothness. "His son shall rue that day, and his soul will writhe as it feels my vengeance on his darling;" and the fiery, vengeful girl grits her teeth in very anger. Her naturally violent temper is rendered still more ungovernable by the power which she wields as queen of her tawny band. In moments of great excitement she is subject to fearful paroxysms of rage, which almost tear her frame asunder, and then woe to the follower who crosses her will or disobeys her slightest command. "I would forego my revenge," she continues, " to make her comfortable!—

I'll send a message to the young lord. If he obeys my commands, I'll forgive the past;" sounding her whistle, Maldran enters.

"Maldran, go to London at once! Find the young lord and give him this message;" she makes known to him the details with which we are already acquainted. "If he agrees, take the money to this house." She hands him a piece of dirty, greasy paper whereon are the words Nelly Valentin and also her address. "Tell her that it is from a friend, but mention no names. If his lordship refuses my offer, return at once." Dismissing him with an imperious gesture, she closes her eyes.

CHAPTER XXII.

Philto.—O my son!
    I would not have you with the profligate
    Hold any conversation, in the forum
    Or in the street. The manners of this age
    I know . bad men would fain corrupt the good,
    And make them like themselves. Our evil manners
    Confound, disorder everything—

Lysikles.—This prudence, as a buckler to my youth,
    I ever had :—
                PLANTER'S TREASURE. II. II.

GENERAL HOLMES, who has taken up his quarters with Philip for the present, is in the front parlor of the house, looking out of the window, and watching the numerous passers-by. He looks on with an amused air at the strained gestures and dandified grace of Sir Welle Kneebend as he pays his devoirs to his fair companion, and loads her with euphuistic compliments and honeyed speeches.

"Pardie, fair Mistress Allstile! Believe me when I tell you that you are the Venus of my thoughts, the Aphrodité of my dreams, and if Cupid will tip his shafts in the fire of your eyes, can I help it if they rankle in my heart?"

She favors him with a pleasant smile as she replies, "As I am virtuous, sir, you are pleased to flatter me to-day." And she manoeuvres her fan with the most dangerous adroitness, artfully leading him on to give her more of his newest compliments and well-turned periods.

The general is interrupted in his observations of London life, as compared to his own quiet home, by a pair of little, soft hands which clasp tightly over his eyes, while a pair of fragrant, dewy lips press his scarred and bearded cheek.

"Good-day, father mine. Truly, I think yon pretty girl, who trips so lightly on the pave, must have bewitched you. I made noise enough when I entered, but you never even turned your head!"

"I was thinking about something, Margery, and I became too absorbed to pay attention to anything else, I suppose."

Pushing a low stool close to his feet, she sits down on it, and rests her chin on his knee, while her eyes look up to his face; they have lost the old look of perfect happiness which once glowed in them and diffused its light over her.

"Well, father," she begins, "you desired to have a long talk with me to-day. I am all ready now, so pray proceed!" and a saucy look sparkles for a moment in her eyes. She adds, by way of parenthesis, "I do trust that there is nothing disagreeable coming?"

"Daughter," he replies, gravely, "I know that the topic will be disagreeable to you; but it is one which must be faced sooner or later; therefore, the sooner the better. Never let the enemy flank you when you can attack him in front!—a good maxim, my dear!" He coughs once or twice to clear his throat, and resumes: "It is about Philip that I would speak, hinny!" At these words she buries her face in her hands, and is very silent. "I have observed a sad change in his demeanor toward you of late. He has not only grown indifferent and careless, but he has often treated you with a cutting cruelty which I will not allow!" Margery shakes her head in denial, but will not raise her face. "His conduct has become the talk of London, and it is confidently reported that he is one of the ringleaders of the Mohocks —a vile rabble who cut, maim, and insult whom they wish in perfect security. It is a well-known fact that his losses at the gaming table are immense, which losses necessitate his raising money among the Jews who invariably get cent per cent. If he persists in this course, or continues to neglect you any longer than this week—back to Bucks you shall go!" He notes how her fingers press tightly against her temples, and his heart yearns for her. Altering his tone of command for one of entreaty, he adds, " You will do as I wish, hinny?"

She shivers slightly, but no answer comes from her, and he feels the hand which touches his own grow cold and deathlike. He raises her head, and to his great alarm sees that she is lifeless and still. "Peggy! ho, Peggy!" he calls in loud tones, but before the servant can enter, my lady herself sweeps in and cries: "Heavens, General! What is the matter? What ails Margery? What have you done to her? As I live the poor thing has fainted!"

In answer to her questions, he replies distractedly: "I believe I have killed her! I told her that if Philip did not in future treat her more like a wife and less like a quean, she must go back again to Holme Grange. Look at her! His conduct has made her grow thin and pale, and I know that if he continues his brutal treatment of her much longer, it will not be long ere I shall lose my darling. The thought almost crazes me!"

Lady Wharton, turning pale, falls into a chair close by her, and cries in stifled accents which seem wrung from her heart, "Philip, Philip! she will not be the only victim," she adds abruptly, "General, I love Philip more than myself, far more, and you can understand my feelings when I can tell you that I think that your advice to poor Margery is good! Philip—my tongue almost palsies as I say so—is already worse than half the rufflers in town. I have had spies who have informed me of his movements—of his disgraceful intrigues and insolent demeanor to high and low; and I have listened to their accounts with an aching heart. Time and again I have tried to reclaim him; but he invariably repulses me with a ribald jest or an impious execration. O God! it cannot be long ere I am laid with my husband."

The General's eyes flash as he listens to a mother's detail of her son's crimes and blasphemies; and he exclaims sternly, "Put him under the control of some one who can master him. Send him away from London and its associations. While he is amid such a crew as the Mohocks, he can never come to anything creditable either to himself or us."

She replies in a firm voice, "Thank you for the suggestion, General; he shall go!"

Holmes, satisfied that she will follow his advice, rejoices accordingly, and replies, "When Philip returns, I will tell him of my purpose, and see what effect it has on him!"

Margery has recovered from her swoon, and she weeps silently. Poor child! she is too heart-sick and wearied to offer any opposition to her father's words. Suddenly she raises her head as though she hears a well-known foot approaching, and looking alternately at her father and Lady Wharton, she gasps, "Philip! he is coming!" The door is thrown open with a crash, and Philip enters. His clothes are all awry, and his tangled curls hang in matted bunches on his torn and rumpled collar; one of his shoes lacks its buckle, and the plumes of his hat are broken and muddy. He looks sullen and haggard, but an amused smile flits across his face as he exclaims, "Que le Diable! here's a pretty spectacle for a gentlemen to view. Let me cast you, i' faith!" he begins in a drawling voice: "Scene first. Room in my own house. Characters: General Surlysides—stern and angry. Mistress Prettypouts, his daughter—tearful but shrewish! Umph! My Lady of the Goodson—imperious, but weak-minded; and last, though not least: Philip, her model son—good-natured and obliging, but ill-used by the other characters. Umph! Time uncertain. Draw up the curtain! The prompter's bell has tinkled." Taking a chair, he twirls it around two or three times, and finally seats himself on it, with his face to its back, which is the approved fashion at the Highway, an inn of unenviable notoriety as the resort of thieves, gamblers, and rooks.

Holmes, giving Margery in charge of her ladyship, desires her to leave him to deal with Philip alone, to which she accedes, and they leave the room without a glance at Philip, who looks on with a smile on his lips and a sneer in his eye. "Hoity-toity" he exclaims, and turns his attention to Holmes, who says in a stern manner, "My lord, it is high time that we arrive at a mutual understanding. Of late your conduct to my daughter has been such as I will not brook. You treat her as though she were your light-o'-love, and not your innocent, loving wife. I have heard of your brave deeds in Drury and the Strand, and also of your reckless gaming and your profligacy, which must in time lead you to destruction and ruin. Where are all your nights passed? I doubt not that you would be ashamed to tell me where you spent last night?"

He is interrupted by a flourish of Philip's hand as he rises, and says, in a cool, irritating manner: "Hark ye, General! your most monstrous curiosity shall be gratified. Last night I passed in a mighty pleasant manner at Dollie Hawke's. Various gentlemen and myself honored her house with our presence. We played several games at whist, and s'blood, I regret to say I lost a few hundred guineas. After that we walked Drury and Newgate till we were tired. After—but you have had enough, General, eh?" and he laughs heartily.

Holmes replies, "My lord, you are not fit to have charge of my daughter. I shall take her back to Holme Grange, and there she shall remain until I hear better accounts of you than at present! Good-morning." And he leaves Philip to think over the turn which affairs have taken.

Now the door opens again, and his mother enters. Whistling a prolonged note, he runs his fingers through his hair. "Egad!" he exclaims; "another battery to open fire."

"Philip," says her ladyship, in a voice which compels his attention, "what I purpose saying to you, and why I say it, require no explanation, nor need you offer any resistance to my wishes; for you *must* do as I desire you. Ere this week is out you will be under the charge of a tutor who will take you abroad in order to teach you to be a gentleman, a Whig, and a Protestant. You have ample time to make all your preparations in the three days which are allowed you ere your departure. Do you understand me?"

"Yes, I think I do," he replies, awed by her determined manner and the steady look which she concentrates on his face. "You are rather peremptory, but what can I do? *che sarà sarà.*"

Surprised at her easy victory, she goes to him and kisses him with a renewed confidence in his nature, and she leaves the room with a pleased expression on her face.

"Scylla and Charybdis without a choice. At one blow I lose Margery, and am sent abroad with, most probably, a long-haired, prick-eared, shambling pedant, of whose didactic propensities I shall have the advantage. At any rate, the rose of my thorns is that I can get to the place where England's anointed king lies perdu," and he strikes up in a low key—

"The king shall hae his ain again!"

CHAPTER XXIII.

Queen.—" I know your projects and your close cabals."
THE EARL OF ESSEX, I. 1.

King.—" O, Gormaz! O, Alvarez! stop not here."
XIMENA, I. I.

THE chevalier had received Earl Mar at Fetteresso with great kindness and affability, and had then taken up his march to the royal palace of Scone. There he expected to find a large and well-disciplined army; instead, he saw crowds of unarmed vagabonds who were rioting and drinking with a sublime indifference to the orders which had been circulated among them. James's soul was not big enough to encounter such a grievous disappointment, and he re-embarked at Montrose, dispirited and hopeless. He landed at Gravelines after a short voyage, and thence he travelled to Saint Germains.

He was tall and slimly built; his countenance was tinged with a gloomy cast, and the Stuart frown was oft bristling in his brows. His presence was imposing and kinglike, but his lack of energy, his vacillating mind, and his distrustful nature belied his looks. The outside white marble and fair to the view—the inside corruption and decay.

His first step was most unwise and impolitic, and surprised at once friends and enemies. Even his sympathizing half-brother, the Duke of Berwick, admitted that " he must have lost his reason to dismiss the only Englishman he had that was able to manage his affairs ;" and he spoke highly of his able management and his astute policy in directing matters. The dismissal of Bolingbroke, which occurred about a year after his disgrace at the Hanoverian court, was occasioned partly by his incautiousness in speaking of state secrets and his irreverent fashion of ridiculing the grand pretensions of the miniature court, and partly by other indiscretions. At any rate, he was deposed from his office, and the seals were transferred to the gallant Earl of Mar.

James then proceeded to Avignon, where he held his court hard by the Palace of the Popes—a sombre Gothic pile of the twelfth century, which was raised high upon the bold rock of Doms. In one of its dripping dungeons, deep down in the solid rock and dark as Erebus, was once immured the Roman Tribune, great Rienzi. It was in Avignon, the favored, also that Petrarca first saw that Laura of Noves, who is as real to our senses as though she stood before us now.

Bolingbroke was intensely piqued at his disgrace, and he at once renounced all connection with the Jacobite cause, and, it is affirmed, made overtures to my Lord Stair for a pardon. To the Queen-mother, who had circumspectly sent him a kindly letter to inform him that "his dismissal had taken place without her knowledge and consent," his answer was prompt and curt: "I am now a free man, and may my arm rot off if ever I draw sword or pen again for your son!" Thus the chevalier created a new and powerful enemy at a time when he was in the direst need of friends.

In England the leaders of this ill-omened rebellion reaped to the utmost their reward for their attachment to the Pretender. Many minor officers underwent a short court-martial and were summarily shot; whilst the more prominent were escorted to London with fifes and drums playing a "triumphal march" to grace their "public entry." They were all tied with their arms behind their backs, not even excepting Forster, the Parliament member—a stern, cold man, whose face was granite, and who held his back as stiff as steel as he scowled on the yelling crowd who pelted him with eggs, apples, and dead cats, after the chivalrous custom of the mob at all times. In the House of Lords were impeached the Earl of Derwentwater, first cousin to the Pretender and a Roman Catholic, either of which circumstances was enough to behead him during the fearful excitement which prevailed in London; and the Earls of Nithisdale and Carnwath, both of whom narrowly escaped the axe; and various other nobles with whom history has more to do than romance.

In the Commons some of the staunchest Whigs inclined their ear to mercy, and regretted the necessity of robbing England of her noble families; but Sir Richard Steele, who had risen and moved some milder measures than the rope or the axe, was violently attacked by Walpole, who cut about in such a slashing style that "Literary Dick" almost swooned to find what a villain he had been—almost an abettor of rebels and parricides! Walpole saw the necessity for a terrible example, and he was merciless, determined that the disaffected should be taught an example which would never be forgotten.

* * * * * *

Philip slowly saunters down Pall Mall, dressed in a suit which makes many a dandy's heart fill with envy as he ruffles by, scented, curled, and pomatumed. In his right hand he carries a thin malacca switch or whip whose head is of gold and incrusted with diamonds. With it he gingerly taps a little girl who carries a bundle of clothes which have just undergone the laundress' operation of cleansing, signing her out of his way with a condescension which is simply overpowering.

As he arrives in front of that resort of wits, fools, and

quidnuncs, the Smyrna Coffee House, he halts at the door for a short time, takes his snuff-box from the pocket of his azure satin waistcoat, opens its jewelled lid with a twist which excites the admiration of the bystanders, and delicately titillates his nose with the aromatic powder—taking especial care, by the way, that a few grains shall fall on his snowy lace bosom. Entering with an easy grace, he lays a guinea on the bar, and entirely waives his claim to any change, while he looks around at the various idlers who lounge at the bar or sit in groups at the tables. "Ah! Swift, how d'ye do?" and he nods across the room to the Dean, who is drinking coffee with Mat Prior at the centre table, which is reserved exclusively for distinguished guests.

"Ah! Wharton, how d'ye do?" Swift irascibly retorts; he is nettled at his rather insolent bearing and the apparent condescension of his manner.

Philip, walking up to the table, extends his snuff-box, which favor the Dean reciprocates, and after the delicate operation of inhaling it is accomplished, Swift says, "My lord, I hear that you are to be shipped off on your travels shortly. Let me see! what is the name of your future governor?"

Philip angrily replies, "Governor? Demme, sir, secretary—secretary!"

"Well, then, secretary," replies the Dean with an ill-concealed smile.

"To-morrow I set out for Geneva. My secretary's name is Monsieur de Savatte, a right worthy Frencher."

Swift cries in affected alarm, "Save me! For your mother's sake, I hope that his principles have been Anglicized?"

A few of the bystanders titter at this remark, for in the time that he has been in London, Philip has contrived to let everybody know how widely different are his views from those of his mother's both as to religion and politics. He feels the thrust, and hears the titter; but he coolly replies, "No, my dear Swift; I understand that he is still too French to believe in the creed of which you are one Christianly expounder; but he is a Calvinist and a loyal gentleman." He turns his back on the Dean as he says this, and facing the group who have clustered near him, he exclaims in a scornful voice, "In what low hole am I that I can see in one lump such a pack of snuffling curs as ye? S'life! but that my sword has been in good blood, I'd e'en have a few passadoes at ye for my amusement!"

Instantly cries of "Stab him! knock him down! cudgel him!" are heard from those who are more concealed from view. Drawing his rapier, Philip whirls it once above his head, a motion which makes the nearest shrink from him in affright, and he stands on the defensive in expectation of an attack; those who surround him, however, are chiefly men of peace—poetasters, small wits, and literary hacks—and none of them offer to molest him. Looking at them for a moment, he bursts into a hearty laugh, and curses them soundly for a pack of cowards. When he has finished his tirade, he shows his back to them, and sheathes his blade with a vicious snap. What now? Mat Prior springing quickly to Philip's side elevates his thick cane above his head parallel-wise. No sooner has he done this when thwack! falls a heavy cudgel on it with such force as to make the protecting stick flatten Philip's hat over his eyes.

Directly he turned his back on the titterers, one cowardly fellow aimed a blow at him which would have certainly broken his head if Prior had not diverted its destination, and returned the compliment by levelling the would-be hero to the ground. The landlord now pushes in and swears, if order is not restored, that he will give the alarm and have them all arrested.

Philip thanks Prior for his good service, and asks the favor of a bottle of wine with him, of which he also invites Swift to partake; but the worthy Dean declines, and pleading an engagement in St. James' Park, he leaves them to discuss it alone.

"It was a lucky ward-off which saved my skull that time, Mr. Prior! Allow me: 'Your health and success.'" And the glasses clink together before they are emptied.

"Thanks, my lord," replies Prior. "You spoke of going abroad. Do you design travelling in France at all?"

"Very probably I shall. I should like to see Paris vastly well."

"Avignon is not far from there?" adds Prior, in a low voice.

"Well, even Avignon has its sights," replies Philip with a smile, which his companion returns. "How is it with yourself and the government now, Mr. Prior? All quarrels settled?"

"Yes, my lord, and I am thankful for it. My long confinement seriously impaired my health." He refers to the two years during which he was kept a prisoner in his own house.

"S'life!" replies Philip, "I'd have run away long before two years expired or a week either, or else I'd have fired my prison. But I must leave you! Bye-bye! I am off for the park and a bit of fresh air." And paying his bill, he goes out.

He has not strolled along very far when he encounters his friend, Sir Harry Hautefort, whose arm he takes and they walk off together: ogling the fair dames as they pass, or criticizing the dresses of the fops and cavaliers.

Sir Harry unluckily steps on a loose stone just as a glistening beau is passing him, and the mud spirts in a dirty stream on his pink silk stockings. The injured cavalier, laying his hand threateningly on his rapier, scowls at the author of his misfortune, but pursues his way in silence, while Philip recites, in a tone loud enough to be heard a dozen yards off, the following consoling couplet:—

> "Oh, bear me to the paths of fair Pall Mall;
> Safe are thy pavements; grateful is thy smell!"

Those who have seen the occurrence enjoy a laugh at the expense of the spattered gentleman, who, however, does not deign to notice Philip's audacity in thus making him a public jest.

"Faith!" says Sir Harry, "if I had been in his position, and he in mine, it is my calm opinion that he would have received a kicking for his carelessness."

Philip laughing, and directing his attention to a couple of well-known Whig noblemen who are conversing together a short distance from them, says, "Harry, drop a few yards behind me, and mark the row I'll raise in St. James!"

Accordingly, Sir Harry lags behind, while Philip advances to within a few feet of the gentlemen whom he had pointed out, and with a few prefatory flourishes he begins to sing in a loud voice:—

> The king shall hae his ain again

All stop and turn in surprise as they hear this treasonous refrain sung in broad day, and in the most frequented part of the park. Still Philip continues his song, while the bewildered Whigs look with horror on the daring gallant who thus openly defies them.

Sir Harry takes himself off as soon as he sees how matters are going, and he is now ensconced behind a tree at some distance from Philip. The crowd is rapidly thickening, still Philip is unmolested, and still his song is heard. But now cries of "Papist! traitor! rebel!" begin to sound from some of the angry spectators. Suddenly the crowd opens and falls back, and the guard appears. Their captain walking straight to Philip, demands his sword, and informs him that he is under arrest. Philip stopping his song, exclaims, "My sword? You'll get it in your vitals if you interrupt me again!" and making a grasp at its hilt, he attempts to draw it; but the officer, striking his hand, knocks off Philip's grip, and drawing it out himself, he commands his men to "lay hold of the prisoner." Philip, seeing the utter futility of resistance, spitefully finishes his song, and says, half to himself and half to the officer of the guard—

"The Earl he drew out half his sword;
The guard drew out the rest!"

Luckily for him, the justice before whom he is taken happens to be Jacobitish in his principles, and has a predilection for the bonnie king who never got his own again; so that he is merely reprimanded and mulcted in the sum of five guineas for creating a public disturbance and then discharged, neither a wiser nor a happier man, but with an idea that home is the right place to favor with his presence after his late wise actions.

No sooner has he entered than her ladyship desires his attendance in the drawing-room, and thither he goes. The occupants are my lady and a tall, cadaverous, pedantic-looking man, whose lantern jaws give an unnatural length to his pinched face. His rusty, cropped wig is pulled down too much in front, for it nearly covers his bushy eyebrows; his dress is faded and sombre, and it has scarce an inch of lace or edging on it from his collar to his square-toed shoes. Poverty-stricken learn-

14*

ing betrays its presence in his every motion or gesture, in every seam and band about him. Philip's first thoughts are, "This must be Monsieur de Savatte. S'life! what a scarecrow! I shall have to dress him decently before I'll be seen with him in public. What an air of Calvinistic morality incrusts his antique person! Even his buttons are precise and formal, and his shoes are actually devoid of buckles! 'Sooth, I have an aversion to the man already."

Her ladyship introduces this personage to Philip as his future governor, with many commendations of his learning and research, which he acknowledges by a stiff bow. Philip shakes hands with M. de Savatte, and says, in incisive accents, "Monsieur de Savatte, I wish you to distinctly understand that in future you are in my employ as private secretary, not as governor. I object to the latter title decidedly."

M. de Savatte replies, with a gesture of surprise, "My lord, may I ask why the worthy title of governor is obnoxious to you?"

Philip says blandly, "Of course, I object on the score of veracity. The title governor would be an untruth, for you will never govern me, though you may advise me."

M. de Savatte extends his hands in amazement at hearing such rebellious words from his future pupil, and turns to his mother with a look of inquiry. Greatly mortified at Philip's words, she forces a smile as she replies, "Philip often says more than he means; he does—"

But Philip ruins her palliative by saying, "In this case, though, I said less than I meant, Monsieur!"

A lackey entering at this instant, hands a letter to Philip, who, bowing apologetically to my lady and M. de

Savatte, goes to the window to read it. He looks perplexed and mystified, as though he cannot comprehend the meaning of the letter. Finally he throws open the window, and calls down to the man, who awaits his answer, "Here, fellow, take your precious scrawl back to your mistress, and tell her that I never honor dead men's drafts. Leave, now, and never trouble me again about matters of which I am as ignorant as the king himself!" So saying, he throws the letter out of the window, and once more addresses himself to his future tutor. "We start to-morrow, I suppose. Where is our first stopping place? Paris, or Geneva, or where?"

M. de Savatte replies, with a stiff jerk of his body, "Geneva was mentioned by her ladyship as the best place for the instillation of the right principles into your mind!"

"Ah!" Philip adds with an incredulous look.

My lady, who begins to fear that Philip's insolence may create difficulties which will be hard to adjust if the conversation is prolonged, now bows the learned man out, with an injunction to be all ready by the morrow, to which he replies, "I have only to pack a few books— my classics and metaphysics, and then I am ready."

As the door closes after him, Philip begins to criticize his looks and his speech; but his mother, good-naturedly defending, beseeches her son to pay great attention to M. de Savatte's teachings, and to profit by his learning.

"Rely on me," he replies with a sudden twinge of conscience: "Hereafter I'll try to be less rackety in my actions. I fear that I have been the cause of many a sad day and night with you!"

She replies: "My son, I cannot deny it; but if you will conduct yourself better in future, you will be the cause of more happiness to me than ever you have been misery."

Philip kisses her affectionately, and a pang of remorse touches him as he sees how wan and worn she looks. Poor woman! as she kissed her darling "good-bye," the next day, she was heavy at heart, and felt an indistinct foreboding that she would never see him again.

CHAPTER XXIV.

Chremylus.—Phœbus protect us! Gracious deities!
　　　Why, what the mischief has this fellow met with?

Chremylus.—Hey day! whom have we here?
　　　　　　　　　　ARISTOPHANES' "PLUTUS."

PHILIP and M. de Savatte land in safety after an uneventful voyage, during which Philip's conduct has been most exemplary, and has agreeably surprised his governor, who thought he had caught a tartar when he saw him for the first time; and in the letter which he wrote to Lady Wharton, the tutor gave her a glowing account of her son's actions.

They do not tarry long in any of the towns or principalities through which they pass, except in a small electorate on the road to Hanover, where Philip insists on stopping for a whole day despite the remonstrances of M. de Savatte. He has seen a pretty German flower-girl pass before the window of his room, and has at once taken a violent fancy for her; he replies to his impatient governor, "Monsieur, she is lovely, divine! I must see her again even if it is only for five minutes! Such a sensation as admiration is not to be sneered at, sir, in my *blasé* condition."

"*Eh bien*, my lord! as you wish; but the sooner that we arrive at Geneva, the better."

Philip finally agrees not to remain here longer than to-day, whether or no he sees the flower-girl again. He occupies his time in going to court and raising a flutter among the punctilious princelings and the court dames who are all agog to see the son of the great English nobleman, whose reputation has extended even to this dull region. He is feted, caressed, and—greatest honor of all—decorated with an order of knighthood, which he is assured by the courtiers will insure him respect in any quarter of the globe, to which modest assertion he replies, "My lords, I do not value the ribbon the worth of a groat on that account. My name is a warranty of respect, as you all know;" and he feels a trifle offended; nevertheless, he is quite proud of his decoration, and wears it in a prominent place on his waistcoat lapel.

Philip does not find his flower-girl, however, as he has forgotten all about her by the following morning; M. de Savatte does not recall her to his memory, and they set out for Hanover, "England's royal nursery," arriving in the capital safe and sound. For two or three days they stop at the best hotel which the town boasts, when they receive an invitation from a German nobleman, who places his house at the disposal of the young lord. Philip accepts the invitation, and he and M. de Savatte are now the guests of Count von Erschlief.

Philip and his host are together in a bright, sunny room, which faces the Platze, whose linden trees are agreeable to the eye and fragrant to the smell. In guttural German, Von Erschlief questions, "How are politics in England, my lord? The mails are so irregular that I am often behindhand with outside news?"

In his own estimation, the count is a great politician —skilful, sapient, and shrewd, but in truth he is as dunderheaded a German as ever waded through musty tomes of metaphysics or dabbled in abstruse philosophies. He is short and stout, and his fat cheeks fall in unctuous layers from his lacklustre eyes to his neck. M. de Savatte is in the back part of the room, where stands a small library of books and MSS., and he is so absorbed with its treasures that he ignores everything else.

"My dear count," replies Philip with a mischievous look, "I am rather ignorant of affairs in England at present myself; but it is confidently reported that Madame Robethon is in high favor with his majesty, and moreover that she has turned high Tory, i'faith!"

The count stares at him in surprise, and, after a moment's silence, he splutters out, "Mein Gott! is it so? This is news indeed!" To which Philip nods affirmatively, with a countenance of regretful solemnity and a deep sigh.

To fully understand the ridiculous nature of Philip's assertion, it is necessary to know that Madame Robethon is a Hanoverian lady of low rank, who has a body so squat and a voice so disagreeably coarse and croaking, that she has been christened at court by the cognomen of Madame Grenouille.* Her principles are Whig to a proverb. Taking his departure, after the above astounding intelligence, Philip leaves the count in a most unenviable state of mind on account of the vexatious aspect of affairs in London.

M. de Savatte has remained so absorbed in the treasures he has found, as to miss entirely the conversation which has taken place at the other end of the room. Philip looks towards him and smiles at his rapt gesticulations. The tutor is grasping in both hands an immense vellum-bound folio, which is protected at the corners with wide strips of tarnished brass; he has not taken the trouble to go to the table and lay it there for easy inspection, but he has placed his right foot on his left knee, thereby forming a projection on which the folio reclines, and he

* Frog.

cranes his neck in a painful manner in order to peruse the top lines. His countenance is serious and earnest. "Right, right," he exclaims; "Cato in his time knew of three kinds of myrtle—to wit, the white, the black, and the Conjugala, so called haply of wedlock or marriage, and peradventure it may!" Philip leaning over to see what it is that interests him so much, reads on the top line, the title: "Plinie's Naturall Historie."

"Parbleu, Monsieur! Plinie seems to engage both your eyes and ears. I have romanced most wonderfully for the last half hour, and have not been once corrected!"

The studious pedant raises his head in bewilderment, blushes and apologizes: "My lord, pardon my rudeness, I pray you. I was so interested that I recked not of time or place!"

"All right," Philip carelessly replies; "I feel as though I should enjoy a promenade to-day. The weather is glorious. Will you accompany me?"

The tutor replies, "My lord, your wishes are my commands!"

"Provided the wishes are of the right sort!" adds Philip.

Monsieur pays no attention to this remark, but launches at once into enthusiastic praise of Pliny and his works, proceeding in learned jargon to explain his system until Philip impatiently tells him to drop the subject and walk out with him.

Whilst they are out, Philip casts his eye on a fine English stallion, whose coat is as glossy and smooth as satin and as black as ebony. The rider bestrides the horse with the ease and grace of a practised horseman, extorting an exclamation of pleasure from Philip, who appreciates his thorough command over the animal. Regardless of his total ignorance of the equestrian, Philip advances towards him and raises his hat, a salutation which the rider returns, at the same time checking his horse.

"I beg a thousand pardons, sir, for this intrusion," says Philip; "I am Lord Wharton of Rathfarnham and Catherlough."

"And I, my lord," replies the stranger, "am Sir Geoffrey Mountairy."

Philip resumes in an abrupt manner, " Sir Geoffrey, I have a desire to purchase your horse. It pleases me mightily. Will you sell it ?"

" Really, my lord," Sir Geoffrey replies, taken aback at the strange proposal, but, as he is rather reduced in circumstances at present, willing to dispose of the animal if a good price were offered; "hitherto the desire has never entered my mind, nor do I particularly wish to sell him; but if you will promise to treat him well, I may be induced to part with him!"

Philip hurriedly replies, "I will give you any sum you may deem him worth—five hundred guineas!"

Sir Geoffrey, rejoicing at the mention of so large a price, closes with the offer at once.

M. de Savatte in vain argues and expostulates. Philip is deaf to reason, and tells his tutor, with a sprinkling of oaths, "I will have the horse, cost what it may!" and resumes to Sir Geoffrey: "Send him to Count von Erschlief's, and I will give you a draft on London."

Sir Geoffrey replies that he will go thither at once, if Philip so wishes; to this proposition Philip agrees, and he hurries his angry governor off home again to await the distinguished arrival.

In due time the stallion comes, and of course, receives its meed of admiration and praise. The count is highly pleased with him, and declares that it is a horse fit for the Czar, an opinion in which Philip concurs.

Philip is in his room glancing through an abstruse work

on the law of nations, which he comprehends as thoroughly, after two or three industrious readings, as an ordinary mind would after a month's hard study; for with a memory wonderfully retentive, he combines reasoning faculties of no common order. Throwing the book from him with a disdainful gesture, he exclaims, "Tut! Savatte told me to devote at least a day to the study of the polemical introduction. Ah, ha! I would wager heavy odds that I already know his theories better than himself! when he—Eh? come in!" he cries in response to a low tap at the door.

M. de Savatté enters with a lugubrious expression on his dried features. He holds in his hand a letter whose edging is black an inch deep—a sign that death has robbed some one of a friend or a relative. Philip turns a trifle pale as he takes the letter, and when he sees his own quarterings on the black seal, it almost falls through his trembling fingers. M. de Savatte considerately leaving him alone, softly closes the door after his exit. Philip reads a few lines, and his hand crushes the paper with a convulsive grasp.

"Mother, mother! I am all alone now! O God! Why did you die?"

His tears patter on the paper thick and fast as he resumes the perusal: "Your property will be taken in charge by trustees appointed as by law. You will be allowed an income of £2000 per annum, until you are of age!" "Trustees, eh? cent per centums," he mutters; "a charge of twelve shillings for their care of a guinea!—Mother! mother!" he cries in a savage, bitter manner! "A curse on the fate which robbed me of you! Mother is dead? dead? My head whirls so I cannot comprehend!"

* * * * * *

He awakes next morning gloomy and taciturn. M.

de Savatte observes his moodiness, and justly ascribes it to the ill news which he has received, for a document has been sent to him from the trustees authorizing him to retain his position as tutor to his lordship. At breakfast few words pass between them, but when Philip has finished he says, in a low voice, "Monsieur, to-day I begin a new course of life. I shall eschew Toryism, and be the Protestant which my—which I ought to have been!"

Monsieur nods assentingly, and with rather a mystified air, for he has not known Philip's proclivities for Jacobitism and the Scarlet Lady.

All the morning Philip is obedient and attentive to the instructions of his really talented tutor, but towards evening he becomes the same irrepressible pupil as before, and instead of working out some knotty problem, or construing some difficult passage, laughs the questions away with a clever pun, or an amusingly inappropriate question, causing his troubled tutor a world of thinking to answer.

Early the following day they depart for Geneva, where Philip is to remain until he shall have completed his education.

CHAPTER XXV.

Cleon.—With all speed I fly—
        SOPHOCLES.

Cleon.—One word at parting—I have left your service.
Who follows me, believe, will prove a knave
Still greater than myself.
        ARISTOPHANES.

PHILIP is far better pleased with his new quarters than he thought he would be. At present he is lazily sauntering through the jeweller's region in company with M. de Savatte, and he examines with great interest the rare workmanship which is displayed in their watches, rings, and bracelets. Gennaro Lemontri's shop he admires most of all, and in return for Gennaro's kindly attention to him during his inspection of the trays of costly gems, Philip purchases three tiny watches, beautifully chased and enamelled, and seven or eight sparkling rings, besides various other knicknacks, amounting, as the bill declares, to 350 guineas and 15 shillings, in English money. Gennaro generously throws off the latter item, and Philip, giving him an order for the amount, requests him to send the purchases to his lodgings.

Philip surveys the rapid torrent of the Rhone, as it dashes under the bridges connecting the several parts of the town, with a vivid appreciation of the beauty of the scene. The glaciers of Chamouni, and Mont Blanc the mighty, fill him with indescribable feelings. M. de Savatte, whose varied knowledge is always useful, regales his charge with romantic stories of the passes of the Tête Noire, and the dangerous foot-paths of the Col du

Geant, which lead into beautiful Piedmont: and he thrills him with graphic accounts of the terrible crevasses of the Mer de Glace, that are so deep and green and cold.

Philip thinks that he would like to live here forever, and he is sure he will never tire of Geneva, asking himself, "Can there be a more beautiful place in all the world than this city of frozen beauties?" He proposes a walk about the environs, to which Monsieur assents; before they have got fairly under way, they are joined by a friend of Philip's—Sir Edgely Warely—with whom he has become acquainted among the riotous crew of the Mohocks, who asks permission to make one of his party, a request which Philip gladly grants.

Although Sir Edgely has openly professed Whig sentiments in England, he has been viewed with suspicion by that party; indeed, there are some who have not hesitated to insinuate that he maintains a treasonable correspondence with the exiled court, and that he is a disciple of the Scarlet Lady. These charges, however, have never been substantiated, and as he is clever, witty, and handsome, he has always mixed in tolerable society. Mayhap his dexterity with the rapier and his quickness to avenge an insult or a slur, have tended to make questioners or accusers wary in their actions.

"Are you in Geneva permanently, my lord?"

"Yes," replies Philip. "This is my resting-place for a year or so."

"Under favor, my lord, may I ask who is M. de Sav—I really forget his name;" adding, with a laugh, "he looks like an ossified epitome of learning!"

"Oh! M. de Savatte? He is my secretary!"

After a short conversation on minor topics, the beauty of the surrounding scenery, and the odd dresses of the Germans, Sir Edgely says carelessly, but with a quick, comprehensive glance at Philip; "Eh! my lord, oranges once more top the gallant oak!"

Philip replies hotly, "Yes; poor Jamie met a crushing defeat both on the field and in the house, when two such gentlemen as Derwentwater and Kenmure were eased of their heads to delight a pack of gaping curs!"

A curious, triumphant-like smile lights up his companion's face as he replies, "Ay, my lord. When King James heard the news, he came as near crying as a king can."

Philip starts as he hears the Pretender called by his Jacobite title, and says musingly, "I should like well to go to Avignon to note how James and his courtiers compare with our head and his creatures at home."

"Compare!" returns Sir Edgely; "the thought is absurd! England's best blood is with his sacred majesty, and all that are chivalrous and brave enough are with their true king awaiting but an opportunity to follow him to his stolen kingdom, there to reap the reward of their loyalty and affection; and those who have cringed to the Dutch glutton and his vrows shall be banished the kingdom root and stock!"

M. de Savatte, who has been engaged in the examination of some pieces of rock or spar a few yards away, catching a few words of Sir Edgely's reply, bustles towards his pupil, fearful lest the stranger may be a Jacobite agent on the lookout for converts. Sir Edgely noticing his approach, however, adroitly turns the conversation to more general topics, and descants admiringly on the grandeur of the scenery and its chastening effect on the mind.

In a little time Sir Edgely announces his intention of leaving; before doing so, however, he slyly slips a small packet into Philip's hand which closes on it immediately.

After this, he returns to town, whither Philip and Monsieur soon follow.

Arriving at the hotel, Philip waits until his tutor is engrossed in the contents of a musty volume called "A true accounte of ye Dryads and Hamadryads." He then takes the packet from his pocket to inspect it. He finds a ribbon within it about six inches long; its color is red, with a white space in the centre whereon is depicted the chevalier holding a sponge in his right hand to signify that if he ever regains his kingdom, he will wipe off the public debt, which debt is the cause of much bitter feeling in England, and affords a great rallying cry for the Tories. Around the sides runs the legend "For our wronged king and our oppressed country." Attached to the silk by a gold pin made in the shape of an oak-leaf, is a white cockade. Philip's heart beats quickly as he unpins it, and he exclaims, with a glance at Monsieur, "It smells Mar-ish!" He holds it in his hand a moment as if in consideration. Finally picking up his coat, he puts it on. Now he proceeds to attach the cockade to the right breast, pinning the ribbon on his inner coat. Thus attired he consults the glass. The adornments *do* become him! The pink lapels of his waistcoat do not accord with the red ribbon as well as they might have done; but taking the effect all in all, it is satisfactory; and for variety's sake he avows himself high Tory and Jacobite.

It is early morning, and the sun's rays scarcely glint on the waters of the Rhone. Philip leaves his room, and walks to the stable, where his new purchase munches the straw in lazy contentment; stepping into the stall, he pats the stallion soothingly on the side. "Oho, my beauty, you belong to a Wharton now. To-morrow you will belong to even a greater than he—a Stuart!" The animal whinnies and paws as though he understands him, and half turns his head to lay his nose on the shoulder of his new master: "Yes, to-day decides me. I'll go to Avignon, and leave that crusty curmudgeon of a pedant to get along without me. Faith! the separation will not kill him. His books are more to his taste than I am, parbleu!"

Laughing noisily as if at the contemplation of a good joke, he resumes: "I'll leave him a companion suited to his nature i' faith!"

He steps out at a rapid pace as though he suddenly bethinks him of an important commission. Yesterday he saw a party of itinerant Savoyards who had with them a led bear, which danced and capricoled to the rude music of their rustic pipes; and he noticed them as they entered a small cabaret in the lower part of the town. Towards this cabaret he goes. He opens the door, and steps inside, to the surprise and joy of mine host, who seldom sees a gallant of such feather enter his humble place; he is almost too overcome to reply to Philip's question, "Are the Savoys who exhibit a bear about the streets lodging here?" after a short pause, he replies, "Yes, milord, I will call them;" and he bawls to them in the peasant patois to come downstairs immediately as milord wishes to see them. Turning to Philip he asks him whether the bear shall come also, to which he replies with a smile: "Of course! that is the animal which I most desire too see." The order is repeated, and shortly Master Bruin is heard treading heavily down the stairs, and he flumps into the bar in company with his masters.

Philip tells them that he wishes to purchase their animal, but they are so sleepy that they can scarcely comprehend him. However, when he thrusts a handful of guineas in the hand of the foremost of them, and grasps Bruin's chain, they seem satisfied, for they nod their acquiescence in a thankful manner, and slowly reascend to their sleeping place.

Philip marches triumphantly along the still-deserted streets, while his prize follows meekly after, his long, scuffling strides compelling Philip to proceed at a mighty brisk pace. As he draws near to his lodgings, he calls to one of the three lads who have joined him on the way, and tells him to hold the animal until he returns. The lad looks at Bruin distrustfully, but as the bear is muzzled, and appears tolerably peaceful, he agrees, keeping a respectful distance from him withal. Philip stepping carefully inside, indites the following polite epistle to his unsuspecting governor, who reposes soundly in bed and has never a thought of the scene which will greet him when he enters the beloved library.

"*Most erudite and omniscient governor:* No longer able to stand your inquisitorial ill-usage, I leave you. However, that you may not want company, I have left you a bear as the most suitable companion that could be picked out for you.

Your long-bearing pupil,
PHILIP WHARTON.

To M. DE SAVATTE."

Philip, chuckling maliciously as he folds and seals it, lays it in a prominent pigeon-hole on the escritoire, where Monsieur will be sure to see it at a glance. Now he packs his most portable things, and puts them under his arm; the coat and waistcoat which he wears are those that are so loyally decorated. He returns to the future companion of Monsieur, and rewards the lad who has held it during his absence, promising him an additional gold piece if he will lead it into the library and leave it with an old gentleman who will enter there in a few minutes. The boy gives the promise, and receives the gratuity.

In order to enjoy the joke to its fullest extent, Philip stations himself at the latticed window of the library. He knows Monsieur's regularity in his movements, and momentarily expects him to enter.

"S' life! he comes," cries Philip.

The tutor enters and gazes at the note with inquiring eyes, and slowly, deliberately puts on his horn-rimmed spectacles. Breaking the seal, he examines the writing; his brow knits, and his lips compress and open alternately. Turning around as if at some interruption, he opens the door: Philip almost chokes with laughter as he sees him jump back in affright. The grinning urchin leads the bear into the middle of the room, and before its astonished occupant has a chance to speak to him he is gone. Monsieur looks first at his shaggy guest and then at his letter, while Bruin rears himself on his hams, and rubs his ears and his nose with a comical clumsiness; Monsieur compromises matters by entrenching himself behind the wide table and keeping a wary eye on the enemy whilst he reads the letter. Philip can surmise what his sensations are by the varied expressions of his face during the perusal, and he enjoys the affair hugely.

"Sapristi! I must decamp, or else I'll be caught," he mutters, and with a farewell look at his governor, he repairs to the stable where his stallion "King Jamie" is ready saddled and bridled.

CHAPTER XXVI.

Saladin.—Here is a windfall, truly! Is there more
   To come?
            LESSING'S "NATHAN THE WISE."

Withal the king——
   With his thin, anxious face and pale,
   Sat leaning forward through the tale,—
      MORRIS' "THE MAN BORN TO BE KING."

PHILIP is at present wandering alone through the streets of Lyons in order to have a look at anything amusing or interesting, for wherever he goes he invariably sees everything that is worth seeing; and as he has heard of the ancient Chapel de Notre Dame de Fourvières, he determines to have a survey of it ere he leaves the city. This chapel is not remarkable for its grandeur or beauty; on the contrary, it is very plain and modest; its richly stained windows alone redeem it from a charge of ugly bareness.

Philip stands in front of the light-flooded altar and takes in at a glance all the gorgeous paraphernalia of the Romish creed; and a feeling of solemnity and awe strikes his senses; yet vague, troubled doubts rise in his mind at the sight, and the prejudices of other days surge in his heart.

He turns to leave, but a sudden change in his feelings decides him to remain, and kneeling reverently before the altar he breathes a prayer—it is his first in the house of the Pontiff of Rome. He rises and seats himself on one of the low stools which stand near the confessional. "I wonder if my mother looks down on me now? If so, she will think I am a most dutiful son; Jacobite and Papist—the one from principle, the other from fancy or —conviction? At all events the one seems to have led to the other, so that I 'll e'en call it a sequence of consequences." Hearing a footstep behind him, he looks around to see who the new-comer is; it is Sir Edgely Warely.

"My dear fellow!" cries Philip, "on my life I am glad to see you! However did you manage to scale this holy height?"

Sir Edgely, who looks as surprised as Philip, replies, "Well, my lord, I chanced to be in the neighborhood, and so I thought I would pay Notre Dame a visit, and recite a few pater nosters for the benefit of my soul!" as he finishes, he glances at the decorations pinned on Philip's coat. Philip notices the direction of his glance, and says: "Let me thank you for these, Sir Edgely;" and he points to the ribbon and the cockade. Sir Edgely starts as if surprised, and exclaims, "My lord, I was sure that your heart was true to his majesty! Do you intend to go to Avignon, where the court is to be held for the present?"

Philip looks perplexed as he answers, "In truth, I know not how he would receive the son of the great Whig leader! No, I will not go. I 'll write a letter to him, and proffer my allegiance! Sir Edgely, do you intend to go there? If you do, let me beg you to be my messenger."

"I am going thither," he replies.

"Good! You will take a stallion which I have bought especially for his majesty, and present it to him with my compliments?"

Sir Edgely, eagerly replies, "My lord, I am only too glad to be able to oblige you. I will set out at once."

Philip replies, "We must first retrace our steps to

town, and I will write the letter; then off you go with lightning speed to our gracious master!"

Philip writes the letter, and the Jacobite agent sets out post for Avignon to carry in the adherence of this most important ally. Philip awaits an answer in great impatience, and can scarcely sleep all night. The next day he is notified that a gentleman is awaiting him in the bar-room. He dresses himself in the violet-satin suit which is slashed with amber-colored silk and heavily laced, attaches the ribbon and cockade to his breast, takes a final look in the glass to curl his embryo moustaches properly, and then walks down stairs in a flutter of excitement to see the royal emissary. He observes a tall, broad-shouldered cavalier who is attired quite as gayly as himself, and who is resting one arm on the oaken bar, while the other clasps the waist of the pretty serving-maid, whose face is as red as a peony. He is speaking to her in the French patois, and calls her by many fond names. He turns as Philip enters, and favors him with a haughty stare, which is returned with one even haughtier and more insolent; but the girl explains matters by saying, "Milord Wharton—Milord Winton!"

The stranger's attitude changes at once; extending his hand to Philip, he says, "My lord, allow me to apologize for my boorish conduct; for which I shall never forgive myself. My name is George Seton, Earl of Winton."

Philip is pleased at James' condescension in sending a peer to meet him, and he cordially responds to the compliments which Seton delivers with the grace and affability for which his lordship is noted. His face is a picture of careless, jovial good-humor and nonchalance; his tawny moustaches surmount a mouth that is delicate enough for a woman; and his eyes betoken a cheery, hopeful disposition. Mad George, as he is called in London, for his many odd freaks and escapades, engaged in the last insurrection in England, and was sentenced to death despite the clever defence which he made, and the manifold tricks by which he tried to evade the law. During his trial, the high steward Lord Cowper, having overruled his casuistical objections with much asperity, he replied with scornful emphasis, "I hope you will do me justice, and not make use of Cowper-law; as we say in our county—hang a man first, and then judge him!" He managed to escape, however, by sawing the bars of his cell with a file which one of his light-o'-loves—a Mistress Wilsome—threw into his window at midnight, after the warden had gone his rounds. Before the insurrection he had lived for some time with a blacksmith in France in the capacity of bellows-blower and odd-jobber; and during that time he did not hold the slightest communication with his family, nor did he send for a penny of the vast revenues which he inherited, and which are now confiscated by the government.

Philip plies the emissary with questions relative to the chevalier and his surroundings, waiting impatiently for him to disclose the royal message with which he has been intrusted.

"My lord," says Seton, "his gracious majesty has done me the honor to appoint me as your conductor. He has expressed his royal desire to see you at court; and has also authorized me to express to you his thanks for the superb horse which you presented to him. If you are ready to set out, we may as well be off for Avignon at once."

"With all my heart," cries Philip, joyfully.

James reclines in his chair of state with dignity and grace, and as he extends his hand for his new adherent to kiss, he looks a proud Stuart from head to foot. Philip rises at his request, and makes a low obeisance, retiring backward until he stands by the side of the Earl of Winton, who is engaged in a serious flirtation with Mistress Arual Dolling, a beauty of sixteen summers, who has been spoiled and petted until she is as imperious and exacting as an eastern despot. Her figure is small, but plump, and in all her motions she is as graceful as a fawn. Her complexion is bright and fair, and she owns a pair of azure eyes which swim in coquettish expressiveness. On the left side of her dimpled chin are two round patches, and the curled, pouting lips above seem made expressly for love's kisses to die upon.

Philip is introduced to her, and at once the fickle beauty bestows all her attention upon him, shamefully neglecting "Mad George," who lifts his eyebrows, and smiles deprecatingly, as if to say, "All right—as you please— it is your nature, and you cannot help it!" Philip exerts himself to please her; and his well-modulated voice, his wit, and his vivacity keep her in a state of piqued pleasure and half-admiration of a man who dares to cross words with her, and even come out the victor, while protesting his defeat, and begging for quarter. It seems that her laughter disturbs his majesty, for he taps significantly on the arm of his chair, and contracts his brow in a frown. Hiding her face behind her sandal-wood fan, she makes a moué of defiance at him, which amuses Philip beyond measure. "S'life!" he says, in a low voice, "I am so angry at your léze-majesté that I must e'en let Seton into the affair;" turning to the earl, who has been scanning the assembled demoiselles and courtiers with a critical eye, he says, "Come, my lord, you desolate us by turning your back on us so coldly. Give Mistress Dolling and myself the benefit of your conversation!"

"Transfix me! but I'll do so right willingly; more for my own sake, though, than for yours."

James, who has been conversing in low whispers with Earl Mar, who seems to have pressed some subject to which he is averse, finally consents, and Mar, after begging permission, steps to Philip's side, and whispers in a low tone, which none overhear except Seton and Mistress Dolling, "My lord, allow me to unofficially announce to you that his most gracious majesty designs to confer upon you the title and privileges of Duke of Northumberland. I have the honor of first congratulating your grace!" shaking his hand cordially he returns to James, who has watched the proceedings from under his eyes with a half-dissatisfied look.

Philip is overjoyed at this new sign of the royal favor, and his blood tingles with loyalty and devotion to James, who is, in this instance, wise against his will, through the diplomacy of Mar, who sees that Philip may be of great use in furthering the designs of the exiled court. Philip's whole mind now centres itself on the idea of doing something to show that he appreciates the honor which has been shown him; but all at once this idea flies to the winds at the recollection that he has left his prettiest snuff-box in his room at Lyons, and he determines to return for it immediately, and get back again in time to take an active part in Jacobite politics or battles. He whispers his intentions to Seton, who stares at his affection for a trifling snuff-box; and excuses himself to Mistres Dolling, who is highly offended that he can leave her for anything in the world, so high an opinion does she entertain of herself.

James beckons to Seton to come to him, an order which he obeys, and stepping behind his chair he awaits patiently any commands that may be given him. After finishing his discourse with Mar, James turns his attention to Seton, saying, with a kindly smile, "Where found you our new subject, my lord?"

"In a dirty cabaret in the lower section of Lyons, your majesty."

"And how did he express himself at our message?"

"He was overjoyed, your majesty, and seemed to feel the great honor bestowed upon him."

James nods his head sagaciously, and says, "We have finished with you, my lord." At this Seton retires from the presence and renews his flirtation with Mistress Dolling, who welcomes him with an enchanting smile.

James, leaning over to Mar, inquires: "Think you it is possible that the heroic Winifred of Nithisdale will be at our court to-morrow? 'Faith we would like to see the woman who is so ingenious as to have deceived the veteran gaolers of our London Tower! Have you the particulars of the affair? It is said that you have received despatches from England lately containing a detailed account of her husband's escape? We would enjoy its recital."

"Your majesty, it will give me great pleasure to tell all I know of the subject," and he relates his story, which reads more like a romance than a stern matter-of-fact recital, in which a gentle head was saved by the fearless devotion of its owner's wife—the beautiful Winifred—who is thus described by one who saw her: "She is delicate and feminine in appearance, and her hair is light-brown, and generally powdered. Her eyes are large and soft; her features regular, and her complexion is fair and pale."

James listens with great attention, and as he reaches that part where Winifred travelled to Traquhair to rescue the family papers, and returned safely to London with them, his majesty claps his hands in great glee; but when he hears how spiteful the king was towards her,

16*

and how he said that "Lady Nithisdale did whatever she pleased in spite of him, and that she had given him more trouble than any woman in Europe," he grinds his teeth, and the Stuart frown mantles on his face. "The boor!" he exclaims; "there is as much chivalry in him as there is in one of his native hogs!"

"Or his mistresses," adds Mar.

James smiles as he answers, "Ay! neither von Schulenberg nor Kilmanseck can boast of much but adiposity, idiocy, and the hatred of our loyal subjects." He remains silent for a few minutes, while Mar occupies himself in running his fingers through his towering wig. "Mar, the Duke of Argyle is said to be tired of this Hanoverian usurper!"

"Your majesty, he is a great friend of the Prince."

"Ergo, an enemy to his father," adds James.

Mar, laughing low, wonders aloud at his majesty's astuteness. "Your majesty, it is surmised that Walpole is being mightily worried by my Lord Sunderland and divers others at court, and it is thought that he will resign ere long, and take his tool Townshend along with him!"

"Ah! I did not know of that!" replies James, and he begins to count the beads of his rosary, and his lips move quickly as he recites a pater-noster or an ave Maria; the while his eyes are cast devoutly on the floor; suddenly he ceases his devotions, and asks: "Where is Mademoiselle Delamour? We would see her." And again his beads occupy his attention, while Mar goes in search of the notorious and beautiful Desirette Delamour, a favored mistress of James—and only a few of his courtiers.

CHAPTER XXVII.

"Let other nice lords skulk at home from the wars,
Prank'd up and adorn'd with garters and stars,
Which but twinkle like those in a cold, frosty night;
While to yours you are adding such lustre and light,
That if you proceed, I'm sure very soon
'Twill be brighter and larger than the sun or the moon."
SWIFT'S PARODY.

INSTEAD of returning to Avignon, as he intended when he set out for Lyons to regain his precious snuff-box, Philip bethinks him that Paris will be better suited for one of his parts and acquirements; and so to Paris he goes. His first act of wisdom in this city is his visit to the Queen Dowager, the consort of James the 2d, residing at St. Germains, surrounded by the exiled or disaffected nobles who still retain the idea of seating the chevalier on the throne and then reaping the reward of their constancy. The papers which endow Philip with the empty title of Duke of Northumberland have been forwarded to him from Avignon, and under that title he now goes, to the surprise and disgust of the loyal Englishmen who chance to be in Paris, and to the immense delight of the opposing party.

He takes a superb residence in the vicinity of the Tuileries, and has it furnished and adorned with such lavish extravagance as to excite comment among even the spendthrift Parisians, who fritter and gamble their fortunes away on the whims of a mistress or the turn of a dice. His equipage is the finest in town; for outriders he has two negroes, whom he calls Mustapha and

Mahomet, in ridicule of George's back-stair attendants. His runners are considered the finest and best-winded men inside of the gates.

Drawn by four large, black stallions, his coach conveys him swiftly down the Boulevard, while he reclines against the cushions in an easy, but studiously graceful attitude. Now he calls to the driver to stop, and the horses draw up with a clattering din before the door of Anatole Cherprix, the famous dealer in pictures, art productions, and articles of *vertu*. Philip has noticed in his window a group of statuary—Circe and her victim—which he thinks would look pretty in his private room; it is carved with high artistic skill, and is, as Anatole declares, "a perfect gem."

"I will sacrifice it for ten thousand francs, milord. Shall I send it to milord's house?"

Philip replies, "Yes. Send it before night to *la maison* Northumberland, and I will give you an order on London;" returning to his coach, he majestically once more displays himself to the admiring Parisians and the resident English as he retires to his magnificent abode.

After partaking of a rich lunch, he sallies out again in quest of amusement or excitement that will pass away the time until dinner. As he proceeds lazily towards the Tuileries, he feels a hand laid familiarly on his shoulder. He turns quickly, and to his surprise recognizes Sir Edgely Warely, who cries, "As I am alive! It is strange how often I meet your grace! I was wandering about disconsolate and friendless, when I thought I saw your grace's form—which I could recognize among a thousand—and I am vastly pleased to find that I was not mistaken in my surmise."

Philip is flattered and pleased with Sir Edgely's speech; moreover he is glad to have some one to whom he can talk, for his residence in town has been so recent that not even the watchful tuft-hunters have had time to run him to earth.

"Sir Edgely," says Philip, in cordial tones, tempered, however, with an almost imperceptible condescension of manner, "I cannot express myself in suitable terms for the pleasure of this meeting."

Sir Edgely bows in acknowledgment, and replies in a careless, haphazard manner: "How would your grace like to call on my Lord Stairs? He is at home now, I am certain!" He knows that Philip will visit Stair before long, and fearing lest he should be regained to the Hanoverian party, he determines to beard the lion at once, and go with Philip to the ambassador in order to counteract any influence which that oily diplomat may attempt to secure over his actions or his thoughts.

Philip replies: "The very place of all places. I have a desire to see his excellency, who, they say, is a marvel of good-breeding and astuteness. I promise myself a little amusement when he discovers these on Whig Wharton's son, eh?" and he points to the ribbon and the cockade; whereat they both laugh heartily, and Sir Edgely praises his boldness and encourages him in his foolish intentions; for he would like nothing better than to produce a complete estrangement between Stair—who is so inimical to his party—and Philip.

Their names are announced, and they are ushered into the hall, in a few minutes the ambassador descends the stairs. Polished and graceful in his deportment, his manners are complaisant and insinuating. Welcoming Philip with great warmth and cordiality, he condoles with him on the recent loss of his mother. He compliments him on his good looks and fine appearance, but purposely neglects to call him by his new title, and Philip is so charmed with his conversation that he does not wish to raise a discussion in which he fears he would be worsted.

Not so Sir Edgely, for as Stair addresses Philip as my lord, he coughs twice or thrice in a very significant manner, and as he finds that his hints are unheeded an angry feeling glows in his breast at Philip's lack of self-assertion.

Stair gives Sir Edgely a very cool welcome, paying little or no attention to him, for he knows him to be a rank Jacobite and a partisan-hunter for the Pretender. After a few observations relative to matters at home and abroad, Stair says to Philip: "Your father was a true friend to his country, and when England lost him, she had one great man the less: I hope and trust that you will follow so illustrious an example of fidelity to your prince, and affection to your country, by treading in the same steps!"

Philip, averse to advice under any circumstances, is, in this case, particularly incensed at what he considers his excellency's impertinence both to himself and his friend; and he replies in a sneering tone and with a spiteful glance, "I thank your excellency for your good advice; and as your excellency had also a worthy and deserving father, I hope that you will likewise copy so bright an original, and tread in all *his* footsteps."

This allusion to his father's disgraceful share in the Glencoe massacre, and his remorseless hatred and destruction of the Macdonalds of that ilk, after the submission of their chief Mac Ian, causes the earl's pale face to burn with mortification and rage; subduing his first impulse of revenge, however, he replies in a tone which makes Philip almost despise himself for his insolence to one so much older than himself. "My lord, my father did what he thought right and just, and it was his unfortunate over zeal which prompted him to an action, at the recollection of which his son now hangs his head in shame. My lord, I thank you for the rebuke conveyed to me so gently."

It is now Philip's turn to flush, and he looks so shame-stricken that Stair involuntarily extends his hand in token of forgiveness, and Philip gripes it with a pressure which is a better apology than a volume of words. Sir Edgely's brow lowers as he sees that the shrewd diplomat has thrust home a wedge which may split his design to pieces, and he bites his nether lip in anger.

Says his excellency, "My lord, can I have a few minutes' *private* conversation?"

At these words, Sir Edgely seems as if he would remonstrate; but if he so intended, he wisely controls himself.

"Certainly, your excellency," replies Philip. "Excuse us for a short time, Sir Edgely."

Stair, leading Philip to his private apartment, requests him to be seated, and continues: "Under favor, my lord, are you aware of the character of this Sir Edgely?"

Philip demands rather warmly, "In what respect?"

"In everything, both his public and private character?"

Philip replies, "Well, no! I met him in London a short time since. He seems to be a good-natured, clever gentleman, and as he rather courts my acquaintance, and yet is neither servile nor insolent, I have taken a slight fancy to him! As for his public character, I know that he is greatly attached to the Chevalier: small blame to him for that, however."

Stair affects not to notice the last remark, and replies, "My lord, he calls himself Sir Edgely Warely; his real name is plain Edgely Valentin; and unfortunately he has never known who was his father. Not his fault, to be sure; but you know the world's opinion in regard to these things! He is a traitor to his king, and a spy and inveigler for the Pretender, and well is he adapted for his offices, for he is crafty, unscrupulous, and daring:— three qualities that make him a dangerous friend and a worse enemy!"

Philip is so astonished at these revelations that he does nothing but mutter in a low tone, something about "insulting his friend—reparation and false charges;" mutterings which Stair ignores, by crossing to the other side of the room, ostensibly to open his window.

By the time he returns Philip is more composed, and he remains sullenly quiet, while his face is flushed and perplexed.

"If the question is not offensive, my lord, why do you wear those gewgaws which dangle on your breast?"

Philip flushes more deeply as he retorts, "Your excellency was once my father's friend, or you should certainly expiate this insult to my king on the field of honor!" and bestowing a haughty look upon him Philip descends to Sir Edgely Warely, or, as he shall be called after this, Edgely Valentin.

Stair bites his nails in vexation as the young "quicksilver" disappears, and utters, "Honest Tom, without his coolness!"

As Philip descends the stairs, he makes up his mind to find out whether or no the ambassador's accusations are correct, so, before he enters the reception chamber, he calls, in a low, indistinct voice, "Valentin! Edgely Valentin!" and watches the effects of his words. The Jacobite turns in an instant, and casts his eyes in every direction with a wild look in them, while his trembling lips enunciate in a thick unnatural voice, "Who calls?"

"I! Philip Wharton, you forsworn liar! Go! Never let me see your face again; never call me friend again, or I'll have your face slit so that your father—excuse me, your mother—would not know you again. 'Tis a pity that I cannot do it with my own hand; but a Wharton never stoops to cross steel with a—" He holds back the last epithet, and half-regrets his cruel words. For a moment Edgely staggers like one drunk, then drawing his cloak over his face, he walks out with staggering, uncertain steps.

"A pest on my scurrilous tongue! Poor man; I turned his head when I spoke so villainously to him;" and he walks home with a slight compunction pricking at his heart.

Philip receives a message from the ambassador early in the day, in which he is invited to call and be presented at court; so, at the time appointed, he dresses himself with elaborate care, and orders his coach. Stepping carefully inside, he cries out, "His Excellency the Ambassador."

Stair receives him with as much graciousness and affability as though he had never passed a disagreeable word with him; and when they arrive at court he guides him through the intricate hallways and amuses him with descriptions of the various people with whom he will be likely to be brought in contact during the presentation to royalty.

After the ceremony is over, Stair renews his character of guide, taking Philip to all the parts of the palace that are beautiful or interesting. He points out the beauty of the *pavillon de l'Horloge*, and tells him a strange story of its architects, Delorme and Bullant, who were matches in impiety and blasphemy. They had impiously placed a statue of Catharine de Medici on the façade, directly over another of the Virgin Mary; and just as they were sending in the last rivet which was to hold it in its place, a thunderbolt from a cloudless sky struck them both, and killed them immediately; while the statue of the queen was nowhere to be seen.

They are promenading the vast gardens of the Tuileries, and enjoying the pure breeze wafting over the clear bosom of the lovely Seine. Stair is saying, "My lord, honor me with your presence to-morrow! I expect to have quite a company at my house, most of whom are either talented, witty, or beautiful; and I'll take my oath on't that you will enjoy yourself. I shall expect you as my guest if you have no prior claims."

"Your excellency may depend on me," replies Philip; "I revel in the anticipation of the morrow."

Stair, who has business within the palace, now excuses himself, and advises Philip to look about him, and enjoy the surrounding scenery.

"Edgely Valentin! Umph! the man is clever and unassuming. 'Tis a pity he cannot speak of a father; but he can console himself with the fact that half the world is in the same quandary; the only difference is that some know it, and others do not."

Philip is already beginning to gain many friends in Paris; for his fine parts, ready wit, and especially his reckless expenditure have begun to produce quite a good effect in the courtly circles of the city. He is known to many by the title of Le Beau Wharton, and if the story of his marriage had not preceded him, he would have been looked on as a godsend by intriguing dowagers with penniless daughters. As it is, his society is eagerly courted by many of the wanton beauties and profligate monseigneurs who make up the celebrated coterie in which the influence of Ninon de l'Enclos and l'Abbé Scarron are strongly felt.

Once or twice he has endeavored to procure an interview with the *ci-devant* " La Belle Indienne,"* who buried herself in the Convent of Saint Cyr on the dissolution of *Le Grand Monarque;* but his attempts have been fruitless, and in his chagrin at being foiled, he perpetrates the following couplet on her, which he sent in to her by the portress :—

> Yes! lie hidden! perverse Indienne,
> You scorn of women and love of men!

CHAPTER XXVIII.

> *Sittah.*—How now, dear Saladin, what play is this?
> *Saladin.*—Indifferent? Yet I thought it good.
> *Sittah.*—For me——
> LESSING'S NATHAN THE WISE.

STROLLING oward the main Boulevard, Philip joins in with the crowd of essenced fops and mincing beaux who hail him with complimentary protestations and welcoming smiles, which he accepts with a calm consciousness of his right to such attentions. One of the nearest fops, a Count Bétenoire, says to him, with a flourish of his cocked hat, which he carries in his hand to show his glossy periwig, " Ah-ha! Your grace has heard of the accident that occurred to his Excellency, my Lord Stair!"

"Accident!" replies Philip. "No, I have not. Tell me all about it, I beg of you."

The Count resumes: " Voici! Monsieur Killmahl, a young English surgeon, who came here to study in our Hospital, and who is a great friend to your King James, had occasion to pass by his excellency's door an hour

---

* Mme. de Maintenon, the instigator of the revocation of the Edict of Nantes.

or more ago, and irritated, I suppose, by his enmity to his excellency's master, he smashed his windows, and nailed a placard to his door, on which was written, 'King James forever! Death to the Dutchman!!' Of course he was arrested, and Monsieur Killmahl is now on his way to the prison of Fort l'Evêque, where he will have ample time to cool down and repent of his rashness."

Philip is amused at the affair, and willingly joins in the laugh at the foolish saw-bones. Turning to Maréchal Tiernan—an Irish officer in the service of France—he says, "Maréchal, give me the aid of your trusty arm, and I will at once repeat M. Killmahl's performance. Then we shall see whether they dare mention Fort l'Evêque to *me* or not!"

The Maréchal smiles at the oddity of the proposal, and answers, "I advise your grace by all means to give up the enterprise. But if your grace is resolved to execute it, I beg you to leave me out of your party; for it is a kind of war-making to which I have not been accustomed."

Philip colors slightly at the imputation. However, he laughs it off as a joke, and the conversation turns on other subjects.

Bétenoire proposing an adjournment to the Salon of la Comtesse de Petitscrevé, a notorious gaming-hell in the fashionable quarter of Paris, the suggestion meets with unanimous applause, and thither they proceed.

Madame's mansion is aristocratically situated, and all its surroundings are *au fait*. The "Grand Chambre" is on the second floor; it is spacious and airy, and richly adorned in the Louis Quatorze style. The walls are divided into oval sections, in each of which is a highly-colored painting, either by Watteau or after him. Between each picture are four delicate clustered pillars of variegated marble, that ascend from the floor to the ceiling, where they spread into the rich Corinthian apex. The vaulted ceiling glows with rich allegorical designs, not over chaste or refined, but artistically beautiful. Two of the most noticeable are the depictions of Britomartis, and the interview between Iachimo and Imogen. The floor is covered with rich velvet, which gives no echo to the tread; but there is not a mirror in the room. The reason is obvious: a gamester who risks his hundreds or his thousands would not care to have his cards reflected for the benefit of his adversary. La Comtesse. is a lovely, sparkling woman, rather inclined to embonpoint. Her eyes and hair are coal black, her glances keen and penetrating. She is known to keep marvellously cool and collected under the most trying circumstances, and she is as crafty as a fox. At ombre, whist, or basset she can successfully cope with the best players in Paris; yet, for all, the young lordlings who frequent her salön are always delighted to lose a few thousand francs to her, merely for the purpose of being able to say to friends less favored, "Parbleu! I lost an odd thousand to Petitscrevé yesterday; good player— very!" For La Comtesse seldom plays with any save distinguished visitors, thus bestowing a certain caste on her opponents. Those conversant with private court scandal aver that on one occasion she won over a hundred thousand francs of his majesty in less than two hours; but such aspersions on the dead monarch must be received with caution.

Philip and his friends engage a table, and they are soon deep in the varying fortune of the blind goddess.

Count Bétenoire, although the representative of a noble family, is unfortunately compelled to live more by his personal ingenuity than by his "flowing coffers," and his game is always safe, wary, and high. Philip is his adversary; and as the game finishes, he finds himself five thousand francs poorer. Though the loss does not deeply trouble him, he is somewhat mortified at his defeat, and he says to the Count, as they are leaving, "Do you care to throw a few mains with me, Count?"

"Sangdieu! yes: as well that as anything else;" and they return to the table.

A servant in velvet livery hands the ivory dice on a silver salver, and Philip sweeps them into the box. At this moment the Maréchal whispers Philip to avoid high play, "for the Count is always lucky at a main." Philip resents this kindly admonition with a haughty stare, and throws his cast.

"Deuce, quatre, deuce—your grace counts low," says Bétenoire, and he throws. "Trois quatres! good!" he exclaims.

Philip raises the box again, saying, "Count, I double the stakes!"

"Doubled it is," replies the Count.

Philip's cast is fifteen. Bétenoire rattles the cubes well before he throws, while Philip leans back in assumed indifference, and exchanges a few words with the Maréchal. The Count taps him on the shoulder to draw attention to his cast.

"Sixteen, eh? You are fortunate, Count."

The Maréchal adds, in an aside to Philip, "Cela va sans dire!"

Philip replies with a shrug, "It is nothing. Golconda is not ruined by a pearl's abstraction!"

CHAPTER XXIX.

—Whom the grea
Choose for companions tête-à-tête ;
Who at their dinners, en famille.
SWIFT.

THE ambassador looks around at his guests with a gratified complacency, and well he may, for within whispering distance of him sit renowned authors and celebrated statesmen, famous beauties and honored soldiers. Philip is distinguished by a seat on the right hand of his host, who is determined to flatter him into being a Whig, if it is possible. On the left of his excellency, leaning over the table and flirting with Mlle. Toutedetruire, a beauty notorious for the duels fought in her honor, is the celebrated, stammering priest Abbé Dubois, son of a Correzian apothecary—once valet to a pedagogue, now a member of the council and the possessor of the two richest abbeys in the country. His ability, wit, and tact are amazing; but his viciousness and selfish profligacy are indisputably more so. He is the most trusted counsellor of the Duc d'Orleans; yet his character is so horribly corrupt that even Philip* was once compelled to say to him, "Abbé, a *little* honesty, for God's sake!"

Farther down Rollin's kindly honest face illumines the board, presenting a fit contrast to the Abbé's flushed, sardonically sarcastic countenance. Philip, who has pleasurably noticed the gay vivacity of Mlle. Toutedetruire whilst she has been conversing with Dubois, is amused

* Orleans.

by seeing her turn her back on him with an angry expression on her mobile features, the consequence, doubtless, of his scurrilous wit; after which she turns her attentions to himself, while her eyes beam in an encouraging manner. She has an olive complexion, eyes dark and expressive, and a straight, narrow nose, whose thin nostrils dilate tremulously as she breathes. Her mouth is a trifle over large, and rather sensual. Unlike the high and weighty coiffures of Madame de Maintenon, her hair is cut short and twisted into flighty little curls which dangle wantonly on her brow. Half a dozen patches adorn her chin and its vicinity, and her deftly-wielded fan is a miracle of delicate traceries.

Says Philip, "Mlle. Toutedetruire, why so cruel to the precisian Abbé?"

"Bondieu! What do you think is my reason for treating him so coldly?"

"I could never guess! May be he called you a Jansenist?" Rollin glances at him at these words. "Or depreciated your perfume's delicacy: or, let me see—surely he did not dare to presume to offer himself as your confessor!"

The Abbé laughs until the tears come to his eyes at this last surmise.

"No!" she replies; "your grace is wrong in all your hazards. Listen, and you shall hear the reason. L'Abbé proposed to settle a benefice on my nephew, with the proviso that he must undergo his pupilage with him! Such an insult, when he knows, too, that I have always intended my relation to be a pious, God-fearing man!" and she casts a mischievous glance at the aspersed Abbé, who is sipping a goblet of ruby wine with evident enjoyment.

Dubois pretends intense chagrin at her insinuations, and in revenge he inclines his head towards her uncovered shoulder, and therefrom blows a tiny cloud of *pèrle poudre*—a fashion to which she conforms more for fashion's sake than for any real need of its enhancing effect. Watteau, who is sitting close by her, quickly draws off his laced 'kerchief and affectedly essays to catch the snowy atoms ere they fall: for which strained chivalry he is punished by a tap of her fan on his cheek.

The atmosphere of the salon is close and stifling with the odors of perfumes, pastilles, and scented cigarettes, that are now the necessary concomitants of a fashionable assemblance. Le Dieu-donnè, as they called Louis, had strictly prohibited the use of all scents or perfumes at court under penalty of his displeasure. Consequently, after his decease, a reaction took place, and now every beau and belle dispels Arabia's perfumes about them as they walk, move, sneèze, or cough; while in every salon pastilles are burnt and fountains of perfume make the atmosphere heavy and trying to the nervous or excitable.

The ambassador drinks to Philip's health and prosperity, and in conclusion says, "And as true a lover of his country and as loyal to the king as was his gifted father!" In responding, Philip says very little beyond acknowledging his excellency's compliments; very soon, however, the heavy wine which he has been drinking begins to fire his head, his tongue wags looser, and soon his wit and bold remarks keep his side of the table in cachinnatory convulsions. Stair, conversant as he is with Philip's ready speech and his biting pleasantries, is surprised at him. The more he drinks the greater seems his thirst, until Stair fears that before the repast is over he will either be under the table or else will have to be carried away to sleep off the effects of his hard drinking. Hammering noisily on the table to attract attention, Philip springs up on the seat of his chair, and places one foot on the table, while the company cheer and applaud with hand and foot.

"Mesdemoiselles et Messieurs, fill up—my toast will suit you all!" and he glances at his host, who begins to arrange a few sentences in order to acknowledge the toast of which he is to be the subject. "May Orleans dare to follow in Louis's wake, and send a diamond hilt once more to England! Until then, long live our exiled monarch James the Third. After—my toast will be: long live our restored king, and death to the Dutch invader!"

For a moment there is a hushed quietness, but Stair is cool and self-possessed; signaling with his hands, a band of hidden music sends out a low, entrancing strain which helps to dispel the restraint and relieves the necessity for any remarks on such an untoward event as has occurred.

Philip has descended from his eminence, and he is at present by the side of Mlle. Toutedetruire, who left the table in order to visit the mirror to inspect her laces, her ribbons, and her countenance. "Ventrebleu!" she exclaims, "your grace has caused a grand sensation with your absurdities! What could have put such a foolish toast into your head, *vous bête?*"

He replies with a smile, "Your own sweet eyes, that betrayed your sympathy for poor Jamie!"

She bestows an arch look upon him as she says, "*Fi donc*, your grace! What would the Duchess of Wharton say if she heard you speak to me in such a gallant manner?"

"Curse me if I care what she would say," he rejoins in an excited manner.

With a cautioning glance from her eyes, she presses a little, plump hand on his lips, and steps quickly to the other side of the room; where she is soon engaged in a witty, wordy warfare with l'Abbé Dubois and his excellency.

Claudine de Tencin, the *ci-devant* canoness and Orleans favorite—now the mistress of l'Abbé, who sustains her in an almost regal style—has been unusually quiet during the evening; but as soon as she observes that Philip is alone, she calls to him to come to her and sit down on the sofa beside her. Philip obeys with as much alacrity and grace as are possible under the circumstances; and as wine and women combined tend to sharpen his wit and render it more piquant, the two are soon engaged in lively conversation. The lady is a mistress of the art of badinage and coquetry, and is moreover an unusually talented woman. Her figure is lithe and graceful, revealing a charming languor in its attitudes. Her eyes are dark brown, sparkling, and intelligent; lips full and red; while the slight down shading her upper lip tells of her southern origin and her fiery nature. She wears her hair in long, loose curls, which fall on her neck and shoulders. She is dressed in a very *négligé* manner, almost as much so as were afterwards Pompadour and Parabaré. Her costume is made of a thin, transparent Indian fabric of a pearl color, studded with golden crescents—the *coa vestis* of the period.

"Your grace," she says, "pray glance at l'Abbé and Toutedetruire! One would say that his very existence depends on her kindness, to judge from the expression of his eyes; poor man!"

"I have had an eye to them, Ma'm'selle Tencin; he is after one of her gloves which she has hidden in her dress!"

She replies: "I have heard—between us—that the Chevalier St. George once made overtures to Emilie, and that she politely declined on account of what she called 'his pious fanaticism!'"

"Faith! if she wants the opposite of a friar, recommend me to her."

"She tries well for an abbé, though, in spite of her worldly scruples!"

"Ah ha!" laughs Philip; "an abbé may be worse than a king!"

"Or better!" replies the Tencin, adding rather abruptly, "Will your grace be in town any length of time?"

"No, *ma belle*, I will not. I must shortly return to England to inspect my estate, and also attend to some vastly entertaining advice anent them given by my family lawyer!"

"Eh bien?"

"A downwright Whig, who will test my orthodoxy, and nasally advise me to 'model yourself after your blessed father, who was a pillar to the state and a prop to the church.'"

"And you will, I suppose?" she says, and casts a quick glance at him while pretending to look at Dubois.

"Sainte Vierge! will I? See!" and he directs her attention to the Jacobite badges concealed under his coat. "You heard my sentiments at table. Do you think that I was joking? No! I was in earnest, and, as for Protestantism, to —— with it and all its exponents!"

"Ingrate!" she murmurs, pressing her fan on his hand.

Already the intoxication of her presence is stealing over him; he whispers in her ear, "*You* could make me Whig or Tory—Protestant or Papist!"

She lifts her eyebrows, and draws down her lips sanctimoniously as she replies, "Truly, I would be a valuable adjunct to Holy Mother Church, if I had the power which you say I have."

Philip's answer is certainly to the point: "Test yourself, and you will be assured."

Philip is not altogether sober, but when he tells her what she can do with him, he knows what he is about, for he is aware that she is a firm Jacobite and a trusted Romanist; while, on the other hand, she does not know that he is already half Catholic in his heart, but ascribes his offer to an excited brain, of which she, as a true Catholic, must take advantage.

She resumes, with a certain degree of gravity, "I am not, as your grace probably knows, the most suitable person in the world to turn converter; but if I thought I could induce you to embrace the only true faith, I would think it a condonation of many guilty words and actions which I have committed;" she looks straight into his eyes with a long, persuasive glance, and purposely lays her hand on his. Its warm, living pressure thrills through him from head to foot, and he takes it up and kisses it in a semi-drunken delirium.

"Dear Claudine, from this moment I am a devoted son of the church, and a true believer in the Holy Catholic Faith!"

She smiles sweetly on him, and tells him how glad she is that she has "made, at any rate, one convert for Mother Church."

We will step across the room to where a party of gentlemen are engaged in dicing—a mode of passing the time of which his excellency is very fond; at present, however, he does not take part in the game, for he is secretly engaged in writing a description of Stanrig Bartoslav, the long-bearded Russian who is now rattling the dice; he has a stern, proud look about him which is far from ingratiating, and his mouth curls in supercilious pride. His excellency overheard a few remarks that he made in the early part of the evening, and he has discovered that he intends to visit the Pretender in order to give him assurances of sympathy from some eminent Russian noblemen, after which he purposes visiting England; and these remarks his excellency is jotting down in order to forward to his royal master.

As the evening advances, and more wine is poured down craving gullets, the noise and confusion increase, and license and freedom from restraint reign triumphant. But we will leave this scene ere the mad intoxication of a Regency supper pollutes overmuch our reading, which is hard enough to keep clean and pure and yet furnish any idea of this period and its morals. Here, as everywhere else, is illustrated the great law of the equilibrium of forces. France, relieved from the gloomy devotions of Louis and the Maintenon, experiences the reaction which breeds wantons and rakes, midnight orgies, and protracted gaming.

CHAPTER XXX.

Portius.—Marcus, the friendships of the world are oft
Confederacies in vice, or leagues of pleasure ;
Ours has severest virtue for its basis.
ADDISON'S CATO, III. I.

THERE is an unusual crowd collected in the Rue Saint Denis, who ever and anon exclaim in admiring ecstasies: "Parole de Dieu! Beautiful! solid silver, on my word! wonderful!" and expressions of admiration and astonishment are many. The sergeants de ville hurry to the scene of confusion, and hustle the bourgeoisie aside with the martial scorn for civilians; but when they see the object which has produced the unwonted disturbance, they become quite as noisy and excited as any one else.

The innocent cause of all this wonder and surprise is a small carriage, the entire body of which is covered with silver filigree work, wrought at intervals into heraldic quarterings, still further enriched with set-in gems. The hubs of the wheels are also decorated with precious stones. There are two vacant seats in front, while in the box behind sit in stately silence two huge negroes, black and ugly as twin Calibans, and as shiny as if they had just been dipped in a candle-tank. They are dressed in azure velvet jackets trimmed with gold, and knee-breeches of the same material. They are without hats of a civilized fashioning, but their thick, crinkly wool is combed into fantastic semblances of cocked hats, retaining their shapes through a plentiful use of bandoline and pomatum. The equipage is drawn up before the door of M. Enivrant, jeweller and perfumer, and from there to the carriage the crowd has formed a narrow pathway of craning necks and wondering eyes. "*Il vient! il vient! le beau Wharton!*"

Philip steps composedly over the threshold in company with a gentleman of peculiar aspect. His dress is white satin slashed with azure; and his knee-breeches tinkle with many oak-leaf buttons, all of which have a small diamond in their centres; the buckles of his square-toed shoes are resplendent with diamonds and sapphires. His companion is almost his fac-simile in dress, with perhaps a shade less of magnificence. His stature is small, his shoulders slightly contracted and stooping. His face seems familiar; but, if we recollect aright, he was in an abbé's costume the last time we saw him. It is Dubois, who is Philip's companion in this new freak which has set half Paris by the ears. Some say that le beau Wharton is doing this on a wager; some, that he is endeavoring to ingratiate himself with the Parisians in order to subvert the Regency; while others maintain that there is a deep policy hidden under his apparent madness. In fact the more wonderful the tale, the sooner it is believed. Dubois has so well disguised his features by the aid of cosmetics and a long, military beard, that he escapes recognition and the consequent censure which he would incur through his complicity in such nonsensicalities; he is at once christened "Le Chevalier Inconnu."

This wonderful carriage and its occupants have been exhibited through all the fashionable streets and boulevards, and wherever they have stopped for a few minutes Philip has scattered handfuls of money to the people, and then harangued them in a speech of Jacobitical tendencies; after which he would throw hundreds of the Jacobite cockades to them to wear as emblems of their sympathy with the cause of the Pretender.

L'Abbé's witty and scurrilous remarks draw roars of laughter from the admiring bourgeoisie, and as Philip rises from his seat to reprimand his friend for his shocking obscenity, in words more shameless than the other's, their merriment knows no bounds, and they scream applaudingly: "Vive le Wharton! Vive le Chevalier Inconnu"—expressions which both acknowledge by raising their hats and kissing their fingers.

Finally the excited people unharness the horses from the shafts, place their own shoulders to the task, and triumphantly drag the carriage and its burden to la Maison Northumberland. Philip rises and steadies himself by holding on to the splashboard, as he says, " My worthy plebeians! we appreciate your great kindness, and are really thankful for your evident admiration of our persons; still, the return of our horses would make us feel yet more grateful for your attention toward us." The crowd clap and hurrah as a burly blacksmith leads forward the horses, and re-harnesses them, and Dubois screams in a shrill, falsetto voice, "Largess—largess!" Philip, thrusting his hand into the box on the bottom of the carriage, whirls a shower of newly coined francs among the expectant crowd, who curse, bellow, and fight like tigers in their thirst for the silver distributed so madly and culpably. After this, Philip grasps the reins and drives rapidly to the Ruelle de Venise, where he jerks the horses up with a loud cry in front of the Tête du Frère, a cabaret of very humble pretensions.

Dubois exclaims, "In the name of all the saints! Wharton, what is your idea in coming here!"

"'Faith, I know not—except—"

Dubois interrupts: "I fear Bacchus reigns in your grace's brain at présent."

"*Et tu, Brute!*" he retorts, and resumes: "Let us load the carriage with wine bottles; what say you?"

Dubois does not reply, but begins to hum a parody on Marlborough *s'en va en guerre*. Philip, springing to the pavement, enters the cabaret, and in a few minutes he reappears with his arm linked in that of the host—a fat, red-faced, vulgar fellow, who is ready to fall to the ground at Philip's condescension. Philip has promised him five hundred francs if he would alter his sign to Tête de Jacques.

Dubois exclaims in surprise, "Your grace!"

Philip replies, "All right, my man of many churches. I have made these agreements with this honest fellow! first, that he shall change the word Frère for Jacques; and secondly stow as many bottles of wine in the carriage as it will hold at a nominal price of fifty francs per bottle!"

"Eh bien!" replies Dubois, testily: "But there is no necessity for you to make a friend of the fool!"

The man wriggles his arm from Philip, and drops behind

in a shame-faced manner, as he mutters, "My lords, it is not my fault! I hope I know my place better than that."

Philip, drawing him forward by his ear, cries, "Here! my red Boniface, put your hands in there, and help yourself;" and he lifts the lid of the money box.

The man, with a dazed expression on his face caused by the sight of so much money, begins to count out the sum agreed upon. Philip watches him for a minute, and then bids him drop all that he has counted, and to hold his apron, which he does. Philip scooping up two handfuls, dashes them in it, and then scrambles over the bottles of wine with which the carriage is filled, and regains his seat beside the Abbé, who exclaims amusedly, "What does your grace intend to do with all this second-rate wine? You are certainly not going to drink it?"

"Drink it! No! I have too high a regard for my teeth and digestive powers to do such a thing, I assure you, *mon abbé*. I have a use for them, however, as you will see in time. Shall we drive to Petitscrevé's?"

Dubois assents, and tries to think what Philip intends to do with the wine.

As they roll along in high spirits, Dubois whispers, "Orleans is coming this way, your grace. If he stops to talk to you, recollect that I am Sir Charles Castle—an English friend of yours; for he dislikes me to have a hand in anything tending to make my memory more respected than it is at present."

"*Tres bien!* pull your hat over your eyes, and draw your collar up to your ears, *mon abbé*, and if you are forced to speak, talk in a gruff, disagreeable way, that will repel any advances which he may make to you!"

"By the calendar! he comes straight towards us!" exclaims Dubois.

"Sure enough!"

The Duc rides a superb animal, which he brings to a

halt before the carriage; he salutes Philip, who rises and removes his hat, while Dubois affects to be absorbed in the gambols of a ragged gamin on the opposite side of the way.

"Your grace is determined to astonish even Paris with your magnificence? Pray, who is your companion? His form seems familiar to me."

"Companion!" returns Philip; "he is my servant Sêche Péteux, and an excessively impertinent jackanapes he is!"

"Ah! a thousand pardons," returns the Regent. "The Duchess of Berry has desired me to invite you to the Luxembourg?"

Philip replies in a flippant manner, which causes Orleans' face to flush: "Thanks, *mon duc.* I will take the earliest opportunity of seeing her!"

Orleans bestows a stiff nod upon him, and rides off so quickly that he almost upsets a group of gamins who are clustered near his horses' heels.

"Duchess Berry—Palais Royal—Luxembourg!" sneers Dubois. "Your grace had better season yourself with a few suppers at Orleans' ere you test your powers of drinking and your competency in regard to filthy wit and meaning oglings in her grace's violet boudoir."

"Come, come, Abbé; her grace and yourself must be at daggers drawn, you talk so bitterly about her!"

"Not at all; but her wild orgies and amours are terrible in their evil influences on Parisian society; for, when the rest of the sex see such a shining example, will they not follow it? and if they do, how long shall we have faithful wives and pure daughters? As for men, they now get drunk from policy, and for the same reason are confessed libertines! What shall we do when women rival them in private life, and participate in what are known all Europe over as Regency orgies, and known too for their profligacy, wantonness, and utter shamelessness? Ugh!"

"Encore! Abbé, encore! It does me good to see you virtuous for once: Ah ha! I take credit to myself for the discovery."

The Abbé rejoins bitterly: "It is a part of my character, which I show but seldom. When I do, it is called hypocrisy! Sure, that is not an unusual trait in church exponents?"

Philip replies: "I am not competent to answer you, Abbé! When I first knew you—or at least before you enunciated your anathema maranatha against her grace— I should have said, taking you as a specimen, that hypocrisy held no place in the church, your peccadilloes were so bold and open. But since—" He shrugs his shoulders, and casts a sidelong glance at the off horse.

By this time they are opposite to Mme. Petitscrevé's, and Philip astounds the Abbé by reaching down for a bottle, and then hurling it through the salon windows into Madame's especial apartment. Crash! and it flies through the thick, stained glass which Madame had imported from Italy at a large expense.

"*Mille diables*, your grace! What do you mean?"

"Amusement, my dear Abbé, amusement. You see there will be an infernal uproar in a few seconds. I shall allow Madame and her attendants to yell and curse for awhile—that you must admit will be amusing?—and then I will pay for all damages—make everybody about drink King James's health, then exit in a shower of blessings."

In a minute all is confusion. Petitscrevé's head is out of the window, and she is talking and gesticulating in a most angry manner; the hall door is opened, and a posse of gentlemen, croupiers, and servants appear, who simultaneously demand the reason of this outrage.

Dubois draws his hat entirely over his face, folds his arms, and vows to let Philip get out of the scrape the best way he can. Philip grasps two more bottles. One he tosses slowly up to Petitscrevé, who dodges it and begins to grow almost frantic; the other he sends through the window above her head. The assembled *habitués* of the salon, although exasperated at his audacity, are yet impressed with the splendor of his equipage and the dress of himself and Dubois, and some call out to him to cease his throwing; none interfere with him, however, until one servant grasps at the head of the nearest horse, whereupon Mahomet springs from his seat and knocks him down with an accompaniment of foreign oaths, and then springs back to his place.

Dubois, fearful of consequences, says: "Your grace! put an end to this affair, or it may end more seriously than we think for."

Philip seems to think so too, for he opens the money-box, and calls out, "*Ma belle* Petitscrevé, what is the cost of your broken window?"

She will not answer him, thinking that he only means to taunt her; but, as he repeats his question, she replies in a troubled voice: "Your grace, this window alone cost me two thousand francs, for which I have Monsieur Chondrille's bill!"

Philip replies: "Send your bill to la Maison Northumberland, and it will be paid, *ma belle;*" and he does not wait for an answer, but kicks the rest of the wine into the street, and drives off homewards.

As they turn into the Boulevard, they pass Edgely Valentin, who throws a malignant look upon Philip, which he returns with an amused smile. Dubois, who has noticed the scowl, says: "Certes, if that man could ever poniard your grace and escape detection, he would most assuredly do it! Did you mind how he looked at you?

His eyes said vendetta as plainly as ever tongue spoke. Pardieu!"

"Oh," replies Philip, "he is an understrapper at court —a spy for my party. He once foisted himself on me as a friend; but when my lord Stair informed me of his true character, of course I declined further acquaintanceship with him, so that I do not think he would injure himself to do me a favor."

As they stop at the door of *la maison*, Philip says abruptly, "Abbé, I return to England to-morrow in order to wind up some little affairs which I had in hand when I left London with your countryman, M. de Savatte;" and he smiles as he thinks of the trick he had played on him, and he tells it to the Abbé, who laughs heartily at the *contre-temps*, in spite of his surprise at Philip's sudden resolve.

"These English!" he murmurs apologetically, as if that title completely justified any amount of freaks or idiosyncrasies. However, he asks: "Is your grace so soon tired of Paris?"

Philip replies: "Well, no, I am not tired of Paris so much as I am of myself; wherever I stop long, I always find myself repeated to a nauseating extent."

"How repeated?" queries Dubois.

"*Mon Abbé*, it is ever the privilege of great men to produce followers."

"Parbleu! You give me a negative answer. So you mean to say that you have created so many would-be fac-similes of yourself that you are tired of seeing them. Is it not so?"

"Right, Abbé," he replies; and his face—I am sorry to say—is disfigured with conceit and arrogance.

Says Dubois: "Do you intend to take your seat in the House on your return?"

Philip colors as he replies: "No; I think not, for the present."

"No!" exclaims Dubois in apparent surprise; "I should have thought that that would have been your primary object."

Philip being under age is of course ineligible to Parliament; this the priest knows, but he also knows how to make a friend by two or three questions or answers; and he is aware of Philip's desire to appear older than he really is.

"We French," continues Dubois, "never could understand either yourselves or your politics. When you arrive at Court I should feel infinitely obliged to you if you would present my compliments to Madame Kielmansegge—a lady who, by the way, might be useful to you at Court; her acquaintance is quite worth cultivating."

Philip replies, half angrily: "Really, Abbé, you are forever telling me whose acquaintance I should cultivate! You forget that a Wharton is to be approached—not to approach!"

Dubois smiles, but agrees with him in every point. "Lord Stair will probably secure the pardon for Bolingbroke?" queries Dubois.

Philip replies: "Pah! the man is a fool. Let him return to his rightful king, and ere long he will need no pardon!"

"What means your grace?"

"I mean that it will not be long ere a Stuart shall again sit on a hard-won throne!"

"Say you so?" replies Dubois dubiously. "How comes it that your grace is so violently opposed to your deceased father's party?"

Philip replies, with a laugh: "Pardieu! I have pawned my principles to Gordon—the Chevalier's banker; and until I can repay him, I must be a Jacobite. When I do repay him, I'll turn over a new leaf, and embrace Whiggery forever."

It is a fact that, even with the immense annuity which he is continually receiving from home, he is always in debt, and that to an immense amount; although he often has the money, he would rather squander it in extravagances than liquidate his numerous bills.

CHAPTER XXXI.

Now change the scene; a nobler care
Demands him in a higher sphere:
Distress of nations calls him hence.
SWIFT.

PHILIP is once more in London, and he is busily engaged in superintending the altering and re-furnishing of his mansion, which he is having decorated in a most fanciful, extravagant manner. He is at this moment in his father's death-chamber, and it is now in a state of confusion and uproar. Artisans and artists are intently occupied in measuring, plumbing, plastering and painting. Philip speaks! Let us listen with respect to this symbolization of economy, who actually superintends his own affairs!—a wonderful thing for him to undertake considering his thorough aversion to business of a practical nature.

"Here—s'death! fellow. I ordered the green screen to be left in its former position, and now you have—tut-tut!" and he pishes angrily, and screams: "Take your vile tools out of my sight! Fool! get you gone! And here, you cabineteer! I want my private room finished in ebony; a type of myself—sombre and inflexible."

To tell the truth, his orders impede work far more than they forward it, for they are so contradictory and confusing that the workmen secretly wish his lordship anywhere but in his own house. A servant enters with a letter, which Philip glances over, and exclaims: "Harry Hautefort!. Ask him to step up at once!"

He scarcely finishes the command when Sir Harry steps gingerly towards him: "My lord, allow me—"

"Ah! Sir Harry, you have come at last! It is high time, let me tell you!"

"True, my lord," he responds, and he presses his scented handkerchief to his brow: "I would have been to see you sooner, but—"

"But me no buts, my dear fellow; it is all right. Have a glass of wine with me, or rather without me, and I'll change my clothes, and go out with you to get rid of these glue-scented, varnish-stuck pack of rascals who are pulling my house to pieces, and nearly distracting yours ever—" and he is gone.

"Rackety as ever!" murmurs Sir Harry. "There are strange rumors about his doings abroad. I question the truth of the report which makes him a Jacobite, but he is so headstrong that all one would have to do to make him one thing would be to persuade him to be its opposite!"

Sir Harry is himself a Tory—or Trimmer denotes his principles better; for, although apparently a violent Tory, he really believes in a middle course. But in these days it is necessary for a public man to be an extremist, or else he runs the risk of being attacked by both parties who unite in the one particular of hating half-way men or Trimmers.

Philip re-enters, and exclaims: "I am a quick dresser, you see."

Sir Harry replies: "As I live, my lord, our London

sparks will groan in envy at your suit; it is glorious! superb!"

"The last Parisian cut!" replies Philip.

"'Sooth, you'll be more successful than ever in your heart affairs with such a covering to help your face."

Philip answers: "Yes, the dress is quite pretty; the quadruple slash on the doublet is my own idea, as is also the bone-lace frill on the outer edging."

"Possible?" exclaims Sir Harry, and he stoops to admire Philip's taste and ingenuity. "It must have taken a deal of study to originate these devices."

"Oh no—not for me!" Philip replies, and he jerks his swordbelt a trifle to the right to make it lie more conformably to his waist.

"Where shall we go?" queries Sir Harry.

"Wherever you wish. Yet stay—I have a message from a friend in Paris which I promised to deliver as soon as possible. Let us to court, and see the great George and his greater mistresses."

"As you say, my lord," replies Sir Harry. "His majesty's ministers hold a levee to-day."

They walk together arm in arm, feathers flying and spurs tinkling. As they proceed on their way to the cockpit at Whitehall, Philip meets many of his former friends, all of whom are delighted at his return, and speak in high terms of his increased good looks and manlier bearing; which compliments he returns so profusely that even were those to whom he speaks enemies they must become his friends; for Philip possesses all his father's powers of cajoling and flattering, and whom he wishes to be his friend, he can make so, often in spite of himself.

"Harry," says Philip, "I think I'll change my mind, and defer my visit to the wiseacres. You will not be offended at it, I know?"

Sir Harry replies with a smile: "Faith! no. On the contrary, I feel quite relieved—as if an incubus were taken off my mind."

They retrace their steps, and Philip proposes a trip to Hampton Court, to which Sir Harry agrees, and they proceed to one of the many water-stairs in the vicinity of the palace, and engage a wherry. The day is delightful, and the sun showers its genial warmth over all. A soft breeze ripples the swelling surface of the water; and the foam which the wherry's prow makes under the strokes of the athletic oarsman flies to their faces in cool, silvery spray. Noble elms and beach trees slope down to the water's edge on either side, and throw a deep shade in by the banks where numerous parties lie in their roomy wherries, and flirt, play on the cithern, dilate on the new brocade, marvel at the fine flavor of Mistress Jonson's tea, or explain the last passado or entréchat brought from Paris.

Away they go—past imposing mansions and modest cottages—past loving couples who saunter the walks so absorbed in themselves that they are ignorant of the amusement which they give to the spectators of their innocent diversion—and past lumbering ships which float the wealth of the prolific Indies to our colder, less productive clime. Both Philip and Sir Harry doff their hats ceremoniously as a gayly decorated bark shoots by manned by three burly watermen. The coronet emblazoned on their right arms evinces that the fair occupant may boast the *sangre azul* of poet's parlance. She is the loveliest woman in all London who has just passed them—Mary Bellenden. Her cheeks are like the mellow half of a ripe peach, her lips as red as the wild sumac of the American colonies. Her eyes are as blue as the sweet wild violet, and her hair is the rich chestnut so usual among English girls. Her virtue and goodness are well known. She is much courted in society and even the prince had made some overtures to her a short time since, which she had indignantly rejected, and told him, with fiery looks and burning cheeks, " Prince! I tell you that Mary Bellenden could not turn Mistress to the man she loves—much less to one she *hates!*"

Says Philip: " S'life! Harry! I saw a few beauties at the court over the water; but Mistress Bellenden pales them all. Even in my dreams, I have never seen such perfect loveliness." He stops, and an angry shade crosses his brow, as he adds to himself: " If I had not been such an arrant dolt, I might have honored Mistress Bellenden myself."

" Yes, my lord!" interpolates Sir Harry; "and her temper matches her looks, as our virtuous Prince found out to his cost!"

Philip adds, in a disgusted manner: " Faugh—the Dutchman! He thought he had a Kielmansegge, or one of that stripe to deal with. He has yet to learn our English women! *Apropos* of women—have you heard aught of Lady Wharton or General Holmes since I have been away? I have not had a letter from them since I left for the continent."

This is false, for he received several, but did not answer them, nor in some cases even read them during his riotous career in Paris.

Sir Harry replies: " No, my lord, but I know that they are both in the country somewhere, and tolerably well!"

" I shall have to run over to Bucks, ere long."

" Hampton! my lords!" cries the waterman, as the boat's keel grates on the clean sand. And now there ensues a good-natured dispute between Philip and Sir Harry as to the right to pay the man; who shrewdly settles it by saying: "Troth! yer lordships can both pay me; d'ye see?" They smile at his new way of settling a dispute, and the fellow receives double his fare for his impudence.

They proceed to the Palace, and are ushered in with the etiquette and ceremony usual in such cases—a description of which would only be tiresome and profitless.

Attracted by the laughter and merriment proceeding from a room to the left of the wide vestibule, they enter, Philip leading the way. There are present about a dozen ladies and fully as many gentlemen, busily engaged in chatting and flirting, talking politics or scandal, and sipping Souchong out of large, shallow saucers, or drinking wine from cut-glass goblets. Philip is at home in such places, and he is soon surrounded by an admiring party. Lady Deloraine congratulates him on his return, and inquires, with a significant glance, about his wife. She is a graceful woman, slightly built, but easy and unconstrained in her movements. Her face is pleasing and attractive, and her prominent chin and bright eyes show that her temper is none of the mildest. As an instance of it, you shall hear of her reply to the Countess of Buckenburgh—a retort which is even now the subject of conversation among a few of the scandal lovers who are here. While she was in the royal presence yesterday, the Countess had said, in the hearing of his majesty and Lady Deloraine: "These English women do not look like women of quality; they ever have their eyes on their feet, and always look in a fright; whereas our countrywomen hold up their heads and hold out their bodies, and they make themselves look great and stately, and more like quality than the poor English women." To which Lady Deloraine replied in a loud voice: "We show our quality by our birth and breeding, madame, and not by sticking out our bosoms, and making the throne shake with our strides!"*

Lord Harborough is sipping Souchong and exchanging bonmots with Mistress Nostitz—the Polish Envoy's lady—a sparkling, witty little body, with very black eyes and a dazzling white skin. M. Nostitz might have felt justifiably jealous if he were about, to notice how warmly my lord regards her, and with what affectionate solicitude his hand rests on her arm; however, as the action is unknown to all but themselves, the lady demurely allows it to remain there, amiably unconscious of the audacity.

"Ha! ha!" laughs Sir Harry, in a low voice. "Behold la Grenouille. Let us go over and talk to her! She is in the sulks, and I'll coranto for an hour if she fails to amuse you."

Nothing loth, Philip steps across the room to where Madame Robethon sits alone with an angry scowl on her low forehead. Her cheeks are fat and shaky, and she has innumerable chins which rest on her almost invisible neck; while the way in which she is sitting is ludicrously suggestive of an immense toad, for her eyes are dull and watery, and her mouth —— Pope! aid me to a simile!

"Ah, Madame Robethon, how is your health to-day? Good, I hope? for, when you are unwell, England moans the illness of one of the few beauties who adorn her sea-girt shores, and cause less favored countries to grow green with envy!"

"Ach! milord Wharton, you speak untruth with me!" she rejoins angrily.

Philip lays his hand on his breast in an earnest man-

---

* The Countess of Buckenburgh was very stout, and her tread was remarkably heavy, while her long strides were the occasion of many a laugh at her expense,

ner as he replies: "Madame, I feel your cold, cutting sarcasm in my very marrow!"

She half bounces from her seat as she exclaims, "Marry? Mein Gott! You haf too good a wife now for—" and the remainder of her words are lost in the peal of laughter which the rest of the company find it impossible to repress; and really her croaking voice, her shaking body, and her squat rotundity are enough to excite the risibles of St. Dominic himself.

After about an hour's conversation with Lord Harbrough—who has vainly attempted to probe his views on the ministry, for Philip has seen his design, and foiled him with double-edged answers which might mean yes or no, and which have perplexed his questioner with their ready wit and nonchalant reprising—he motions to Sir Harry, and they retire from the room. He says in a careless, off-hand manner: "Well, Harry! I feel as if a trip into the country would do me good! I think of going to Bucks, and rusticating amid the Phillises and Corydons of my native village. Town dissipation is telling on my nerves; I need solitude and fresh air to recuperate my flagging energies."

"Recuperate! my lord. 'Faith, if I had half your energy, I would count myself a lucky man! Your face is fresh and rosy, and your long, quick step half kills me."

Philip replies: "Yes, my constitution is good, I admit; but it could be better: moreover, I want to see her ladyship and her stern old father, who once on a time gave me a mighty severe raking."

"For some practical joke you played on his venerable person, I presume, or an intrigue that shocked his ideas of morality and virtue. Speaking of intrigues, did you ever hear the story of your respected father and a Nelly Valentin?"

Philip thinks a moment, and replies: "Nelly Valentin? I have heard that name before; but my memory fails me in regard to the circumstance. Yet when I think of it, I recollect that I once received a vile scrawl signed by a gypsy—whom I permit to live on my estate—who demanded a thousand guineas or threatened me with some vague but dire vengeance. I was mad at the time it came, and I paid but little attention to it, except to order the scaramouch mercury to depart."

"The same, probably, but of that particular incident I was ignorant; but I may as well tell you the whole story as we go along, unless indeed you have something better with which to pass the time. This Nelly Valentin—"

A man soberly clad, whose face is partly concealed by a broad-brimmed hat, and who has appeared to dog Philip and his friend for some time, now draws closer to them.

"Was a rustic beauty," continues Sir Harry, "whom your father saw and—"

"And God's curse on him for the vile deed!" hisses rather than speaks Edgely Valentin, who has heard Sir Harry's every word; and he throws off his hat and reveals himself to the astonished gaze of Philip, who thought him in Paris; while Sir Harry half draws his rapier, and glares in a puzzled manner at the insolent intruder.

"Nelly Valentin!—Edgely Valentin!" exclaims Philip, and a sudden light breaks in on his mind. "This man must be a relative of hers, who is rightly enraged at our jesting over Mistress Nellie's disgrace: particularly as I am the son of her betrayer!" He exclaims haughtily: "Master Valentin, your insolence deserves a severe chastisement. However, if the lady of whom we spoke is any kin to you, we apologize, and promise you that we will not renew the conversation until you are without earshot."

"Any kin!" he sneers, and his face grows livid with his great passion. "I would give up my life if her seducer could appear before me! He should know what a gall-hearted, lying villain I deem him!" and he gripes the pommel of his heavy sword until his hand is white with the strain.

"A God's life, sirrah!" exclaims Philip; "this is insolence with a vengeance! A good thrashing from my servant would cure the ill humor that plagues you!" and Philip looks sternly at him; but he proceeds in a softened strain as the thought passes through his mind, how he would feel under like circumstances: "Come, my good man, you have now aired your opinion of my dead father —an opinion which he doubtless merited; and your best plan now is to decamp with a whole skin and be thankful for my forbearance."

"Yes," chimes in Sir Harry. "If I had thought you were a gentleman, you should have felt the new Italian passado tickle your scandalizing gullet. As it is—I leave you your life."

Edgely Valentin looks scornfully from one to the other as he replies: "Good lack, my lords! 'Tis a pity I have no title to stick to the front of my good name, or I should, as you desire, be gratified with a sight of your steel; and more pity 'tis that my blood would disgrace your weapons." He picks up his hat again, draws it over his face with a savage jerk, and walks rapidly away.

"S'life, Harry!" says Philip, with a laugh, "we must tear reputations to pieces in a more secret manner, if we would avoid a repetition of such scenes, for which, to tell the truth, I have but little stomach."

"Umph!" grumbles Sir Harry: "if we cannot talk of a far-away country lass but a defender springs up in the shape of a sad-garbed clown, what shall we do in town, where every woman has so many relatives—right-handed or otherwise?" And he finishes the story that had been interrupted, and Philip chuckles admiringly at his father's adroitness. An erring son can find a real consolation in the *faux-pas* of his lamented sire.

CHAPTER XXXII.

"Then all for women, painting, rhyming, drinking,
Besides ten thousand freaks that died in thinking.
Blest madman, who could every hour employ
With something new to wish or to enjoy!"

DRYDEN.

PHILIP does not enter by the usual gateway, but leaps his horse over a low stone wall, and lands in the forest a few yards distant from Elm avenue, pushing forward toward the old trysting-place—once the loadstar of his thoughts; he draws rein and springs from his saddle:—

"Margery Holmes—Margery Wharton!—I did not think the difference had been so great, or I would not have dispelled my love-dream by such a common-place means as marriage. Poor girl!" and a remorseful pang shoots across his heart as he rests his hand against the same seat on which they once sat by the hour together and where she had leaned her dear head on his shoulder which had trembled with its precious burthen. Here, he pressed her soft lips with kisses that sunk down to her heart, and left their traces in a deep, unchangeable love. He thinks of the night when she sprang into his arms with that little sob of joy and grief, and told him with a tearful smile that he could do with her as he wished; and every little circumstance and incident of that meeting—even to the tearful glisten of her eyes in the moonlight—surges up in his mind. He gulps down some obstruction in his throat, and mounts his horse in a slow, dispirited manner. Suddenly he strikes the spurs deep into her sides, and the animal leaps so violently that she nearly unseats him, despite his perfect horsemanship; "Steady—steady, Het!" he exclaims, and at the sound of his voice she calms down, but still proceeds at a quick pace until he checks her at the Weird's Cave, where he takes a long look around before he again sets off toward the Castle.

His home appears desolate and cheerless to him now, for there is neither a father nor a mother to welcome him with a grasp of the hand or an embrace. He looks wistfully at the window where his mother would have been, and his eyes grow brighter, and their lids grow tremulous. He glances cautiously about to see whether there are any watchers; then, satisfied that he is unobserved, he angrily dashes off his cheek a tear, which would come whether or no; for his young heart yearns for his dead parents.

A minute, and he is at the lodge-door, and he draws a long, deep breath, places his hand to his mouth in hunter fashion, and screams in piercing tones the view-halloo. The door opens with wonderful rapidity, and Shem's honest face and curly pate protrude in questioning wonder. "Well, Shem!" exclaims Philip, and he grasps Shem's hand with a hearty shake.

Shem is thunderstruck for a moment, but finally releases Philip's hand, bends his knee, and begins to address a welcome to his master in the words of an old formula which is customary on these occasions; Philip interrupts: "Up, Shem, up! Never mind your welcome. Your face is a better index to your heart than the words of a musty old parchment. Where's Debbie and Brad? Call them at once!"

In spite of Philip's command Shem remains stolidly in the same position until he "has had his say," then he hurrahs with a rare good-will, and quickly reaches for his hunting horn, upon which he performs such a shrill, far-reaching call that the very lodge shakes with the air's vibrations. "That 'ull bring 'em, my lord! Rebeck me, but your lordship has grown tall and big sin' you left for furrin pairts."

"Good sakes, Master Philip! have ye come back at last! Gie me a buss for the sake o' old times when you an' Brad were dandled on the same lap! good sakes! how weel-favored ye 've grown, to be sure!" exclaims Debbie in a breath; while Brad stands in the background with his mouth opened in a smile, and his eyes sparkling an eager welcome to his former playmate and yet dreading to come forward for fear of "makin' a fule o' himsel'," as he afterwards explained. Philip notices his hesitation, and with kindly tact he goes up to him and shakes him by the hand, and inquires about his wife Meg Throck, the former Meg Busbie, who is well and happy. He then says: "I must leave you now, for I want to run over to Holme Grange!"

"Ay, do!" adds Debbie; a warning glance from Shem, however, and she holds her tongue.

"You must consider my visit as a secret not to be divulged, for I return to London to-morrow, and I have no time to spare—not even enough to sleep one night in my former chamber; and as I shall not be able to see you again before I go, I 'll bid you—' good-bye,' and my blessings on all of you. And Brad! give my love to Meg, and tell her that when I come again I shall pay her a visit!"

As he approaches the Grange, he rides more slowly

until his champing, restless horse proceeds at a pace more in accordance with a funeral than a proposed meeting with a loving wife. He is now behind the bushes whence he looked out on her one well-remembered night; and with an exclamation at the uneasy movements of his horse, he springs from the saddle. At first his step is slow; now he strikes out at a quick step straight up to the low window where Margery used to sit, and play with her spaniel or converse with her father.

No one is about, and the room is very dark; for the heavy curtains are drawn, and they keep out the light. He steps inside and remains motionless for a moment until his eyes have become accustomed to the darkness. Now he can see distinctly; and his quick, stifled breath shows that he recognizes the form which lies on the blue-velvet lounge under the bay window. Stepping noiselessly to the window he half draws one of the curtains, and a broad ribbon of pink light falls athwart Margery's face. She looks more like a marble effigy than a living, breathing girl; the lily has vanquished the roses on her cheeks and left them pale and waxen. Her lips are tightly closed, while the corners of her mouth are drawn and curved as though she dreams of some sorrowful thing. Her sunlit hair falls in fragrant tresses on the dark velvet, and undulates and glitters golden-like on her fair neck and bosom, which rises and falls in irregular starts as though she has a half-consciousness of the presence of an intruder.

Philip kneels down by her side, and looks at her long and tenderly, until, no longer able to control the power of his newly-awakened love, he put his arms around her waist and draws her to his breast, while his lips touch hers with a kiss so passionate that she screams in affright, and wakes to find herself in Philip's arms. "Philip!" she exclaims, and her body becomes cold, and heavier than before, and she is unconscious; at this juncture Philip hears the General's well-known step coming toward him, and he awaits the denouement in some anxiety.

"Margery! Margery!—I'm sure she called—Margery!"

Philip, disengaging himself, faces Holmes, and says calmly: "Well, General! Philip has returned, you see!"

"Bilboes and lobedoes! my dear, dear boy;" he exclaims, in excited gladness. "Why did you outflank me in this manner? If I had known, you should have been met with all the honors of Holme Grange. Have you seen Margery?" he goes to the lounge and endeavors to rouse her, thinking that she is still asleep, and Philip does not undeceive him. "Wake, Margery, hinny! Here is somebody—Heavens! she is dead! Philip, Philip! come here! Have you—"

Philip adds: "She knows I am here, General! She fainted when I showed myself to her."

Holmes looks relieved at the explanation, and replies: "That's all, eh? All right, then; here—" and he calls for a servant to bring in the lights and iced wine for "Mistress Margery."

For a time ensues confusion worse confounded by the General's impetuous movements, and his excitement at the return of his daughter's husband. Margery has recovered, but she is still too weak to stand, and she is half reclining on the lounge with eyes all ablaze and a glorious color in her checks; whilst Philip gives an outline of his wanderings abroad, and as he finishes, she says pleadingly: "You will never go away again, Philip? I have been so lonely here, even with father."

The General adds: "Yes, stick to home and us now. You are surely tired of travelling by this time."

"Yes, I am," replies Philip, "but I really must set out for Dublin in a few days. I have political business to attend to there which I shall shirk as much as possible, you may be sure."

Margery's face grows troubled as she hears this intelligence, and the color slowly fades away from her cheeks.

By this time Philip has recovered his equanimity, and he begins to blame himself for having a hand in so theatrical a display as he has himself created. The General goes to the door, and apologizes for his departure, and now Philip and his wife are alone together. She rises from the lounge, and sits down on a footstool close beside him. She looks up into his face so long and anxiously that Philip begins to feel guilty and embarrassed, and to break the painful silence, he says: "Sweetheart, tell me what you have done during my absence."

The old smile momentarily dimples her cheeks as she replies: "Always call me sweetheart, Philip dear! It sounds like Rooksnest and the dark, cool avenue. The time has dragged—but never mind, darling! You are with me now, and I am happy—so happy." And she hides her face on his knees to conceal her tears of joy.

Philip elevates his eyebrows, shrugs his shoulders, and mutters, " As bad as ever, curse me!"

She lifts her bright eyes to his face, and says, in a voice which is deep and thrilling with repressed emotion: " Did you speak, darling?"

"No, Margery; I was but thinking!"

"Of me?" she asks.

"Yes, Margery, of you!"

CHAPTER XXXIII.

―――Took proper principles to thrive :―――
SWIFT'S " LIBEL."

THE gypsy queen still holds her court in the forest's heart, but Maldran Gudru is there no longer. He has been disgraced, and expelled the camp for two years as the penalty of insulting his royal mistress. When he returned from his errand in London and told her of its fruitlessness, she reproached him for his lack of energy and idleness, to which he replied in an insolent manner which angered her so much that she struck him on the mouth with her hand, and he caught her by the neck in his blind rage, and tried to throw her down. In return she drove her four-edged poniard through his traitorous arm, signalled for help, and Maldran was disgraced.

Philip feels a passing desire to view once more the forest camp, where he gambolled and played at hide-and-seek with his tawny, ragged playmates; and he is now walking thither. The day is clear, cold, and bracing, and the keen north wind rushes down the lungs icy-cold and nipping. He enters the camp, and unperceived walks to the queen's tent by a back path with which he is familiar, and he calls in a low voice, " Queenie! queenie!!" The door opens at the summons, and the queen ejaculates in surprise, " My lord!" " Yes, queenie!" he replies, and he catches her in his arms and salutes her with rather more fervor perchance than friendship alone calls for, and so she thinks, for as she disengages herself, she exclaims, " For shame, my lord;

you almost squeezed the life out o' me. Recollect that ye are not the little Philip of other days now, but a grown gentleman, an' ower old to kiss an' hug me as ye used to do!"

He laughs at her remonstrance, and replies: "You are in a bad temper this morning, queenie!"

Her face clouds with a moody expression as she answers, "Am I? Mayhap I have cause."

Philip is about to put his arm around her waist, when she shrinks from him with a gesture of dislike, and cries: "Stop, my lord! I care not for such fooleries!"

"The more fool you!" he retorts, nettled at her petulance. "I thought you would like to see me ere I left for Ireland; but as I am not welcome I'll go away as quickly as I came!"

"One minute, my lord!" she says, and she lays her hand on his arm. "I have something to say which ye must hear before ye leave queenie."

Philip is a little surprised at her words, and ascribes them to some whim or freak, but willing to humor her, he waits for her to proceed.

"My lord, I did not ask ye to break bread or sup wine wi' me when ye came in. This is the reason. Your father—"

But it is useless to narrate her words, for we know her story. As she finishes Philip cries: "A plague on these Valentins! Wherever I go, it is Valentin!—in Avignon, in Paris, in London, and now here on my own estate. A thousand guineas were a small sum to be rid of this tiresome persecution. Send to Shem Throck's for it to-morrow, and it will be there. I pity the poor woman; but s'life I do not see why my father's peccadilloes should be punished through me! A fico for your 'vengeance,' as you so maniloquently term it. I give the money out of pure charity to Mistress Valentin. I can go now, I suppose—eh, queenie? Come! give me a kiss for my good-nature; I deserve one!"

Her face is brighter now, and she smiles demurely as she replies, "My lord has a right to poach on his own manor when he chooses!"

Philip requires no other permission, and he presses his lips on hers again and again until she repulses him with a good-natured scolding. "Good-bye, queenie! I am going over to your Irish cousins, now, and maybe you will never see me again."

The General is up and walking briskly about in the garden for the sake of his health, and, as he expresses it, "to keep my sword-belt from growing too small." But Margery still sleeps, for it was very late ere she could compose herself after the exciting event of the previous day. Philip informs the General of his intention to start for Dublin at once, and bids him good-bye amid his half-angry protestations and entreaties; and he tells him that he will go up to see Margery in her room.

"Well! if you will go, bless you, my boy, and let your shadow darken my gate again as soon as possible."

Philip steps lightly to the bedside, and sees that Margery is sound asleep. He opens his escritoire, and hurriedly writes a short letter in which he tells her that he "leaves her in this manner in order to spare her the pain of a parting, and that he will soon return, or else send for her;" he finishes with, "Good-bye, wifie! I kissed you adieu whilst you slept, so that you might dream of me: for Debbie used to tell me that 'a sleeping person kissed will dream of the kisser.' Hoping that the saying is true, I bid you good-bye for a short time."

He lays the letter gently on her bosom, touches her lips very lightly, and goes softly down the stairs and through the hallway to the front of the Grange, where his horse stands ready saddled and bridled. He shakes hands with the General once more, vaults into the saddle, and off he gallops at full speed! Away—down the avenue, through the forest, across the meadow lands and hunting-ground—he flies, fearing that Margery may awake and send after him; for tearful partings are "mightily apt to disturb one's equanimity and enjoyment!"

While in London Philip had endeavored to take his seat in parliament, but being under age he was ineligible, and to his extreme chagrin and regret he found that his aspirations for political honors were foiled, at least in England. His fertile mind had other resources, however, and he determined to go to Ireland, and see whether the more hot-blooded, mercurial Shamrockites would have the same objection to receive him as their English brethren, for his Irish peerage entitles him to a seat in their house. Of course he is ineligible there, also, if his peers see fit to make him so; but he is hopeful and sanguine, and he has great confidence in his powers of persuasion over the impressionable people whom he purposes to honor with his person. As he pushes forward at a quick gallop, which sends his young blood tingling joyously through his veins, he soliloquizes: "If I cannot gain my point there, I am beaten for a couple of years! But I cannot, will not fail, for, young as I am, I feel certain that I can topple over half the arguments and decisions that are given there, provided they are no better than are those delivered and registered by our London orators and judges. They say in Ireland that a steel point must prop a hard word, which is certainly a point in my favor; for if such is the case they must all be gentlemen, either from nature or necessity." His mind gloats on the future when he will be, as his father and Harley and Stanhope were before him, the cynosure of an admiring people, and the leader of an enthusiastic parliament who will applaud his tactics or compliment him on his wit, learning, and bravery; and his heart throbs an *Io Triumphe* in the glorious anticipation of the future.

CHAPTER XXXIV.

> Thus, with each gift of nature and of art,
> And wanting nothing but an honest heart.
> POPE'S "WHARTON."
> He must be greater than his sire ;—
> SWIFT.

PHILIP is soon a great favorite in Dublin, with both Whigs and Tories, for his daring, his generosity, and his great powers of drinking, frolicking, and conversing. He is unanimously admitted to the House, where—to every body's surprise and possibly his own—he turns sides and becomes as violent a Whig as before he was a Tory.

He finishes his maiden speech with these words: "My only thought will be to support the ministry, the government, and to advocate the Orange cause." It abounds in terse reasoning, strong arguments, and scathing sarcasm against the Opposition; and it is adorned with all the flowers of rhetoric and fancy. Cheer upon cheer bursts from his excited listeners, which he acknowledges by a graceful bow, and he takes his seat. His hand is grasped "many a time, and oft" before he receives all the congratulations which are poured in on him. Says Lord Carnbregh, a well-known orator and lawyer: "My lord, I heard your father when he was quite young, and he was wonderful; but, if you continue as you have begun, you will eclipse his achievements altogether."

Philip's eyes glitter, and his cheeks flush as he replies: "My father led his party in London. Sure I can do the same in Eblana?"

His words sound prophetic, and as his audacious answer is circulated around, it is received with cheers and laughter. A few veterans among them shake their heads doubtingly at his words, but they are not heeded in the general hubbub and brouhaha.

That night Philip retired with his head in a whirl of exciting and ambitious thoughts, engendered by his triumph at the House and the hearty applause of its members. His sleep is broken and restless, and the sun still slumbers as he arises, dresses himself, and strolls down to Liffey's banks. The river undulates dark and dismal in the gray morning light, and he compares its dull, heavy surface to his past life, which has been spent in riotous debaucheries and enervating excesses that, for the time being, deadened and saddened him, mind and body. Now ambition's sun lifts him above his former life, and makes him worthy of commendation and admiration, as heaven's sun will brighten and beautify the now murky Liffey.

"If I had been by his death-bed, I know that his last words would have been: 'Philip, sustain my party!' And I will. I would rather see the Chevalier on his throne; but as he is not there, and doubtless never will be, it is my duty as a true Briton to uphold the government and stand by the ministry. No more shall it be said of me that—

'I see the right and I approve it too,
Condemn the wrong, and yet the wrong pursue!'

Now I'll pursue the right as well as see it, i'faith! 'Tis a pity though that his majesty is so mightily Dutch, and keeps two such frowsies as Kendal and Darlington continually by him—duplicate Grenouilles, devoid even of her sense and passable acquirements—"

"Your lordship is up betimes," interrupts Lord Hintflam, who has approached him unobserved.

Philip turns to him, and they converse on different subjects, the beauty of the far-stretching bay, or pass remarks on the weather, until Philip, whose whole mind is now absorbed in politics, says: "My lord, do you think it possible that his majesty and the prince will ever be better friends than they are? Their bickerings disgrace the country and scandalize its statesmen."

"They will never be in amicable relations with each other. His majesty views the prince with the deepest aversion. Do you recollect, when he set out for Hanover, how he tried to prevent the prince from assuming the regency, and also his dismissal of Argyle?—No, they can never be friends."

Philip replies: "I recollect; his majesty's hatred and jealousy of him were the talk of Paris."

"Speaking of Argyle," continues Lord Hintflam, "the prince's connection with him is indiscreet to the last degree, and only tends to widen the rupture!"

Philip replies approvingly: "You are correct, my lord."

A favorable criticism at which Hintflam seems rather nettled, and rejoins rather pointedly: "I am glad you think so!"

Philip nods assentingly, and resumes: "What do you think about Townshend?"

"The prince's cat's paw," returns Hintflam.

"Yes, he deserves his dismissal for his weakness and his utter lack of diplomacy. It is unfortunate for us, though, for our only support now is Stanhope."

Hintflam rejoins: "And he should have resigned on Townshend's dismissal."

"Certainly not!" replies Philip, "Stanhope is right. Why should we lose two supports because one is fallen?"

"He ought to accept of Ireland. He will only increase bad feeling against him by a refusal!"

Philip replies: "Well, well; we must all do our best

to keep our Tory friends within bounds, or else they may send us under again."

Philip's reason for ending the discussion so quickly is that he has just caught sight of a very pretty girl crossing the muddy street which compels her to expose a foot and ankle worthy of a Gaditana of sunny Spain. He is desirous of viewing her at a closer distance, and hurriedly excuses himself to Lord Hintflam, and he follows after the object of his desires at a leisurely pace in order not to attract attention. She is tall, and magnificently proportioned. Her eyes are dark hazel, and delightfully expressive; and her cherry lips look very inviting, while there is that nameless grace about her which seems more fitted for the saloon than the street—more suitable in a countess than in a lonely girl strolling about Dublin at an early hour in the morning.

She walks briskly on toward the cathedral—a noble structure of great antiquity, and a mass of historical incidents, from the spire on the high sloping roof down to the lowest dungeon of its underground vaults. As she enters the arched doorway, she turns round and smiles coquettishly to Philip, who salutes her, and signs to her to wait for him; but she declines to obey him, and goes inside. Nothing daunted, Philip follows after her. The interior of the cathedral is solemnly grand. The lofty ceiling is an immense, azure vault, dotted with golden stars; while at regular distances the holy fathers look down from the dizzy height with a saintly calmness on their grand faces. Around the extreme circle of the ceiling—almost trenching on the walls—are rose-windows of warm, glowing colors, which fleck the stone floor with mingling dashes and splashes of all the rainbow colors and suffuse the quaint, crumbling, oaken stalls with a delicious mellowness.

Philip never asks himself why the unknown comes

here. There is no service to-day, and the cathedral is lonely and deserted. He walks up the centre aisle, and casts his eyes about in search of her; but she is nowhere to be seen: "Faith! this is a good joke!—a woman hiding from me in a church! ha-ha!" and he calls in a loud voice, "For mercy's sake! my unknown siren, tell me where you are?"

"If my Lord Wharton wishes to see me—lo, I am here!" she answers in musical, mocking accents; and she walks towards him. Her face is concealed by a black silk vizard, which she holds on with her left hand, extending to him her right. He raises it to his lips, but she snatches it away, and exclaims: "My lord, I give you my hand as a friend, not as a conquest! Your tour abroad has rendered you conceited. You doubtless consider me as a prize whom your very good looks have captivated—eh?"

He is rather taken aback at her words, but he replies, with a look of profound devotion, "Fair lady, such insolent presumption could not find a place in my thoughts."

She laughs as she replies: "Hoity-toity! Who dares to accuse his grace of Northumberland of presumption?"

Philip starts as he hears himself called by a title which he has not claimed since his return to England: "None could lay such a charge to him merely for following a lady in the streets, and then inflicting his presence on her in the house of holiness." Rather piqued at her sarcastic manner, he angrily replies, "S'life, I'll not *inflict* it any longer!" and he turns to leave her. But she starts forward, and lays a little, white hand on his arm, and says, in a half pleading manner, "Pardon me, your grace, I—"

He turns so quickly that he strikes against her, and, to keep herself from falling, she catches hold of his arm, whereat he is rather pleased than otherwise; and, as an attentive cavalier, he thinks that he can support her better by putting his arm around her waist. This little attention she declines, and she removes his hand, and says, with a mischievous twinkle in her eyes, "For shame! you a married man, and I a wife—perchance!"

He replies with a sigh: "The first is unfortunately true, but under favor the last is false!"

"Many thanks for your grace's courtesy. Since you know so much, maybe you can tell me who I am—my name, pedigree, and country?"

"Madame," he says, "that is an impossibility, which is my misfortune, and which will be your fault unless you enlighten me;" and he raises his hand to remove her vizard; but she anticipates the movement by drawing back a step, and she holds her taper finger up warningly as she exclaims: "Not yet! but I may tell you my name, if you promise not to reveal it!"

Of course he gives the promise, and a low, rich laugh displays her pearly teeth as she replies, "Madame Grenouille!" He laughs aloud at the ludicrous images which the name brings before his eyes; but his companion appears highly offended, and she conducts herself in such an absurd manner that he is well nigh out of patience with her. Finally she says, in a graver manner: "Let us seat ourselves in this stall, and I will tell you truly about myself, and about others whom you may know." He obeys her, and she proceeds: "Before I say any more, your grace must give me your word of honor that all I say or do in our interview will go no further than ourselves?"

Philip hesitates a moment before he gives her the promise, for he resolves to stop her if she has anything to reveal to him that is inconsistent with his honor to keep secret.

"My name is Nora O'Beirne;" here she pauses, removes

her vizard, and draws a packet from her bosom. "I have but just arrived from Madrid. You will find in this packet a letter of introduction from my friend Mr. Bubb,* and also a message from his eminence the Cardinal Alberoni!"

He looks suspiciously around, but she reassures him with a gesture. He opens, and reads the letter from Mr. Bubb first. In it the minister highly extols Mistress O'Beirne, and praises her loyalty to the government— a recommendation well enough by itself, but rather peculiar when coupled with a message from Alberoni—a man whose gigantic mind and daring courage did not once quail when he singly defied the combined powers of England, France, and Holland, and coolly insulted the haughty court of Vienna.

As he finishes reading the Cardinal's message, his head hums with vague thoughts and half-formed projects. The wily priest, who is tolerably conversant with Philip's character through the accounts of his emissaries in London, broaches to "His Grace," in the most delicate manner, the advisability of "His Grace" resuming his allegiance to "His Majesty James III.;" enlarges on the sufferings of the exiled monarch; sneers at the "happy Dutch family;" and offers him, if he will support the Jacobite cause, the command of a large Spanish troop, an order of knighthood in the highest order of Spain, and a large amount of money and jewels.

As Philip opened the message, Mistress O'Beirne leaves him, apparently to examine the many tombs on the opposite side of the aisle; but she momentarily casts stealthy glances at him, and anxiously waits for him to finish. She looks perplexed and doubtful, and her fan trembles slightly in her hand. Philip's good resolutions almost melt away at the Cardinal's promises, and he

* The British Minister at Madrid.

tries to balance the advantages of the two positions with strict impartiality—a loyal Whig, or a traitorous Tory? On the one side his estates and future wealth will be confiscated, and his name attainted. On the other, he will reap glory at the head of an army, receive a coveted order of knighthood, and a large sum of ready money— an important item, for he cannot yet have full control of his properties, and, although his allowance is large, his expenses are far beyond it.

For nearly an hour does he think over the Cardinal's proposition without coming to a decision. "If I but loved George more and James less, my mind would be easy in quick time; but one the —— S'life, I'll leave the issue to Dame Fortune in the shape of Mistress O'Beirne." And he calls to her, and says :—

"Mistress O'Beirne, Mr. Bubb's letter is a blind, I suppose?"

She nods assent.

"Alb—, the other, is the real cause of your embassy?"

Again she nods.

"Very well! Now I will take my dagger, and scratch two marks on this flag;" she looks surprised at his manœuvres, but follows his motions with watchful eyes. He continues: "My opinions are so exactly balanced, Mistress O'Beirne, that I intend to let fortune decide whether I shall be Hanoverian or Jacobite." She is amused in spite of her anxiety to secure him for her employer, and she laughs nervously. Philip resumes: "One of these scratches will turn me Jacobite; the other will keep me Hanoverian. I will be that which your pretty foot shall first touch." He scratches two long lines on the stone flag, and moves a few steps backward. She replies: "I entreat your grace to consider the question more seriously! you—"

He shakes his head and points calmly to the scratches.

She flushes, as she resumes with a forced smile: "Really, your grace affects an odd way of determining a choice in which loyalty, fame, and pecuniary rewards are pitted against a fancied attachment to a Dutch usurper! But if you will have it so—Holy Mary, help me to save your grace from an inglorious disloyalty to your true king!" She places her foot on the scratch nearest Philip.

"Is that your choice, Mistress O'Beirne?" he asks, with a half relieved expression on his face.

"Yes, your grace," she replies, and her face becomes slightly paler and anxious.

"Then long live —— King George, and success to the Hanoverian line!"

She turns scarlet at his words, and exclaims: "Lost! and Alberoni foiled by a farcical 'chance' —— His Eminence's message, your grace?"

"Here it is!" he replies, and he turns to pick it up from the seat of a stall on which he left it; but it has disappeared. She notices his start, and exclaims: "Your grace, that letter must be found! Your have dealt fairly by me, and I have lost, and I would not like to see your grace impeached for high treason, as you certainly would be if that letter were to fall into the hands of an enemy to you."

He replies earnestly: "Yes, it must be found; it cannot be far away!"

But it cannot be found. High and low they seek for it, but all their efforts are in vain, and finally they are forced to come to the disagreeable conclusion that it is lost.

"Your grace," says Mistress O'Beirne, in a bitter, regretful tone, "it is useless for me to urge you further. His Eminence has explained to you all the advantages that you can gain by returning to your true allegiance;

and as my unlucky mission is accomplished I will return to Madrid, and encounter his reproaches for my unfortunate failure. I shall probably never see you again; so I will bid you good-bye, and wish you every success in your mistaken future."

She extends her hand, which he presses kindly, draws her veil over her face, and walks slowly down the aisle and disappears through the open doors.

In consequence of the triple alliance, the Pretender was forced to cross the Alps and reside in Rome under the shadow of the Pontifical cloak. While there, Alberoni corresponded directly with him, and urged him to rouse all his energies for another invasion of England, which should be headed either by himself or Ormond, and he also sent him many assurances of the king's warmest sympathy and assistance. In Spain Philip is governed alternately by his confessor and by his mistress, the black-eyed, laughing Señorita Dona Inez, who in turn are the queen's tools, whom Alberoni moves to his will like a jointed puppet. In disposition and temper Philip is very like the Pretender, but with even less honor and energy. But even if he had more energy and self-reliance, the former country curate would doubtless absorb them in his own impetuous genius, except indeed he possessed a Cromwell's iron mind and unswervable will.

CHAPTER XXXV.

Pro tempore.

PHILIP's career in the Irish Parliament reads like a romance. Never, in the annals of Irish history, had there been an admission under age except in this instance. His winning address, oratorical powers, and his wonderfully precocious talents are the talk of London as well as Dublin. Wherever he goes, he is sure to meet with a flattering welcome and the attention of old and young; for his power of adapting himself to the capacity of those with whom he is thrown in contact causes all to respect and love him, from the enthusiastic lad still in his teens to the veteran politician or lawyer. The Whigs speak of him as their future leader, and prophesy great things of him. His past offences are now regarded as the mere coruscations of the too forward intellect, and are condoned accordingly. In various discussions in which he has taken part in the House, his arguments have been so clear and conclusive, his delivery and reasoning so admirable, that the side on which he has thrown his voice has been uniformly successful.

The government, anxious to show its appreciation of his services in defending a bill of vital importance to them, has created him Duke of Wharton, and moreover set forth in the patent that "this is but an earnest of still further favors which you may reap if you continue in the course you have begun." His private life has been almost irreproachable. Margery has been living with him for the last year and a half in an uninterrupted state of domestic felicity. To Philip's great joy she promises soon to be a mother. Under these circumstances, he proposes to her that she shall return to Bucks for awhile, where he will follow her in a week or so—a proposition to which she unwillingly acquiesced for she dreads to be away from him.

We will enter and view our reformed rake in the light of a good husband and a steady Whig. The room is fitted up in the most expensive, even extravagant manner, and the different ornaments and curiosities in it evince an oddly fantastic, but refined taste. It is not cold, but a glowing fire crackles on the hearth and diffuses an aromatic odor of sandal-wood and cedar—woods which Philip is fond of smelling, and burns accordingly. A round, ebony table, whose surface is a clear, polished slab of steel, is drawn near the fragrant blaze, and beside it sits Philip and Margery conversing about her intended departure. He passes his hand down her cheek, and says in an anxious voice: "Margery, you look unwell—feverish. Let me ring for a dish of tea!" and he taps on a little silver bell, and the summons is answered immediately by a liveried lackey. "Her grace wishes a dish of tea; and, hark ye, bring a decanter of brandy with it!"

"Yes, your grace!"

"Philip," says Margery, as the door closes, "why do you drink that fiery stuff? In time it will surely make you nervous and irritable."

He answers with a laugh: "In that case, wifie, I shall be reduced to the dire necessity of physicking myself with a decoction of hiera-picra and aqua vita. But I'll risk it for the sake of the grapy flavor the brandy leaves in my throat."

"I never knew you were so fond of the grape before, Philip. I'll get you tons of them if you will give up the brandy!" And she looks triumphant, as if her point is gained; but he replies:—

"You argue well, my little lawyer; but your case is lost! I prefer my brandy and grapes together, for, as the axiom says, '*In toto et pars continentur!*'"

The lackey returns, and carefully spreads a damask cover on the steel surface before he lays on it the waiter, on which stand in company the brandy and the tea with a dish of caraways. Philip swallows a glass of the former, nibbles at a cake, and stretches himself lazily back in his chair. He is more manly now, and his moustaches have some pretence of visibility and tangibility.

"What have you been doing all day, Margery?"

"Everything," she laughingly replies. "Let me see! I was dressed—I breakfasted—oh! do stop asking me tiresome questions, Philip. I want to enjoy my tea quietly."

"Ah, I see; you've been as usual busy about nothing."

She replies pettishly: "You were not admitted to the sight, at any rate, so you need not laugh!"

Margery looks very lovable as she nestles in the cosey arm-chair and extends her slippered feet to the crumbling logs. This night she keeps entirely for Philip and herself, and her instructions to the servant are to let no one disturb them short of his majesty or her father, and of these she expects neither. She is in an enchanting dishabille, and her hair tumbles in a mass on her bare shoulders.

"What did *you* do in the House to-day?—But never mind! I am afraid you will give me some long, wearisome descriptions of a speech from my Lord Prosy this, or his Lordship Tiresome that, or—"

"Never fear, saucebox. I'll tell you about my fling at Lord Kellmoll, who had the audacity to insinuate that I was overbold for my years!"

"As I live! what an ill-bred fellow!" she exclaims, angrily. "What did you say to him? Quick—tell me! How you must have punished him!"

He replies calmly: "Certainly. I never allow insolence to go unchastised. I told him that 'if age constituted wisdom, and youth folly, I succumbed to him.' At the same time, I prayed to the gods I might always remain young, or at least never be able to ascend so high on Minerva's mount as had his lordship."

"You served him right, Philip; only you should—I mean, how crestfallen the poor man must have been!"

"Well, little one, he provoked me to it, you know."

She acquiesces in the force of his reasoning, and looks intently among the smouldering embers to discover omens of births, deaths, or marriages; and lo! in the corner nearest Philip she sees as plain as daylight, a cradle! "Oh! Philip, come here! Look! look! see the —" and she stops. He hurriedly rises from his chair to discover the cause of her exclamations. She does not conclude her sentence, but blushes as red as her own English roses, and buries her face in the chair. Philip sees no cause for alarm, and replies: "Margery, I think I shall order a dose of hiera-picra for you instead of myself, if you persist in this nonsensical conduct;" and he reseats himself, and laughs loudly at her attitude, for she is cuddled up all in a lump, and her hair hangs over the arm of the chair, and falls to the floor in a wavy, shimmering mass.

After this episode, they pass the time very pleasantly in discussing questions of literature and the fashions, and of the most "modish" style of dressing the hair—whether the small steel shoe-buckles are superior or equal to the richer and more elaborate jewelled ones; and in mutual remembrances of dear old Bucks.

Early the next morning Margery set out for Bucks

under the protection of Count Hussite and his lady. The day was bright and clear, and the water shone resplendent with the sun's warm rays, and everything promised a safe and speedy voyage.

CHAPTER XXXVI.

"Persuasion tips his tongue whene'er he talks."
Graced as thou art with all the power of words,
So known, so honored, at the House of Lords.
POPE.

PHILIP is standing on the floor of the House busily engaged in arguing a point at law with Lord Hintflam— a veteran speaker and parliamentary tactician. Says his lordship: "Your grace, it would run counter to the statute which was framed to correct that very evil." Philip is about to reply, when he is interrupted by a messenger who whispers in his ear the intelligence of the birth of an heir to his name, and he leaves the House immediately.

Philip's heart beats high as he walks rapidly homewards, and he feels himself to be a greater, nobler man than before, and the future programme of his son's life is already laid out. "It shall not be like his own in every respect; but he shall be a Whig, and a great man of course!" Finally his thoughts end in a determination to visit Bucks again to see with his own eyes the infant scion of a noble sire.

* * * * * *

Philip shakes the General by the hand in the most violent manner, and they joyfully congratulate each other on the happy event. The head-nurse—a fussy, testy body, arrayed in a black cap of portentous size and stiffness—leads Philip, with all important gestures, to *the* room. Margery is overjoyed to see him, and she proudly shows him their son. "Philip, darling, the nurse tells me that she never saw in all her life such a pretty baby."

"She is a sensible woman; and her services must be well rewarded," replies Philip; and he kisses the end of its little nose in admiring happiness, and then beats a retreat from the severely watchful eye of the head-nurse.

That night Philip and the General sit up very late, and consume uncounted goblets of well-spiced punch. I will add that the standing toast was: "The young one's health, and his future prosperity."

Philip stays at Holme Grange for nearly a month, during which time he amuses himself in hunting, fishing, and various other pastimes, not forgetting the dandling of the baby. Then he begins to tire of rustic happiness, and to long for the gayeties and excitements of town life.

They are eating supper, and Philip has just declared that he has important business in town which must be attended to at once; to which Margery replies, with a pleading look: "Am I to go along with you, Philip?"

"No, Margery," he says, regretfully, "it is impossible; I must post with the utmost despatch; but I will return in a few days—at least, I hope so!" She replies:—

"I hope you will. I always feel lonely when you are away, for father is always busy about his own affairs, and he has no time to spare with me. If I had not my little darling to keep me company, I should certainly not let you go without me; but come back as soon as ever you can."

"S'life! Margery, you can rely on me, I'll not stay in London any longer than I can help." She looks half-doubtful; but drinks her tea in silence. Philip continues in fatherly tones: "Take great care of the child, wifie!" She indignantly tosses her head at this piece of unnecessary advice; as if it were possible she could be careless of his—their son.

We will precede this unwilling traveller to London, and look about us for old sights and familiar faces. Philip's mansion is now finished and ready for occupation. The decorators and cabinet-makers have left their little mementoes on the table in the ebony room, where he will be sure to see them when he enters. The sides of this room are panelled with polished ebony, and the ceiling is ornamented by fretted rafters picked in with gold as a relief to the sombre black. His arms are carved in every panel, while the violet windows also display his quarterings. This peculiar apartment he designs to keep sacred to himself alone, "not even the housemaid shall enter; he will keep it in order himself." Its minor decorations may in a measure account for his aversion to visitors. Underneath the centre window is a Prie-Dieu and a hassock of black velvet to kneel upon. On a curiously carved pentagonal table behind the Prie-Dieu is a Parian statue of the Virgin Mary with hands extended in the act of invoking a benediction. Philip bought it in Paris. Its workmanship is perfect; a halo of mild piety seems to burst from the white face, and in the sightless eyes there is a vague expression of purity and holiness. Around her, long white tapers stand out in bold relief against the rich dark windows. There is also an amber rosary; and a Latin missal incongruously leans against a toy that Philip also bought in Paris. It is a flesh-tinted copy of Praxitele's Cnidian Venus—the immortalized form of the courtesan Phryne, and the wondrous work which alone rescued Cnidus from obscurity and gave it a history.

To this room there is apparently no means of entrance; no door is visible. How, then, can Philip enter this, his sanctum sanctorum? Click! rings the noise of an opening spring, and a small door concealed in the panelling falls down, and Philip enters. "Faith! it's solemn enough!" he exclaims, with a shrug. "The darkness strikes a chill through me with its depressing gloom." He throws off his hat and cloak, kneels down before the Prie-Dieu, and recites a paternoster in a low but sonorous voice. This finished, he makes an inclination to the Virgin, and rises. He attempts to light one of the tapers, but his flint fails to do its duty; and with a half-uttered curse he relinquishes his intention, and sits down on the hassock to consider what he will do, where he will go, and on whom he will call to help him to enjoy the pleasures of which he determines to taste quite freely before he returns to his humdrum life at Bucks.

"There's Harry Hauteforte; he will do if I can think of none better; or there's Peterborough—wofully conceited and arrogant, but a jolly dog and vastly clever in his ways! I must see him—I wonder whether Mr. Young is in town! I would wager fifty guineas he is either dangling at St. James's, or else puffing some influential idiot with fulsome flattery. At all events, I'll run down to the Rainbow, and watch who lays his penny on the bar," and he rises, creeps through his secret doorway, and emerges into the street, where a chair soon carries him to the Rainbow coffee-house in Fleet Street.

He lays his fee on the bar, and orders the particular dish for which this house is famed—stewed cheeses and oat cakes. Charon Skewer, the noted highwayman who has eased the pockets of half London in his time, and who chances to know Philip by sight, cries: " Ah, your grace! 'tis a plaguy long time since I have had the pleasure of a canary cup with you!" Unluckily for Charon, Philip is aware of his character, and he answers not a word, but draws himself up scornfully, and with a right-about turn he gives him the expanse of his back to look upon. "A murrain on his ill-breeding!" mutters Charon, and he strikes up a conversation with the barmaid to hide his discomfiture; while an elderly man, whose appearance betokens wealth and refinement, exclaims, "Well done, your grace! served him right." Philip looks toward the speaker, and says, "Sir James, this is an unexpected pleasure. I thought you were at Ipswich among the hawthorn lanes?"

"I was there," Sir James replies, "but London has charms which never pall, and I have returned again to my old haunts."

"For which I am thankful, as I find so good a companion, and so merciless an enemy of Madame Ennui, of whom you have probably heard?"

"Yes, but never experienced her attentions."

"Fortunate man!" replies Philip.

Sir James Thornhill is sergeant painter to the king. He was once very wealthy, but fashionable excesses have reduced him considerably, and it is his daughter who is Hogarth's future wife. Beside him sits a gayly dressed cavalier whose handsome face is tinged with a grave sadness. He salutes Philip in courtly phrases, and flatters him in the most unconscionable manner. This is Edward Young, who not only composed "Night Thoughts," but also wrote the most fulsome, adulatory poem which ever disgraced any age, "The Epistle to Lord Lansdowne." 'Though nominally his friend, Philip openly shows his contempt for the poet's truckling servility. Philip's hand is now grasped by the erratic genius, Charles Mordaunt, Earl of Peterborough. Mordaunt is small, and singularly spare in person; his features are attractive, and his nose is prominent; his eyes are lively and penetrating, and his face is rather long and meagre. He has come to town to take part in the debates of the session. He addresses Philip with the bluff heartiness and jovial good nature of a soldier.

They all sit down together, and order a plentiful supply of canary. In the course of the conversation, Peterborough says to Philip: "Your grace, I hear that Alberoni is to assist the Chevalier in another attempt. He is even now fitting out an immense armament at Cadiz, and he is said to rely greatly on friends in England. It will be a hazardous matter for any one to have aught to do with this next effort. It will be a short thrift and a long rope; I should be loath to see any of *my* friends favor a scheme so foolhardy as that of the Cardinal's."

The Earl says this so meaningly that Philip begins to wonder whether he conveys the warning as a hint to himself or not, and he regrets the loss of the message in the cathedral at Dublin.

Peterborough now calls out: "More wine, fair Hebe! more wine!" and he trolls out

> "That which most doth take my muse and me
> Is sure a cup of rich canary wine."

"Ah ha!" laughs Thornhill, his whole body shaking with his merriment. "Peterborough's muse! I appeal to your grace whether he should not be fined an additional bottle for mentioning impossible monstrosities?"

Young, who is invariably the last speaker, laughs at Philip's answer of "Certainly!" and adds, "It left him when his majesty came in."

The earl flushes as he replies, "Yes, Mr. Young, and I went out along with it to make room for one who has since managed to scrape his way into decent society and ape his betters."

Young feels the taunt, but, true to his policy of ingratiating himself, he only smiles and requests the "favor of a cup with him."

"Come, gentlemen," says Philip, "let us take a stroll through Fleet Street;" and at his request they rise and walk out. As they pass by Dick's coffee-house, the Earl notices a friend of his at the bar, who is both wealthy and miserly; and he throws a shilling through the window to the maid, and exclaims in a loud voice, "For my Lord Sansor! Take out your penny, and give him a custard for the change;" a remark which creates a laugh against the cavalier pointed out, who lays his hand on his rapier hilt for a moment, but instantly withdrawing it, however, when the Earl notices his movement. Philip proposes a visit to that hotbed of Toryism, Saint James' Coffee-house, and thither they go.

They enter in a noisy, careless manner, which causes some of the quieter frequenters of the place to scowl disapprovingly. They indulge in several glasses of punch, and sandwiches of prime Yorkshire beef, and before they leave, Peterborough mounts a table, takes off his hat, and whirls it above his head while he exclaims: Oyez! oyez! my lords and gentlemen, attend all to the great Mordanto. He intends to recite to you a selection from a great divine's greatest poem—the subject, to be sure, has something to do with its sublimity." The inmates of the house direct their attention to this address, and many crowd around the table in expectation of amusement. He enunciates with dramatic gestures and grandiloquent airs the following squib of Swift's:—

> Mordanto fills the trump of fame,
> The Christian world his deeds proclaim,
> And prints are crowded with his name.
>
> In journeys he outrides the post,
> Sits up till midnight with his host,
> Talks politics and gives the toast.

> Knows every prince in Europe's face,
> Flies like a squib from place to place,
> And travels not, but runs a race.
>
> Heroic actions early bred in,
> Ne'er to be matched in modern reading,
> But by his namesake, Charles of Sweden.

He is listened to in silence until he finishes, when there ensue roars of laughter at his tipsy rendering of the poems. He adds gravely: "The only thing which I find fault with in the poem is the comparison between myself and Charles! I protest against being reduced to his level!"

As the uproar subsides, Philip fills a cup, and exclaims, "Gentlemen, to his grace of Shrewsbury and Alberoni—the one an enemy to the world, the other to England; may—" Loud cries drown the rest of the toast, and the crowd begin to hustle Philip and his party quite roughly until the Earl, Sir James, and Philip draw their rapiers and form a front which does not invite too close quarters. Philip, who is half tipsy and reckless, swears to finish his toast, and resumes: "May they be bound together in h—, and be doomed to gnaw at each other for all eternity!"

Symptoms of a dangerous fracas now begin to appear. Belts are tightened, and swords half drawn by many who were favorable to Shrewsbury while living, and who are enraged at the wanton insult to his memory, and hisses and curses resound through the room.

Philip cries to Young: "Draw, man, draw! We shall have to fight our way out of this. There is no end to the Jacobite fire-eaters amongst yon pack o' fools."

"A Mordanto! a Mordanto!" yells Peterborough, and, maddened with rage and wine, he thrusts viciously in front of him. "S'blood! if ye do not make a path for us out of this den of thieves and cut-purses, we'll slash one." And he draws back his arm.

How it would end if the watch did not push in and separate the crowd, it is hard to say. Their leader orders everybody out of the room except those with drawn swords—a command which produces sundry clicks and raspings as rapiers are hurriedly sheathed. None of Philip's party follow this wise example, however, except Young, who slips behind the watch, and leaves the room in a hurried manner. The honest guardians of the peace now begin to remonstrate with their "Ludships," and "regret the necessity of taking them to the round-house; but it is their duty, and must be done;" protestations which Philip silences by thrusting two or three gold pieces into the hand of the spokesman; a never-failing stratagem, and they leave perfectly contented.

"Egad!" exclaims Peterborough, "we raked them up, Wharton!"

"You say truly, Mordaunt; and it shall not be the last time, eh?"

Sir James asks, in thick, hiccuping tones, "Where's Young? Has he made wings unto himself and flown?"

"Yes," replies the Earl; "'tis an old trick of his. When steel shines, Young leaves."

The landlord unbars the door, and lets his noisy guests out again, and they are greeted with groans and hisses by the crowd standing on the pavement. They answer with scornful jeers, and dare any gentleman to a few passadoes with them! but none respond to the invitation, for both Philip and the Earl are known as thorough experts with the rapier; and Sir James, though not so famous, is yet a dangerous opponent.

They ruffle it gallantly back to Fleet Street, where they are joined by Sir Harry Hauteforte, who has been "biting Bacchus" a bit himself, and he is about as boisterous as any of the party. A cavalier, who is walking on the opposite pavement, happens to look over at our party, and he smiles amusedly, which so rouses Philip's ire that he calls over to him in an insolent manner: "Sir, the scent of your wig offends me greatly! I pray you step here, and give me the satisfaction of a gentleman, for I call you arrant knave and jackanapes!" and he handles his rapier. The cavalier thus roughly accosted, instead of coming over to avenge his wounded honor, passes on with a flushed face and a quick step; while Philip calls after him, "Coward! braggart!" and he reels after his companions who have gone ahead.

CHAPTER XXXVII.

"For he was a lord's own son."
BALLAD OF GLASGERION.

Some in clandestine companies combine;
Erect new stocks to trade beyond the line;
With air and empty names beguile the town,
And raise new credits first, then cry 'em down."
DEFOE.

Though wondering senates hung on all he spoke,
The club must hail him master of the joke.
POPE.

His majesty has returned from his German states, and has opened Parliament in person. The most important measure discussed is the celebrated Peerage bill. Once before, the creation of twelve peers was inserted in the articles of a peer's impeachment; but the bill is expected to pass in the House of Lords without the slightest opposition, and although the Tories in the Commons fight against it, the Whigs have a large majority. It is on this bill that Addison and Steele, once firm friends, take opposite sides as the "old Whig" and the "Plebeian." To everybody's surprise the Commons reject the bill almost unanimously, and Stanhope and Sunderland are foiled in their darling project; while Walpole, who opposes it strongly, is highly praised for his share in its defeat. Philip carefully watches the progress of the bill, and when it is defeated, he speaks admiringly to all about him of the "Independence of the Commons," whereat many are astonished to hear such suspicious sentiments from so warm a Whig as he has been.

Philip received a blow at this time which almost broke his heart. Margery had become lonely and nervous at Bucks, and fearful lest Philip might go back to his old courses, or be taken sick and lack proper attention, she had come to London, and brought the child with her. Philip reproached her for the step, and ordered her to return at once, for fear of infection from the smallpox, which was raging at that time. She obeyed him; but it was too late. In a few days he received the news of his son's death. He shut himself up for nearly a week, and refused to see any one; indeed, he would scarcely eat; but instead he drank large quantities of brandy which deadened his grief as well as satisfied his hunger. His servants denied all visitors: "They are his grace's orders!" was the only answer that inquiring friends received. His grief was very poignant. He had set such great store on his boy, and he hated poor Margery with all his heart as the cause of his loss. He did not once write to her, but sent his commands to the steward to have the body buried with all the honors, and he would not go down to superintend the burial. When he re-entered society he firmly repulsed all offers of sympathy, and sternly forbade all mention of his loss within his hearing.

He is now the President of the Hellfire Club—a set of blasphemous profligates. He was solicited to be a member, but he declined except he should be made president, and sooner than lose him the club agreed to his demand, and he is now publicly known as the leader of "the most shameless, impious crew that ever existed." He is far more reckless and heedless of all restraints now than he ever was before; and he brings things to a crisis by avowing himself a Tory and a Jacobite, an avowal which requires a bold heart and a steady hand to support.

Harley has been zealously advertising the great scheme which is to make England the richest country in the world, and his partisans are loud in their praises of his South Sea Scheme. Its origin and progress are too well known to need any recapitulation, and "the idea that is worthy of Sully or Colbert" is gradually working itself into favor among merchants and traders, nobility and gentry. Philip, who is now of age, and in Parliament, enthusiastically favors it, and fails to see the ruinous future which lurks within it. "John Law! Rue-Quincampoix! actions and shares," entirely supersede the ordinary scandal and topics of the day. The Scotch adventurer is all powerful in Paris, and when he and my Lord Stair quarrel, his Excellency is recalled and Sir Robert Sutton is installed in his place.

As soon as the scheme bill has received the royal assent, subscriptions are opened, and they are taken with such avidity that another and another follow in quick succession. In a short time stocks rise from 130 to 1000, and this wonderful success produces fifty other schemes, many of them of the most absurd nature. The Prince is head of "The Welsh Copper-Mining Company," and in two days he gains forty thousand pounds, then wisely withdraws and thus escapes the subsequent consequences.

Change Alley begins to rival the Rue Quincampoix. Here alone do Whigs and Tories, churchmen and dissenters mingle in amicable agreement to effect transfers, or open new subscriptions. London's noblest dames go masked and hooded to the alley to buy and sell, like any broker. Behold a few schemes selected at random from a crowd of similar absurdities:—

"For importing a number of large jackasses from Spain."

"For a wheel, for perpetual motion."

"For an undertaking which shall be *revealed* in *due* time."

London is crazy. Let us mingle with the mad crowd which roars and surges in the alley. Here is a man with his hands, pockets, and hat full of papers, yelling in shrill, cracked accents the peculiar merits of his scheme, while a near rival vaunts his above all the others, and glances around in search of buyers; and all are either buying or selling with the lust of greed flushing their faces, or making their hands tremble. There is a beautiful woman whose mask has fallen off, and whose hair is rumpled and disordered. She is bargaining with a vulgar wretch for some rising shares. Her name is Lady Winifred Rabie, and she is endeavoring to gain enough to sustain her in her extravagant manner of living. Yonder is Dr. Radcliffe, who has already lost £5000; he is busy calculating the odds on a new scheme which has just been offered to him. The Duke of Chandos is also engaged in the same occupation. "Way for the Earl of Westmoreland!" and his lordship takes his accustomed place as buyer or seller. The king's favorite, Bernstoff, glides in and around the fevered speculators, and warily watches his chances. Now we can distinguish Philip's fair curls and handsome face. He is conversing with an aged cavalier, whose peruke

tells of other days. He is tall, and not ill-favored, but
his neck is too low between his shoulders, his countenance
is furrowed and haggard with his long career of intrigues
and cares; it is the crafty Mr. Craggs. He is persuading
Philip to invest in a few hundred of his shares at
five thousand, to which he finally agrees, and the transfer
is made. Philip pockets the slips, and Craggs chuckles
over his gains. At this moment Philip is joined by
Peterborough, and simultaneously he is accosted by a
masked cavalier who offers to sell him five hundred
shares of a company, which at present ranks high in the
Alley, for a hundred guineas the share. Philip, who is
sure that he can dispose of them at any time for one
hundred and fifty, closes with the offer, and the stranger
exchanges the shares for a draft for the amount. Peterborough
tries to dissuade Philip from buying, and
Philip laughs at his ignorance of their value, and calls
out to the Earl of Westmoreland: " My lord, will you
take five hundred ' Arabian' at one fifty ?" " No, your
grace, nor at a shilling apiece ! 'Arabian' is sunk—president
absconded, and treasurer invisible." At this
startling news Philip at once vindicates his powers as
President of the Hellfire Club, and tears the worthless
scrip to pieces. His first thought is to send a messenger
to stop the payment of the draft, but it is too late for
that now, for the man who has shrewdness enough to
make such a *coup d'état* would certainly cash the draft as
soon as possible.

" Peterborough," says Philip, with a grimace, " that
makes about fifty thousand* I have frittered away in this
foolery !"

The Earl replies: " I suspected the fellow, but I had
not the slightest idea that Arabian was totally worthless."

" This collapse is the beginning of the end, Peter-

* Fact.

borough. During the last few days, I have thought what an unstable foundation all of these schemes rest on, and I fear Change Alley will be many a man's ruin, as it would be mine if I kept at it much longer."

The Earl says, musingly: "Your grace, it strikes me that the fellow who sold you the 'Arabian,' is the same who was once implicated in a Jacobite plot which nearly cost him his life! If I were not sure that Sir Edgely Warely is in Rome, I would swear—"

"Edgely Warely," interrupts Philip, in an excited manner. "Ay, now I recall his voice and his figure, I am sure it is he—the treacherous villain!"

The Earl is a little surprised at his emotion, but he does not ask any questions, and they stroll off together.

CHAPTER XXXVIII.

<blockquote>
They reel and stagger to and fro,
At their wit's end, like drunken men.
SWIFT.

"The swan-feathers the arrow bore
With his heart's-blood they were wet."
THE HUNTING OF THE CHEVIOT.
</blockquote>

PARIS and the Rue Quincampoix have repeated themselves in London and Change Alley. Crash after crash of the various companies has ruined thousands who foolishly invested their whole wealth in the delusory hope of a hundred-fold return. All London and the adjacent towns are in a ferment. The train-bands can scarcely keep order or prevent many riots and disturbances. Parliament has met in alarm, and the members are frightened at the aspect of affairs which greets them. The Commons present a curious, but dreadful scene:

Whigs and Tories change places, while the watchful Jacobites note the embarrassed state of affairs with open delight, and add all in their power to the general confusion, hoping to take advantage of the occasion to improve their plans.

In his opening speech his majesty laments the sad state of affairs, and presses on Parliament the necessity of finding a remedy. His speech is received in the House of Lords in deep silence — the presage of the storm; but in the Commons a member, who has lost very heavily, rises and with excited gestures and white lips reviles the South Sea Directors in the most violent terms, and calls them: "Miscreants! scum of the people! and enemies to the country!"

In the Upper House Lord Mólesworth says: "My lords, I admit that the directors cannot be reached by any known laws, but extraordinary crimes call for extraordinary remedies. The Roman lawgivers had not foreseen the possible existence of a parricide, but as soon as the first monster appeared, he was sewn in a sack and cast headlong into the Tiber: and as I think the directors of the South Sea scheme to be the parricides of their country, I should willingly see them undergo the same punishment." Not a dissentient voice is heard until Walpole replies with his usual calmness and suavity, "If the city of London were on fire, wise men would be for extinguishing the flames before they inquired after the incendiaries."

A bill is brought forward to "punish the authors of our present misfortunes," and it is carried *nemine dissentiente*, for those who have been guilty do not dare to oppose it for fear of being found out, and the innocent for fear they may be suspected. After a short recess for Christmas festivities! Parliament reassembles angrier than before, and with a determination to be avenged on the company which has issued over half a million fictitious stock to bribe their king and his mistresses—her grace of Kendal and Madame de Platen.

General Ross states, with angry mouthings: " We have discovered a train of the deepest villany and fraud that Hell ever contrived to ruin a nation;" and at the conclusion of his speech, four of the directors —members— are expelled the House and taken into custody.

In the Lords the excitement is intense: John Blunt, a sturdy, independent man, is interrogated, but he refuses to answer any questions put to him relative to the South Sea Directors. This occasions a debate which soon branches into more general topics, and scurrilous personalities take the place of cool discussion. Philip, who has hitherto been restrained by Peterborough from taking an active part in the discussion, now rises and claims his right to the floor. The assembled peers, who have long expected a speech from him, now subside into temporary quietness, and await his views in anxious silence—all except a few vehement Whigs who heartily hate him for his renegade conduct. His speech ranges over the whole administration, and he adverts to the dissension in the royal family, and more than hints that "Stanhope has done his best to feed the flames of so unnatural a fire." He cries in trumpet tones: " Look to his parallel in Sejanus : that evil and too powerful minister who made a division in the Imperial family, and rendered the reign of Tiberius hateful to the Romans!" As he sits down a murmur undulates through the House like the wind in autumn branches, and a crowd of hungry eyes turn to Stanhope for his answer to this bold Philippic.

From the time Philip mentioned the dissension, Stanhope has been on his feet, his lips tightly closed and his hands clutched so strongly on his breast that he has torn his lace cravat in two. He draws a long, broken breath, and turns yellow with passion and hatred as he looks directly at his accuser. In his reply he ably vindicates his own conduct, and justifies every act of the administration. He extends a trembling hand towards Philip, and exclaims, in an ominously calm voice: "Such virtuous sentiments and patriotic thoughts sound most strange coming from the lips of the president of the Hellfire club, whose godless schemes, wild excesses, and suspicious political tendencies are the scandal of England; and now, most noble duke, allow me to compliment you highly on your studies in Roman history, and I hope that you have not overlooked the example of the patriot Brutus, who, in order to assert the liberty of Rome, and free it from tyrants, sacrificed his own degenerate and worthless son! Moreover—ah!" His utterance becomes choked, his face turns to an unearthly livid color, and his eyes close with spasmodic twitchings. He sways to and fro like one drunk, and his eyes open and he surveys the house with a vacant gaze. My Lord Townshend rushes to his support, and grasps him by the shoulders. Stanhope slowly turns his face to him, and opens his lips as if to speak; he cannot! A thin black stream trickles through his lips, and runs slowly down his gown, and falls softly, splashing on the floor. A cry of horror bursts from all, and he is immediately assisted outside. While being carried out, the dying man throws a revengeful glance at Philip and his friend.

Philip and Peterborough converse about the terrible incident in the house, and Philip regrets his attack on the Secretary of State, an attack which produced such dreadful effects, and he says: "If I had thought Stanhope was so vastly sensitive to a little bluster, I would not have pricked him so smartly. I trust he will soon recover—he looked mighty unwell when he was carried out."

The Earl replies: "I'faith! I think he gave you as good as you sent, and he gave me a dig as well—small thanks to him for it. But I forgive him, 'he knew not what he did;' but if he had not been taken ill, Mordanto would have buckled on his armor."

Philip says: "Yes, 'tis a pity you did not get a few words in: it would have made additional amusement."

CHAPTER XXXIX.

Hel.—I do beseech you, sir,
    Since you are like to see the king before me,
    Commend the paper to his gracious hand.
        "ALL'S WELL THAT ENDS WELL."

WE must retrace our steps to the cathedral at Dublin, in order to discover where Alberoni's message disappeared so mysteriously. The case is very simple. As soon as Philip and Mistress O'Beirne left, Edgely Valentin darted out from behind the altar, where he had been concealed, and shook a paper or letter in the air with frenzied gestures. He then exclaimed: "At last I have an opportunity to fulfil my vow!" This letter was Alberoni's message, of which he had unseen taken possession. His face was pale but triumphant, and he read the contents of his stolen prize repeatedly.

"Ah ha! Mistress O'Beirne, this pays me for dogging! I thought your errand was to him. Thanks to his carelessness, his life is now, to a certain extent, in my power: London is in no mood to trifle with traitors, and to London I must go and await a fitting opportunity to present this document to their high mightinesses in the Lords." And he took off his left shoe, and ripped the leather lining from the side, enough to allow the letter to slip between it and the outer surface. That accomplished, he drew it on again, and walked rapidly to the banks of the Liffey, where a fishing-smack—whose owner combined fishing and smuggling in a very profitable manner—was to sail for London in a few hours.

In a vile den in Wapping is a rag and junk-shop, kept by an old woman who is a sister of the notorious Dame Brett.

"When Wharton's just, and learns to pay his debts,
And reputation dwells at Mother Brett's:"

She is known to all the foot-pads and cut-purses of London as Dame Grab-all, for she willingly purchases everything that is brought to her, from a diamond set of the first water down to the dirtiest rope's end. On the second floor of this house and in the front room is Edgely Valentin. He is standing by a grimy, latticed apology for a window, and he taps abstractedly on the mouldy walls, whose plastering drops off in a little cloud at every touch of his knuckles. On the sole piece of furniture in the room, a bed, lies a woman, whose face is drawn and wan; and she has great hollows under her glistening eyes and in her flushed cheeks—hollows which tell of fast-running sands. She must have been a lovely girl once, for in spite of the ravages of time and sorrow, her features are still prepossessing and delicate: her hair is very thick and long, and it lies in a tangled mass on the whitey-brown pillow.

He turns to her, and says in a kindly manner: "Have you heard how Lord Stanhope came by his death?"

"Yes!" she replies in a hesitating voice.

He says: "He befriended me once, and saved me from being set on by a crowd of springalds who thought fit to taunt me with my birth—a birth which it strikes me is very generally known in town!" and he clenches his teeth till his jaw-bones harden his features.

The woman replies, in pained accents: "Edgely, drop that subject, I entreat you—it is worn threadbare between us."

He does not answer her, but resumes his tapping at the wall. She casts a stealthy glance at him, and draws from her bosom a tiny miniature portrait, and exclaims in low tones: "God! that he might know all! But my promise—I cannot—will not break it—yet awhile at least;" and she secretes it, and sighs deeply.

He suddenly exclaims: "I will go to the Tower! A large meeting of people will collect there to-day, to mob Parliament and hoot the Houses for their leniency toward the Directors—a worthy set of gentlemen, and more sinned against than sinning—" A rumbling sound like distant thunder is heard, and he continues: "St. Jago! there they are! good-bye! I'll return shortly."

Valentin mixes with the crowd of 'prentices, traders, butchers, and watermen who are yelling and roaring in angry confusion, and he helps them in their outcries. "Hang them! hang the cannibals!" "On to Parliament, and we'll see to matters ourselves." The mention of any name known in connection with the South Sea scheme is greeted with curses and execrations. "Stanhope" seems to be the rallying cry. Valentin clambers on top of a huge hogshead that is close by, and cries in a voice which rises above the tumult: "Friends—fellow-victims! let us demand justice now—at once. On to Parliament! we will let them know that we are men. On, on to Parliament!"

"Ay, lad! on to t'Lords, and make 'em return us the money they've robbed us on!" exclaims a tall, grimy smith who flourishes a gigantic hammer as though it were a cane; the mob echo his sentiments, and Valentin leaps to the ground and places himself at their head.

As they come in sight of the object of their ill-will,

they salute it with a perfect shower of yells and groans. Valentin thrusts his hands into his breast, apparently to search for something, and assured of its safety, he carefully rebuttons his coat, and his eyes blaze with a baleful expression.

The Houses are in session. Harley's "master-piece" is still under discussion, and penalties and imprisonments are still the rule rather than the exception. The king has been spoken of in terms far from flattering; and it shows the general exasperation and angry feelings which reign in the house, that, when his majesty asked them for a large subsidy to Sweden for the trade in naval stores, Lord Molesworth protested strongly against the measure, and finished by saying: "I own hemp is a very necessary commodity, especially at this juncture, but in my opinion we can be supplied more cheaply from our plantations in America."

Philip, whose renegade conduct and determined opposition to the government and all the schemes of the ministry have incurred the ill-will of both his majesty and those in power, is attacked by a special proclamation issued against the Hell-fire Club and its president. The subject is now being debated. Chesterfield's son—Lord Stanhope—is speaking in grave, earnest tones: "This club, which his majesty so justly rails against, is a disgrace to our city. Its members are, with scarcely an exception, notorious for their blasphemy, riotous living, and violent conduct. It is said—God forfend that it is true!—that many of our worthiest families have sons who do not scruple to avow themselves aiders and abettors of this most scandalous and godless organization. If it is true, then will we do a good deed if we can destroy it, and pull from the fire the burning brands!" and after a few more observations on religion and morality, he takes his seat.

Philip rises amid an ominous silence to answer this scathing attack, while Peterborough stands by his side. He casts his eyes slowly around the expectant assembly, and with a sneer on his lips, he whispers to the earl. He begins: "My lord has chosen to attack the honored president of a club, whose door he is not worthy to guard, and also to reflect on his want of godliness, as well as all the other members." Here he pauses, and turns to Peterborough, who hands him a small Bible with a great affectation of reverence. Philip then turns his lips down in a sanctimonious manner, as he resumes: "I am no patron of blasphemy, as I shall prove out of this holy book, which my saintly friend"—he points to the earl—"invariably carries with him in order to controvert the arguments of the ungodly."

"Amen!" snuffles the earl. But Philip's answer is so utterly shameless and impious that I dare not give it to you.

As he finishes, Peterborough rises, and in reference to a theological point which Stanhope has raised, replies: "Though I am for a Parliamentary king, s'life! I'll never have a Parliamentary religion."

Philip says: "Mordanto! you are an honor to the H. F. C. If I were not Duke of Wharton, I would certainly be Earl of Peterborough."

"S'life," he replies, "but your grace is unjust; the exchange would be uneven. How ever could I live with your debts and reputation pulling on me? how would you remedy that?"

"Easily enough," Philip says with a laugh; "I would throw my duchess and her good qualities into the scale."

At this moment there is a noise in the hallway which attracts Peterborough's attention, and he leaves his seat to inquire into the cause of the disturbance.

CHAPTER XL.

I am no love for you, Margaret;
You are no love for me.
BALLAD OF "FAIR MARGARET'S MISFORTUNES."

THE earl is surprised to find a man struggling with the doorkeeper, and is still more so when he recognizes the intruder to be Edgely Valentin; he says to the keeper: "What is the matter? What ails the madman?" But the doorkeeper is too busily engaged in attending to the infuriated Valentin to answer the earl, and he merely nods. The earl, whose strength is wonderful for such a slightly built man, grips Edgely by the nape of his neck and shakes him so fiercely that he drops his hold on the keeper, and endeavors to free himself from the new assailant. The earl exclaims: "What means the insolent fellow? What do you want here? Speak, or I'll choke ye black in the face."

"My lord," he exclaims, "An infamous plot—Alberoni —wait till I gain my breath!"

Peterborough notices a paper in his hand, and he snatches it away from him and then releases him.

"To his grace of Northumberland—Alberoni?—" exclaims the earl, and he crushes the letter into his pocket.

Valentin sees his motion, and he gasps: "The paper— my lord, if you—it must be read before the House. It is part of a treasonous correspondence I have discovered."

The earl asks quickly: "Ah! you say you have more!"—

"Yes, my lord, and I can produce them at any time."

"Do the others criminate the duke as much as this?"

"No, my lord, but they are from well-known Jacobites in Paris, Rome, and Avignon."

"Have you them with you! quick! We are beginning to attract attention."

"No, my lord; but I can get them in a few days!"

"Speak low now—from whom are the others?"

This question perplexes him, and he hesitates. The earl looks sternly at him and says: "Look ye, Sir Edgely Warely! If you—who are such a stern patriot—do not bring me all the letters in your possession which can do any harm to the Duke of Wharton, I'll see that you receive lodgings in the Tower. Now you can go! You know that I always perform what I threaten."

Valentin's countenance assumes a frightful expression, and he stamps his foot in a mad paroxysm of rage as he comprehends that his plans are foiled, while Peterborough smiles at his impotent mouthings. Suddenly he rushes on the earl, who is too quick in his actions to be caught unawares, and as Valentin grasps at his throat, Peterborough hurls him headlong out of the doorway

As the earl takes his seat again Philip says: "My lord, you left me so suddenly, that I feel half justified in asking the reason of your absence?" Peterborough replies in a careless manner: "I heard a noise at the door, and went to investigate the cause. I found a friend of yours there who requested me to give you this document, and to advise you to be more careful in future where you leave your letters."

Philip opens the document, and he is astounded to find it is Alberoni's lost letter. He eagerly requests a description of the person who brought it, and asks Peterborough whether he was suitably rewarded.

"Yes, I amply rewarded him for his trouble; but as to describing him, I am very bad at descriptions. I did not especially observe him."

Philip replies: "Well, if you have rewarded him, it matters little who he is."

The Earl dryly replies: "Umph! sure?"

Philip's answer is lost in the terrific yell which shakes the windows, and makes the Spanish Armada tapestry tremble with the concussion.

Philip thrusts the letter in his pocket, and runs to see the cause of the tumult; Peterborough follows, as do most of the peers. The mob which collected at the Tower has been swollen with hundreds more of men and lads who have joined them along their route.

"Look!" exclaims Philip: "There is Edgely Valentin at the head of the mob! S'life, the fellow looks like a modern fury. He is all awake for mischief."

"'Faith," says Peterborough, "he looks as if he has just escaped from a mad-house or the tender mercies of the Mohocks! and 'faith, he must have a spite against you, Wharton; he has just favored you with a particularly disagreeable look!"

Philip shrugs his shoulders disdainfully, and laughs at the idea of such a foe.

Philip and Peterborough do not return to their seats after the dispersion of the mob by the guard. They proceed to the Rainbow in Fleet Street, and there they remain until late in the evening, when they adjourn to the Pope's Head, in the alley of the same name. The bar is small and clean, and the floor is nicely sanded, while the walls and ceiling are hung with pewter mugs or blackjacks. The landlord Jack Hood is a stout, florid man, and he is so good-natured that he was never known to be angry but once, and that was on an extraordinary occasion; and as Peterborough, who was present at the occurrence, is telling the story to Philip, we will listen: "I'll tell you about it, Wharton. Bowen—that fiery-blooded Irishman—whom you have probably heard of as a clever, handsome actor—was in this very room about four years ago, and I was talking to him about Quin of whom he was vastly jealous and hated like—well, like Congreve does the great Sarah.* I jestingly told him that Quin was universally considered as his superior, whereat he waxed mighty wroth and sent for him. Quin no sooner entered than Bowen cursed him and commanded him to draw, at the same time he brandished his blade in his face. At first Quin refused to·fight, but Bowen gave him no alternative; so he drew, and—egad! there's the mark on the panel where Quin's point touched after passing through t'other's midriff! S'life! he played prettily! a stramazorm, a half whirl with a passado, and the blade fleshed home."

Philip passes his finger over the cut in the door, and says: "Better Bowen than Quin, for if he had gone where would our Falstaff have come from? A sight worth a year of any man's life to see."

They loiter here until Jack intimates it is closing time, so they settle the score, and each wends his way homeward with unsteady steps and bewildered brains.

Philip feels cynical and unwell as he opens his eyes after the night's debauch, and he calls for a goblet of iced canary to clear his muddled head. He glances towards his escritoire, and there among various other letters is one from Holme Grange. He groans inwardly as he imagines its probable contents, and he takes it up and tears it open in a pettish manner. It is quite lengthy, and he is fully ten minutes in learning its contents. This done, he tosses it aside, and exclaims wearily: "What I expected! Fatherly objurgations, marital pleadings—and general persuasions and entreaties—heigh-ho! a ridiculous waste of time and paper. She disobeyed my

* Duchess of Marlborough.

orders—killed my son, curse her! and she shall never—what nonsense! Philip, you will certainly destroy your calm quietude by such frenzies. The only item of interest is the paragraph about Brad and Meg; the rest reeks of Margery and her troubles. S'life, as if I am in fault!" And he thrusts his head down in the pillow, and falls asleep.

CHAPTER XLI.

> "His learning none will call in doubt;
> Nor Pope would dare deny him wit."
> "I own he hates an action base,
> His virtues battling with his place."
>
> SWIFT'S LIBEL.

IN front of the quaint little house known as Dan Button's, are two persons who whisper together in low tones and seem desirous of secrecy. The elder of the two is smaller than the average of mankind, and from his thin, bony neck, down to his diminutive feet, his body has a curious resemblance to a large S. His hands are small, pallid, and very thin; but his eyes compensate for his deformities—they are piercing and eloquent, and they seem to shine with a mute appeal for sympathy, blended with the sarcastic expression of a defiant, scornful wit. He is well known at Button's and Will's as a vastly clever man and a fine scholar, but he is not over-popular at either place, for he is too fond of retort and repartee. His companion is Mr. Morice, who is dressed in a frock suit of brown and silver lace; he is the son-in-law of Francis Atterbury, Bishop of Rochester. As their conversation seems of some interest, we will turn eavesdroppers and listen to it in spite of Pope's keen eyes or Mr. Morice's steel hilt.

Pope exclaims: "All England cries shame on my Lord Walpole for his severity toward the best and wisest man living!"

Mr. Morice adds: "The pigeon-pie which I sent him yesterday was opened by the dirty turnkey to see whether or no I had secreted a letter or a ladder in it, in order to assist him to escape."

"Escape!" says Pope angrily; "Francis Atterbury attempt to steal from prison like a common felon? Never! His soul is too lofty to stoop so low. When he leaves the tower, it will be amid the huzzas of a million tongues which will chant a pæan to his greatness! Pah! this is the first time that *dead* pigeons have been accused of carrying messages."

Mr. Morice says: "Think you that my Lords Orrery and North will say aught to criminate Atterbury?"

"Criminate, man! I must misunderstand you! What can they say to criminate him?" and he anxiously awaits an answer, but Mr. Morice only shakes his head.

Pope resumes: "His grace of Norfolk will probably be honorably discharged?"

"I doubt it, sir," he replies.

"Your reasons, Mr. Morice, for doubting his acquittal!"

"I will give them inside," he replies, and they go in and take a bench in a remote corner of the bar. Mr. Morice proceeds: "In addition to the letters signed 'Jones,' and 'Illington,' which I fear me will be proved to be his, there is this wretched 'Harlequin' affair. You are aware that Mar sent Mistress Atterbury— before she died—a little spotted dog which she named Harlequin. About a month ago, I unfortunately trod on its foot and broke it, so that I had to send it to Mistress Barnes in Houndsditch to be cured. It seems that this dog has been mentioned several times in the letters. Mistress Barnes was examined by the council, and was asked the question: 'Does the dog Harlequin which you have belong to the Bishop of Rochester?' To which she replied immediately: "Yes, it does.' Slight and ridiculous as this evidence may seem, it is really a strong link in the chain of circumstances with which it is connected."

Pope listened in silence, and he murmurs the bishop's answer when he was brought before the council: "If I tell you, ye will not believe; and if I ask you, ye will not answer me nor let me go!" And he recalls Atterbury's well-known hostility to the Hanoverian succession, his offer to head an army in his lawn sleeves, his haughty and ambitious temper, his refusal to sign the Declaration of Abhorrence of the rebellion of 1715, and his turbulent spirit, and he begins to fear that the government may be able to furnish strong proofs of treason and disloyalty when the bishop is put upon his trial.

Mr. Morice says musingly: "They say that seven cardinals presided by the pope's orders at the birth of Charles Edward. This future pretender has pleased our Jacobites mightily."

Pope replies, with a twinkle in his eye: "Yes, and they had a chance to show their feelings in safety on Lord Mayor's day by calling: A Stuart, a Stuart—high church and Stuart, for the mayor's name is Stuart; rather a disagreeable coincidence," and he smiles as he recollects how pleased his mayorship had been at the unusual rejoicings and acclamations which took place on his election.

"I believe you are the bishop's solicitor, Mr. Morice?"

"Yes, and Sir Phipps and Mr. Wynne are his counsel."

"But is it not against the order of the House for a lord to appear by counsel before the other House?"

"Yes, but he has permission to appear either with counsel or without, as he pleases!"

"I am glad to hear that; but Mistress Barnes? what a witness against a bishop—Rochester *versus* a Houndsditch quack!"

"Bad enough! It is reported that his protean Grace of Wharton intends to defend Atterbury in the Lords. Do you know whether there is any truth in the assertion?"

Pope replies scornfully: "His grace is constant only to inconstancy; he is an antithesis, a consistent inconsistency. I doubt that he will belie himself. If he defends him before the trial, during it he will be his opponent. But it would be well if Atterbury could secure him; he is a powerful speaker, and he is fuller of tricks and legal subterfuges, than any man in London."

Suddenly Pope pushes his companion to one side, and a smile of welcome lights his face as he discerns a familiar form standing at the bar in conversation with the bar-maid. The new-comer's countenance wears an expression of jollity and good fellowship. He is clothed in a faded cinnamon coat, whose huge lappels and pockets are adorned with very coppery silver-lace, which tells of long service and hard wear. His ruffles are torn and dirty, and his whole air bespeaks the Grub Street hack who has seen better days.

Pope scrambles quickly towards him, and exclaims: "John, John! this will never do! idling at a pot-house, instead of being at the labors which are to enable you to scale Parnassus' heights!"

He replies: "Hallo! is it you, Mr. Pope? What were you saying? Labors—Mount Parnassus—rubbish! I earn as much talking with pretty Polly here, as I do in my attic, and that is—nothing."

Pope remarks: "Fudge! John, come and have a jack

of canary with Mr. Morice and myself; you are acquainted with him?"

He nods assent, and the three sit down together.

The trial of Francis Atterbury is at present the great topic of conversation and discussion among all classes of society, and especially literary and theological circles. The treasonous correspondence which Walpole intercepted deeply embroils the bishop, and although the people in general side with the imprisoned prelate, it is feared there will be too many proofs of guilt for him to escape a sentence of exile—may be death.

"For my part," says Gay, "I concur with the opinion of several learned gentlemen who frequent my spare chambers, that his lordship's correspondence and conduct are at least worthy of censure, if not of more stringent measures."

At this, Pope presses his friend's foot and glances at Mr. Morice as he remarks: "Marry, Mr. Gay, we will take your opinion on Ma'am'selle Scuderi or Hanover scenery, but on this subject you are in the clouds."

Mr. Morice adds: "Yes, give us your opinion on Scuderi's Grand Cyrus; you have read it, I suppose?"

"I have, sir," says Gay, "and I can assure ye that she is another Sappho—the most proper tenth muse that has, as yet, illumined the literary horizon!"

Pope replies, with a perceptible curl on his lip: "Bravo! John! One would think you had been to the Hôtel Rambouillet and been patted on the back by that Olympian novelist."

"No, Mr. Pope," says Gay; "should any one pat me, the act signifies a—" And he stops in confusion.

Pope maliciously adds: "A superiority in the patter, and you, John, are at least equal to the tenth muse."

Gay reddens, and Mr. Morice says: "To change the conversation, Mr. Gay, what is your opinion of this

Erasmus Lewis who is engaged to prove the handwriting of the bishop. Is he a man of good character, and honest?"

"Too much so for the bishop's good, I fear," is Gay's curt reply, at which Pope looks anxious and troubled, for Atterbury is a very demigod to him.

CHAPTER XLII.

*"Though small the time thou hast to spare,
The church is thy peculiar care."*
        SWIFT.

PHILIP is sauntering down Ave Maria lane in company with a cavalier of commanding presence and distinguished bearing, whose name is Lord William Cowper, alias Will Bigamy, alias Cowper-law: the first pseudonym he has acquired from an absurd story set afoot by Voltaire; the other was given him by his political opponents for his impartiality and severity in awarding punishment to malefactors and criminals. They intend to pay a visit to Dolly's, in Paternoster row, a tavern famed for its juicy steaks and gill-ale.

As they enter Paternoster row Philip chants, in a doleful voice, "Sancta Maria, ora pro nobis," and casts a glance at his companion as he finishes; and Cowper exclaims: "Your grace seems affected by the associations of the row."

Philip replies: "Yes, my lord; it reminds me of Avignon and the holy fathers."

"Tut-tut," says Cowper; "drop the subject, your grace. It ill becomes me to listen to aught pertaining to papistry."

Philip promises not to offend again, and they enter

Dolly's tavern, which has a portrait of Queen Anne as its sign.

"Prithee, Master Dolly," says Cowper, "let us have a pipe of sotweed apiece and a jug of claret;" an order which is promptly filled, and they are soon involved in a cloud of the soothing and enervating Oronooko, which rises in blue wreaths to the raftered ceiling. Philip is a good smoker, and he ejects the smoke from his nose marvellously well, and he can send it expertly from his mouth either in balls or circles; but Cowper is not so dexterous; he contents himself with simply inhaling it and puffing it out again.

Philip sententiously observes: "A blessing on Sir Walter! King James' fulmination and his counterblasts did little good, thanks to the power of common sense."

"Ay, and a most proper and good measure it was; but unfortunately his fulmination is now more honored in the breach than the observance. By the way, the trial will soon take place."

Philip answers quickly: "And then we will see whether Parliament dare deprive a minister of God. S'blood, the sacrilege!"

Cowper gravely remarks: "I agree with you, and rejoice to hear you are against that most unjust measure."

Philip replies in a settled manner: "My Lord Atterbury may count on me as his friend and defender."

Cowper is about to reply, when Philip is startled by a tap on his shoulder, and he turns his head and sees behind him a stalwart, morose-looking man, whose black hair and eyes and brown skin show conclusively that he is a gypsy.

"S'blood, what do you mean by laying thy filthy finger on a gentleman, eh! What do you want?" cries Philip fiercely.

The gypsy answers, in a humble manner, "Your grace, my master, I am Nanar the son of Ma-Krillac. Queenie gave me this for you; I want an answer." And he hands Philip a dirty letter sealed with black wax.

Philip tears it open and reads it, and a smile comes to his face as he finishes its perusal. He turns to Nanar, and says in a milder manner: "Oh! Nanar, I recall the circumstance. One moment, and I will write you a draft for the money." And he borrows a quill and a sheet of paper from Dolly, and writes as follows:—

"Pay to the order of Mistress Nelly Valentin the sum of one thousand guineas (1000) for value received.
PHILIP WHARTON."

A grim smile crosses his face as he gives the draft to Nanar, and says: "Here, and never trouble me again." Nanar takes it and leaves the tavern, and Philip says explanatorily: "A promise to a woman which I forgot to fulfil."

Cowper shrugs his shoulders, as he remarks: "Wharton, you are a sad rake. I fear you will have many of those drafts to write out before you die, if you are not more circumspect."

Philip replies: "You are wrong, my lord. This is one of the punishments that descend from father to son."

Cowper nods his head, and says: "Your grace is justified, and now let us have a turn at ombre."

"With all my heart," answers Philip, and they draw their chairs closer around the table.

We will leave them for a while, and turn to Nanar, who is walking rapidly in the direction of Wapping; nor does he slacken his pace until he arrives before Dame Graball's junk-shop, where he walks in and asks the woman a question, to which she nods affirmatively and points her thumb toward the stairs, which he mounts; he knocks at the first door which he sees; it is opened, and he steps inside. As you doubtless guess, its inmates are Edgely Valentin' and Mistress Nelly. Nanar says, in a monotonous voice, and as if he is repeating a lesson: "The gypsy queen sends Nanar with a duke's recompense for Mistress Nelly Valentin."

Valentin replies with an oath: "Gypsy queen. You lie! the Duke of Wharton sends it; take it back to him and tell him that the only recompense Edgely Valentin will receive is a clear field and no favor!" and he crushes the draft into Nanar's hand again, who quickly smooths it out, and he glides towards the bed where lies the woman, and he says to her: "Sweet lady! queenie begs you to take this draft as a payment for some money which you once loaned her, and also to show her that you still think as well of her as you did long years ago when she was a wee child and you spoke so kindly to her!"

She shivers, but says never a word, and Nanar stands there until Valentin, no longer able to restrain himself, takes hold of him by the shoulder and pushes him out of the room.

Nanar appears quite contented and unruffled, and he philosophically returns to Dolly's with the draft carefully held in his hand. Again he taps Philip on the shoulder, and at the same time he lays the draft on the table.

Philip exclaims angrily: "A pest on you, Nanar! What do you want now? and what do you return the money for?"

He replies: "Your grace, a fair-faced gentleman who was wi' the lady would not let her take it, and he gave me this message for you:—the only recompense Edgely Valentin will receive is a clear field and no favor!"

Philip is astonished at the insolent message, and he

glares angrily at the gypsy, but he makes no impression on Nanar's stolidity and calmness; finally he says with a curse: "Take it to your queen; I told her she should have it; and now get you gone ere I juggle your head with a claret-decanter!"

Nanar carefully secretes the draft in a pocket of his jerkin, and again bows himself out.

"Egad!" says Cowper, "the fellow has a spirit."

Philip answers: "He is a low, nameless hound! and he shall have his nose slit for his insolence if he is not careful. But, come, we'll go down to the House and see whether Walpole and Mr. Yonge are behaving themselves. They are both bitter against our friend Atterbury. I wish Peterborough was in town; we could rely on him."

Cowper says, "Mordanto is a wonderful fellow; he is never quiet, and he has seen more cities, theatres, bagnios, princes, and kings than any man in Christendom."

"And fewer priests and church interiors than any man in heathendom," adds Philip, an observation to which Cowper replies regretfully: "I fear that inattention to church matters is not peculiar to Peterborough alone, your grace."

Philip returns warmly: "How could it be when a Kendal and a Darlington rule the country through a senseless, miserly usurper?"

Cowper is startled at his language, and he exclaims: "Your grace, I must demand that you speak in more respectful terms of his sacred majesty, or else I will have to leave you. Consider that you are talking treason, and as long as I suffer treasonous language in my presence I am to a certain extent a sharer in your guilt."

"Pardon me, my lord; I did not mean what I said; but my feelings are hurt at the recollection of the women who sit on either hand of his majesty, they are so peculiarly ugly—they are a disgrace to us!" and he laughs and kisses his hand to Sir Charles Hellwell, who is passing on the opposite side.

CHAPTER XLIII.

My soul no longer at her lot repines,
But yields to what your providence assigns;
Though immature I end my glorious days,
Cut short my conquest, and prevent new praise;
My life, already, stands the noblest theme.

LUCAN.

THE space in front of the Houses is thronged with an anxious crowd who are all agape for further news of the trial; the watermen are jubilant at their increased profits, for since early morning thousands have been ferried from the opposite side of the river, and from the various suburban towns along its banks. Just at present the silence in the Lords' is intense and impressive, and its members are anxiously awaiting Walpole's answer to the previous speaker. Some look stern and implacable; others appear ill at ease and troubled: Walpole, the accused Bishop, and Philip alone seem calm and tranquil. Atterbury is dignified and unmoved, and his eyes are sharp and penetrating, yet kindly; his forehead is broad and expansive, and his nose is well-shaped but rather coarse: his double chin—which is almost hidden in his clerical tie—evinces his fondness for high living and epicurean dishes, and his wig is large and curling. Philip holds in his hands a mass of notes and jottings connected with the trial, and he reclines in his seat in a careless attitude.

A whispering buzz runs through the chamber, and Walpole rises. In clear, concise tones he reverts to the posthumous testimony of Mr. Neynoe which accuses him of bribery in order to make sure of the Bishop's crimination, a charge which it is of vital importance to his interests to prove false. He entirely disavows all knowledge of Neynoe, and indignantly repels the accusation of bribery and corruption. As he sits down, Atterbury rises, and questions him, in a soft, modulated voice, in regard to a few facts and dates which have an important bearing on the case. All pay breathless attention to this conflict between the two great masters of language and oratory. Atterbury almost exhausts his powers of twisting and turning sentences and words in his endeavors to make his wily enemy contradict and falsify his own assertions; Walpole, however, is cool and wary, and every word he utters is carefully weighed before it is spoken. They are battling for a great stake, and they both know it and appreciate to the fullest extent the ignominy of failure; Walpole fights for power and his reputation—Atterbury for his acquittal.

At last Atterbury comes to the conclusion that his examination of his accuser is a failure, and in order to hide the important end in which he has been foiled, he puts a few trifling questions to him, which are of no real importance, and signifies that he has finished with him: Walpole sits down, with his face as immobile as iron, but the palm of his right hand is cut and scarred with the hard pressure of his nails against it while under the raking fire of the Bishop's inquisitorial examination, and he thanks Heaven that he has passed through the ordeal safely. Atterbury's design in questioning Walpole so closely was to crush the testimony of one witness and injure the reputation of another, to prove Neynoe a perjured liar and Walpole a corrupt and interested enemy.

All his brother bishops have treated Atterbury with great virulence and hatred, and they have hitherto shown anything but a Christian spirit during the trial. Wynne, of St. Asaph especially, has been uncompromising and violent, and he now rises and animadverts on his conduct with such blind, acrimonious hostility as to cause Philip's face to smile in pity at his warped judgment. Unluckily for the reverend man he has accused Atterbury of some misdemeanors impossible to be proved—mere hearsay in fact; and directly he has ended, before he has time to settle his holy person comfortably, Lord Bathurst stands up; with a sneer on his flushed face, he extends his left hand in front of him, while the other rests on his sword-hilt, and he exclaims in angry tones against the mode of procedure in the trial; he denounces it as illegal and without a precedent. He turns to the Bishop's bench, and thunders: "I can hardly account for the inveterate malice some persons bear the learned and ingenious Bishop of Rochester, unless they are possessed with the infatuation of the wild Indians, who fondly believe they will inherit not only the spoils, but even the abilities of any great enemy they kill!" The bishops color under the sarcasm, while a murmur of applause greets the speaker—and Atterbury thanks his defender with an eloquent glance.

* * * * * *

Lord Cowper is speaking in a warm, spirited strain, that shows how deep is his love and reverence for the accused, his hatred and disgust at his enemies; he winds up by saying: "The old champions of our church used to argue very learnedly that to make or to degrade bishops was not the business of the State, that there is a spiritual relation between the bishop and his flock, derived from the church, with which the State has no right to interfere; what the thoughts of *our* reverend prelates are upon these points does not yet fully appear. Something of their conduct intimates as if our old divines were mistaken." Atterbury looks mildly towards the bishops as Cowper says this, as if to ask them to stand up and vindicate themselves, but none would or could meet his searching, questioning eye; they occupied themselves in arranging their robes or looking another way.

Philip, who has thus far taken no active part in the debate, now rises, coughs twice or thrice, meanwhile glancing rapidly through the mass of papers crackling in his hands, then drops them on the floor. He is a focus on which all eyes centre; a hum of expectation buzzes through the chamber as the assemblage await the opinion of the talented scapegrace on this important case. Walpole coughs, Philip looks toward him, and they exchange a very significant glance, which does not pass unnoticed by Atterbury and various others, particularly Cowper, who wonders at the cordiality between the two.

It is necessary to explain the reason of this seeming cordiality between two men who have previously been at total variance on the question of the trial. Yesterday, while Philip's head was full of wine, he had gone to Walpole, and " regretted his wickedness in opposing the just punishment of the bishop," and " begged his lordship to forgive him," with many sighs and groans; "if his lordship would be so kind, so obliging as to take him on his side in the debate, he could conscientiously promise to do his best." The young scamp seemed so earnest in his behavior that Walpole believed him; he joyfully consented that Philip should aid him in crushing the prelate; gave him all the arguments *pro* and *con*, and dismissed him with his blessing. Philip spent the rest of the night in drinking, and now—

Philip's speech is too long to give in detail. However, in the first place, he attacks the testimony of several witnesses who have been examined, utterly annihilating their credit and trustworthiness by exposing their duplicity and perjury; not a fact, a word, or an incident of the whole trial has escaped him, his wonderfully retentive memory making everything subservient to his ends. In particular does he dwell with withering sarcasm on the episode of the dog Harlequin, which is really an important witness for the prosecution; he indulges in keen ludicrous personalities, varied with thrilling flashes of forensic grandeur which chill the blood, and make the heart still with its fiery eloquence. Now he is calmer, and he sums up in a methodical, lawyer-like manner the evidence which has been given. Master Richard Lieface he proves to be an arrant liar and a perjurer, much to Walpole's dismay. He exhausts sacred and profane history for parallel examples, cites all cases which bear the slightest resemblance to the trial, deducing from all of them the wrongfulness of the whole proceeding from the first bill passed against the accused down to the present moment. Although some of his examples are far-fetched and strained, he gives them a gloss of probability, and a semblance to truth which is staggering to his opponents. His voice is loud, sonorous, and penetrating, impassioned and angry, cool and convincing, intense and subdued, whispering and sibillating, while its every syllable pours sharp and distinct into every corner of the room.

Most of his arguments are conclusive and impregnable. As he approaches the beginning of the end, he winds up facts, testimony, incidents, witnesses, bishops, and lords in one great cloud, whirls it around and around with the impetuous force and enthusiasm of his wonderful genius, and sends it crashing and striking amid the accusers of his friend. For an instant there is a dead silence; then from every lip bursts a deafening cry, long and continuous. Atterbury's lips are clenched tightly, and his eyes are glistening with emotion, while Bathhurst and Cowper shake hands with violent energy. Meanwhile Philip is almost overwhelmed with congratulations and plaudits; he is excited and very pale; he exclaims to Cowper, in a careless manner: "Egad! my lord, Dolly's and a beef-steak would do me good after this last eruption."

Astute and collected, Atterbury rises before the excitement is over, beginning the vindication of his conduct. After an ingenious though sophistical explanation of his behavior and his motives, he concludes in the pathetic words which strike a chord of sympathy in all our hearts, even for this arrogant, unscrupulous churchman: "If after all it shall still be thought by your lordships that there is any seeming strength in the proofs produced against me, if by private persuasions of my guilt founded on unseen, unknown motives, if for any reasons or necessity of state, of which I am no competent judge, your lordships shall be induced to proceed on this bill—God's will be done!—naked came I out of my mother's womb, and naked shall I return; and whether He gives or takes away, blessed be the name of the Lord." He can continue no longer, his eyes become full almost to overflowing, while his words grow broken and indistinct.

CHAPTER XLIV.

Oriana.—As I live, Mirabel turned friar! I hope in Heaven he's not in earnest.
Bisaire.—In earnest; ha, ha, ha! are you in earnest?
THE INCONSTANT.

PHILIP has hit upon a new idea; he will turn journalist and edit a second "Spectator" or "Tatler," make himself a popular man with the honest cits, enact the part of a patriot to his country, and be a friend to the people. It requires but a short time to put this idea into operation after its birth. "The True Briton" shall be the vehicle of his thoughts and opinions. Let us to Grub Street, where he is at present engaged in jotting down divers effusions of disguised Jacobitisms, startling political views, discussions on the general aspect of England and her rulers, whom he handles with irreverent boldness. He is perched on a high stool, before a grimy, blackened desk; the room is so narrow and confined that the ink darted from the quill prior to writing unavoidably lights on some side of it and leaves black splashes and spots which have a vague resemblance to myriads of long-legged, bloated spiders rather the worse for wear. The single window is sooty and dilapidated; the straggling rays which manage to crawl through the Lilliputian bull's-eye panes, fall in blurred dimness on the many blots, initials, and scratches on the desk, and cast a sickly light on the opposite wall.

Philip has a sheet of paper before him on which he is scribbling with amazing rapidity. His face is impassive and emotionless. If it were not for the quick motion of the quill and the rustling of his ruffles, one might judge him to be in a brown study. His dress is certainly out of place here; his peach-colored coat is of ribbed silk, heavily laced and broidered with gold; the hilt of his rapier is extravagantly decorated with bands of diamonds and rubies, while a sapphire gleams and glitters in the top. He has apparently finished his task, for he throws the quill down, exclaiming exultantly: "Another stinger for the ministry. I'll rouse their ire before I have done with them. This must to press at once, then; from John-o'-Groat's to Land's End shall they be circulated." He rubs his hands together, while a smile comes to his lips. "Now that I have descended to the ranks and taken arms against my order, faith! I ought to complete the farce and join some worshipful London company—the Rat-catchers or the Wax-chandlers? speak in terms to suit the *mobile vulgus*—not that I love George or Walpole less, but my country more Ah, ha! quite theatrical, but it will doubtless pass for frenzied patriotism with my beloved brothers, the greasy chandlers. However, whether they believe me or not when I announce my new convictions, it will be a new sensation to grasp their democratic palms and call myself one of them!"

He stuffs the MSS. in his pocket, then runs over to John Incink to have it put to press as one of the articles in "The True Briton." He now steps over to Gay's lodging-house, mounts the rickety, old staircase, gropes his way through the close, foul hallway, and opens the door which guards the spendthrift poet from duns and bailiffs. As he enters he exclaims: "Good-day, my plague of moral chamberlains. I have just finished my labors, and I have dropped in to help you if you need—"

"Thanks, your grace," Gay responds with mock gravity; "but any spare ideas you may possess you had better keep to yourself, for the work on which I am now engaged is to make my reputation for life, or else I'll turn usurer and fleece elder sons of their future patrimonies."

Philip replies: "Ah—what is this great work? Another version of 'Three Hours?'"

Gay reddens at the remark, for it calls to mind how his play "Three Hours after Marriage" had been hissed off the stage for its immorality and indecency. "No, your grace, neither crooked Pope nor Jolly Arbuthnot shall have a hand in this. It shall be exclusively my own production."

Philip exclaims: "My dear man, do tell me what it is, then. You keep me on the rack with your—"

Gay interrupts: "One moment, and I will get it. You

must know that it will not be finished for some time—may be three or four years."

Philip adds: "Not until your last fiasco is forgotten, eh?"

Gay laughingly assents, meanwhile drawing a roll of stiff, dirty paper from a pigeon-hole in his desk, which is dusty and rickety. Philip sits down on a pile of worm-eaten folios which happen to be convenient, while Gay, after a preliminary clearing of his throat, begins to read the names of the *dramatis personæ* of his new production: "Captain Macheath—a jolly dog by the way, Peachum, Lockit, Mat-o'-the-mint, Ben Budge—"

"Hold! pardon me for interrupting you, Gay; but the ladies—I am more interested in them!"

Gay replies: "Whichever you like—Mistress Peachum; Polly, her daughter, Dolly Trull, Mistress Vixen—but I'll not read them all, you would be too much wearied."

"What is it? a farce, a tragedy, a pastoral?"

Gay answers: "If your grace will attend to me for a few minutes, I will tell you all about my play. It came about in this way. Mr. Swift and I were at the Rainbow some few days ago, and were discussing Tom Clincher's probable ending, when he suddenly remarked: 'Gay, I think a Newgate pastoral might make a pretty sort of a thing! Try your hand at it; try your hand at it, man.' His suggestion stuck in my head, and egad! this is the consequence." He points to the roll: he pursues in an excited manner: "However, it is not as a Newgate pastoral that I intend it to be known, but rather as a fling at that most nonsensical thing, the squawking, Italian opera, with which all our fashionables are smitten."

Philip says: "Pelt them out of the country with your own airs; I am with you in your hearty detestation of those soft, unnatural airs, fantasias, and conceits which distinguish the Italian school. I prefer our own dear English ballads to all their high-strained warblings. Which is your chief character?"

Gay answers with an air of perplexity: "Now you ask me a question I cannot yet answer. Captain Macheath disputes the palm with Nimming Ned, Peachum, and Polly—faith! I would like to have them all chief characters, if it were not for the violation of dramatic rule!"

"You have not given me its name yet, John, and this is the third time I have asked you."

Gay replies: "Pardon me! I had forgotten—'The Beggar's Opera.'"

"Perfect, perfect! 'Tis both original and striking."

Gay's cheeks color at Philip's approbation. He draws his ragged, faded dressing-gown about him with a satisfied air.

Philip exclaims abruptly: "Good-bye, John. Success attend your labors!" He leaves the room, and leaves also a well-filled purse for the needy poet.

Since pardoned Bolingbroke's return to England, it has been his constant aim to have the bill of penalties formerly passed against him repealed. Unfortunately, a strong party are greatly averse to the measure, among whom is Philip, who looks with detestation on the double renegade, and wonders how a man could become so abandoned and traitorous! The case comes on to-day in Parliament. Thither Philip goes to throw his voice with the opposition. As he enters Lord Harcourt the Trimmer is speaking of the returned exile with feeling and pathos, and he is defending his conduct with much skill. Philip rises as he sits down, and he strongly protests against the measure. He imitates Harcourt's gestures, manners, and pathos so ludicrously that he keeps the house in a continued smile. This finished, he does not wait for the division, but leaves, satisfied that he has done his duty as a man and a patriot.

Strolling toward the Rainbow, where he purposes to spend the rest of the day, he observes Edgely Valentin on the opposite side of the street. He exclaims: "A plague on the sour-faced rogue! He is worse than the Scot's dagger—always in sight! If he ever insults me again, he shall certainly have his nose slit for his pains!"

CHAPTER XLV.

> O Waly, Waly, up the bank,
> O Waly, Waly, down the brae,
> And Waly, Waly, yon burn side,
> Where I and my love were wont to gae!
> I lean'd my back unto an aik,
> I thocht it was a trustie tree,
> But first it bow'd and syne it brak—
> Sae my true love did lichtlie me.
>
> WALY, WALY.

MARGERY is listlessly wandering in the darksome forest, carelessly stepping through the damp grass and the tangled underwood; her face has a look of tired weariness and broken happiness. Her movements are languid and heavy; she has lost her former buoyant gayety and spirit, lost the intense interest the world once had for her; and —God help her!—she sometimes thinks that the black, icy tarn may be her refuge, where her trustful, loving heart will be at rest. Philip has written but one letter to her since the death of her babe; it was so cruel, so harsh, that although she has read it over and over until it is nearly worn to pieces, yet every time she looks at it, it seems to wind a circlet of tightening steel about her heart. She does not cry when she reads it;

she never cries now; tears will not come to ease her throbbing head. All day and all night long, day after day, week after week, month after month, there has been no thought in her mind but of Philip and his—cruelty?—no, his former love and tenderness; none would dare to mention his name to her coupled with cruelty. "He will come back some day—he cannot always be away!" This thought is the star of hope which keeps her from going mad. She often lies on the velvet sofa, where she was sleeping on that day when he came back and awakened her with a kiss and folded her in his arms.

Never since that fatal day, when she carried her baby boy to London, has she known peace of mind or freedom from remorse, nor ceased to reproach herself for disobeying his commands. Her daily walk is through Elm avenue, the old trysting-place. Here she will stay the live-long day and dwell in the memories of the past; she will imagine Philip by her side, and grow less unhappy as his loving words and ardent looks come back to her. See! she turns this way; a dash of sunlight breaks through the interlacing branches overhead, and falls athwart her face; her cheeks have fallen away, and their soft roundness is gone; they are pallid, colorless, all is a wan white except her lips, which are still as red as an autumn leaf, and her eyes are subdued and saddened. She says in a low murmur: "I will go to Queenie. May be she has heard of him by this time." She proceeds toward the gypsy camp.

The white thorn and the honeysuckle vie with the sweet cherry blossom, while the lilac breathes a fain perfume through the dim pathway: the bright peony and the jonquil add their charms and delight the eye with rich tints and varied colors.

Margery has reached the camp; it is just as we left it, except that there are a greater number of brown-skinned, black-eyed babes crowing and playing in the furzes, and on the soft, springy moss; as her eyes fall on them, she puts her hand to her side, as though to still the numb pain gathering around her heart, and her lips are drawn tightly together. As she enters the hut, Queenie bends low and kisses her hand, while Margery tries to smile, but it can find no resting-place on her lips.

"Have you heard aught of him, Queenie?" she asks in a low voice.

Queenie looks pityingly at her as she replies: "Only that master—his grace is well, and so busy wi' court affairs that he can scarcely call a minute his own. These politics, Mistress Margery, are woeful things."

It is an old tale; although she knows that Queenie can tell her nothing of Philip, yet she finds a bitter pleasure in hearing it repeated.

Once there had come a cavalier from London who told Margery that he knew Philip well, and he told so many venomous lies about him in reference to an actress whom he said her husband loved, that she had turned on him like an enraged tigress and commanded him to leave her at once, or she would call for help and have him whipped. Although she disbelieves the story, yet it is constantly recurring to her mind and increases her unhappiness. After a long silence, Margery says: "Queenie, tell me my fortune. See if you can tell me how long it be ere he returns, how long I am to live, or, better still, when I can die." She smiles as she extends her hand.

Queenie takes her hand within her own; she looks steadily at it for a few minutes, then says in a grave voice: "Sweet lady, I would rather bite my tongue off by the roots than tell what your hand shows me." She gently releases her hand and resumes her seat on the deer-skins.

Margery takes no notice of her words, but looks out

of the half-open door and notices the flying leaves which are blown here and there by the shifting wind. Now she bows her head in her hands, and her eyes close. Queenie goes to her, puts her arm about her waist and leads her to her own couch; here she soothes her with endearing names and gentle caresses: "Queenie, you are very kind —hold me tighter in your arms!"

She replies, coaxingly: "Mistress Margery, queenie would be very glad to keep you here all night, but your father would be troubled at your absence. The evening is coming on, there will be no moon to-night; had not Nanar better go with you as far as Rooksnest?"

"Not yet—not yet: I am happier now than I have been for many a day; let me stay here a little longer." She seems to fall asleep, while her breath comes in a series of short, broken sighs, and her eyelids quiver aspen-like. "Oh!" she suddenly exclaims with a long gasp: "how my heart aches! it is—"

"Is Margery here? Margery?" breaks in the General's voice in inquiring accents.

She tries to answer her father's call, but she is unable. Queenie replies: "Yes, Mistress Margery is here!"

"Pistol me, girl! you have led me a pretty chase! I was sure you had met with some accident. What ails you? You look like a broken lily lying there."

She opens her eyes, replying: "Father, forgive me! I am sorry I have given you so much trouble;" attempting to rise, she falls back into queenie's arms. "Father, wait, a few minutes—I am too sick—you—"

The General is alarmed at her evident illness; he kneels down beside her, and rubs her cold, damp hands. She exclaims faintly: "I am dying, father! I would I could breathe my last in the room where Philip kissed me—my heart is easier now; I think it is what is called broken." A shadowy smile flickers and dies on her lips. "When you write to Philip, tell him I died happy; tell him not to grieve; but if he will think of me sometimes when I am gone, I shall know it, and I will be with him though he know it not. Cut off a long braid of my hair; then put it behind his portrait in my locket! Hold me tighter, queenie dear! Kiss me, father."

The owl hoots in the woods, the wind sighs drearily around the hut, while the shades of night are fast wrapping all things in a darkling mantle. The lilacs and the white thorn still dispel their perfume, but the fragrance which is strongest now is the rosemary.

CHAPTER XLVI.

> "For where high honor is the prize,
> True virtue has a right to rise:
> Let courtly slaves low bend the knee
> To wealth and vice in high degree:
> Exalted worth disdains to owe
> Its grandeur to its greatest foe."
>
> SWIFT.

PHILIP's course of life for the last three years has been immoral and profligate to a high degree. His actions have been so licentious and unrestrained by fear of God or man, that we shall pass them over in sorrowing silence, merely premising that he has burdened his estate so heavily with debts and mortgages, that it has been seized by a decree of chancery; which has vested all his property in the hands of trustees who allow him three thousand pounds a year: "scarcely enough to furnish him with snuff and pomatum," as he declared. Retrenchment was necessary, and for that purpose he has gone abroad.

He is in Madrid, the oasis of the Spanish desert. Prior

to his arrival here, he had written three letters from Vienna. One was to the Pretender, in which he expressed sentiments of the "greatest devotion to his cause," and "begged that he might be permitted ere long to reside at his court to watch and cherish his majesty and the Stuart interest." Another was to Horace Walpole, the ambassador at the Tuileries; it was a duplicate of the first, except that in place of the Stuart cause he wrote the Hanoverian dynasty, a slight difference. The last was to the exiled Atterbury, with whom it is treason to either speak or correspond.

He has carefully dressed himself, in anticipation of the many conquests certain to ensue before he returns from his promenade; he really does attract an unusual share of attention from the stately promenaders, both men and women, who turn to look at his handsome face and his fine figure. A discolored, inflamed face is thrust close to his own, and a hoarse voice exclaims: "Hallo, Wharton, I expected you would be in Madrid ere long."

Philip replies blandly: "Ah! my lord, I am overjoyed to see you; how is your health?"

"Passable, but Spanish wine tells on my constitution. By Saint Jago, I get an attack of blue vapors every second week." It is Lord North, the apostate traitor, who turned Roman Catholic and Jacobite to please a man who has since forbidden his presence at his court.

Clinging to North's gold-laced sleeve, and balancing himself first on his toes, then on his heels, is the prime minister, the Duke di Ripperda: an arrant braggart and an imbecile coward; the man of whom Spain has such high blown expectations and the avowed future restorer of the Stuarts; he is capricious, fickle, and a clumsy liar; but for all, his unblushing impudence has secured him many partisans and admirers who have not as yet seen his true character. Stanhope, the British minister, is

probably the only man in Spain who sees through him
and weighs his talents and worth correctly.

Ripperda is of the medium height; his face is heavy and
swollen with excesses and debauchery; his long moustaches are waxed to sharp points; he is attired in a rich
dress of violet satin, slashed with black; his looped hat
is cocked to one side; take him altogether, he is a good
specimen of a fighting, bullying, cowardly Spanish
Dutchman. As Philip grasps his hand after the introduction, he feels a loathing for him he cannot suppress;
he says to himself: "Saugh! a combination of Caliban,
Silenus and Thersites."

Ripperda is smoking a short red clay pipe tipped with
gold, whose bowl is carved so prettily that Philip asks
him whether there are any more like it in town?

He replies: "Ay, more! I always carry a couple for
my friends. Have a pipe, North?" he says, and he
hands one to each. He gives Philip his tobacco pouch,
from which Philip fills his pipe, then passes it to North,
who does the same.

Philip, turning to Ripperda, says: "Your grace,
during my stay in Vienna, I heard some rumors about a
reconciliation between—"

He interrupts him with: "My innocent Duke, I know
what you intend to say; this is my reply: I swear by
the holy Virgin that France and Spain shall never be reconciled as long as I live. England's usurper shall not
only have his German domains wrested from him, but he
shall lose the English crown he wrongfully wears!"

North growls: "I hope so."

Turning to Philip, he resumes: "I trust your grace
echoes that wish?"

"Yes, with all my heart," he replies, wondering at
Ripperda's ravings, certain that he is drunk to talk about

important state affairs in such a loud voice while in the most frequented part of the city.

As they walk along, an open coach passes them in which sits a dame whom Philip thinks he has never seen equalled. She wears the coquettish lace veil of the Spanish ladies, which falls on a pair of white, plump shoulders. Philip exclaims hurriedly: "Ripperda, tell me, before she passes, who is that lady?"

"Which one?" hiccups the minister. "There are so many around that I am unable to answer your question."

Philip points her out; he replies: "Saint Jago! that is the O'Beirne, maid of honor to her majesty, and a very dragon of virtue she is, as I have found to my cost."

Philip mutters: "Conceited jackanapes!" then in a louder voice: "I have seen her before, somewhere! Was she ever in London?"

Ripperda replies: "No, never to my knowledge. She was born here, and I do not believe she has ever been out of Spain."

North says: "Excuse me, Ripperda. If I am not mistaken, she was in Dublin a few years ago. During Alberoni's time, he sent her there as a spy or an agent. She is talented and shrewd, but she failed in her mission —a failure which has done her more good than harm, for her dismissal by Alberoni was the cause of our friend's interest in her."

Ripperda adds, with a chuckling leer: "Yes, that and her good looks, with perhaps a trifle of pity, for she is as poor as a Carmelite; her father was killed in our army. Her mother's pension would barely keep them from starving, if I had not secured her a position as maid of honor." He puffs forth a circling volume of smoke which envelops the party.

"O'Beirne—Dublin—Alberoni?" Philip, thinking over these three names, soon recalls the circumstances with which they are connected. She is the same who brought him Alberoni's letter, the same whom he kissed in the cathedral. " Mistress Nora, I must renew that acquaintance begun so strangely and ended so abruptly!" Raising his eyes at this moment, the coach again is passing. Looking intently at her, he lifts his hat and bows; his heart bounds as she returns the salute with a distinct nod and a sweet smile.

CHAPTER XLVII.

Lyconides, what shall I do now?
PLAUTUS.

THE house is Mr. Keene's, the British consul; the company in the salon consists of two or three loyal English, a few Spanish hidalgos, and a sprinkling of French noblemen. Conversation is carried on in subdued tones, while various couples are promenading. Mr. Keene is attending to his guests, and welcoming them with the well-bred cordiality for which he is distinguished. Suddenly there is a scuffling noise heard on the stairs outside, which draws all attention thither. The consul goes to inquire the reason of the unseasonable uproar.

Here we must stop for a moment to inform you that Philip has received an answer from the Pretender empowering him to act as ambassador to Spain, and also to assist Ormond in organizing an expedition to invade England, and, above all, to vindicate the separation in the Pretender's family; for James has seriously offended both the Queen of Spain and the Emperor, by his treatment of his consort, Clementina.

Arriving at the head of the stairs, the nostrils of the consul are saluted with a strong smell of tobacco, which is his special abhorrence. The servant announces: " His

Grace, the Duke of Wharton and Northumberland!" A hiccoughing voice adds: "Prime minister as well, fellow!" And Philip slowly staggers up stairs. Reaching the top, he exclaims: "Well, Mr. Consul Keene, how are you? I shall supersede you before long for your confounded impudence in being disloyal—disloyal, d' ye hear?"

"Yes, your grace. Will you come in and sit down? You look unwell," he replies in a conciliating manner, adding, however, under his breath, "Talking, tippling knave."

"Keene, I tell you that his majesty's interests have hitherto been managed by her grace of Perth, and three or four other old women who meet under the portals of Saint Germains. His majesty wants a Whig, and a brisk one, to put them in the right train, and I am the man! You may now look upon me, Sir Philip Wharton, Knight of the Garter, and Sir Robert Walpole, Knight of the Bath, running a course, and, by Heaven, he shall be hard pressed! He bought my family pictures when those infernal chancery men griped me; but they will not be long in his possession. That account is still open. Neither he nor King George shall be six months at ease as long as I have the honor to serve in the employ I am in now." Puffing a globe of smoke in the consul's face, he leers insolently at him.

Keene, reddening at his visitor's language, replies: "Your grace, though I am not a duke, I am a gentleman and a true man. I will not allow such expressions to be used in this house. They are an insult to my king and myself. My servant will show you the door."

Philip, steadying himself by an effort, replies: "S'blood, Keene! I'll lower myself to your level for the pleasure of showing you the *punta riversa*, as practised by Don Sabrat and myself with the three-edged blade!"

"Thanks! I shall be at home all day to-morrow. It will give me unbounded satisfaction to cross blades with you, spite of your un-English name for an un-English weapon."

Philip replies: "Adieu, Keene; I am off for Ripperda's levee. He is a man after my own heart."

"And your manners also," adds Keene, contemptuously.

Arriving at Ripperda's, Philip is ushered in, and presented to the minister, who exclaims: "Carramba, Wharton, I am glad you have called! These stilted, solemn dons and impregnable donnas horrify me. However, greatness implies care and trouble, you know."

Philip answers: "I agree with you, Ripperda. We are both in the same boat. Only an hour ago I went to Mr. Keene's—"

"Insolent dog!" interpolates the minister.

Philip resumes: "Curse me, but the fellow was so insolent that I thrashed him before the whole company."

Ripperda chuckles at this; he hates Keene with all his heart, for on one occasion, when he had called out, "Keene, Keene!" the consul refused to answer him, totally ignoring his presence. "You ought to have choked him, Wharton."

"I'll pink him to-morrow."

Ripperda, throwing up his hands, exclaims: "Your grace will certainly not fight a plebeian."

Twisting his thumb and his finger through his perfumed curls, he replies: "Yes, I want to teach him a lesson."

"By the way, O'Beirne is sitting to your left there; she is convoyed by Donna Lospiratos—a rigid duenna, a very Diana."

Philip adds, "Guarding a Venus; I intend to speak to her, though, duenna or no duenna. Help me along by engaging your puritanical friend until I have finished with Mistress O'Beirne."

Ripperda sneeringly replies, " Friend! *Malditos perros!* I have six very good friends*—God, the Holy Virgin, the Emperor and Empress, and the King and Queen of Spain. For enemies every man in Christendom and the Spanish nation. You see they are all my servants, and never was a servant yet that would not be master if he could, but they lack the talent."

Interrupting him with a half-serious, half-joking expression, Philip says, " Ripperda, if you but knew it, you are like myself—not worth a Spanish groat. You have no character, man!"

" Santa Maria purissima!" cries the offended minister; " our rich grapes have their usual effect on an unseasoned head."

Philip retorts: "Not so, Ripperda; not Spanish grapes, but Dutch-Spanish rhodomontades and braggadocio."

Ripperda flushes, but does not reply, keeping his eyes toward the doors where several notabilities have just made their appearance.

Stepping toward Mistress O'Beirne, Philip pays his duties to her with much cordiality. She returns his greeting with a courteous freedom and vivacity which charm him. He sits down beside her, and they are quickly engaged in an interesting conversation. Philip broaches the topic of her past mission to Dublin. Stopping him at once, she forbids him ever mentioning the subject again under pain of her displeasure. Turning to her companion, she says, " I must return to court, now; I will thank your grace to personate my *preux chevalier!*"

He replies with an ardent look: " From this moment I am your most devoted attendant."

* Fact.

She glances inquiringly at him from under her drooping lashes, and, as Philip thinks, leans on his arm more than is absolutely necessary. Bidding her good-bye, he asks: "I can see you again before long?"

"Your grace will not find it very difficult to see me when you wish."

Kissing her hand, he returns to Ripperda, his heart beating with a new sensation. "Ripperda, I love that girl! On my life, she is lovely! Her wit is sparkling, her conversation is fresh and piquant; she is superb!"

"Make her your duchess; then you will find her faults; now you see nothing but her virtues."

"Sage man!" replies Philip, adding, parenthetically, "She cut you once, did she not, Ripperda?"

The minister ignores the question, however, leaving Philip to speak to a friend who has just entered, an emissary from Berlin.

CHAPTER XLVIII.

They are preparing evidence against thee.
THE BEGGAR'S OPERA.

THE consort Clementina has left James in disgust, alleging that she was treated by the Earl of Inverness and his wife—an arrogant coquette—with such intolerable insolence that she would not endure it any longer. She is now in the convent of St. Cecilia at Rome, where the ambitious priest Alberoni is often closeted with her for hours. By thus supporting his favorites at the expense of his consort, James has roused the ire of the emperor at Vienna, who is justly indignant at his cool treatment of a kinswoman of his house. The Queen of Spain is likewise displeased at his uncourteous conduct. Thus, this true Stuart makes enemies of two powerful sovereigns at a time when their friendship is of the most vital importance.

In Spain, Ripperda has ignominiously failed. He has blustered and bragged like a second Bobadil, and has given the most opposite assurances in different quarters. To the British minister he has professed the greatest love toward England, and palliated his warm endeavors for the Stuart cause, by vowing that he assisted James merely as a blind. He has culminated his career by his double dealing with the Austrian ambassador, Count Königsegg, and the Spanish court. To the former he has protested that Spain would not be outdone in her exertions to help Austria, while immensely exaggerating her power and resources; to the other he alleged the readiness and impatience of the Austrian court as regarded affairs in France and England. When both sides were undeceived, Ripperda found that, like abler men before him, he had stumbled between two stools. He has been dismissed with a miserable pension—a gratuitous and merited insult. Madrid is in a terrible state of excitement; Ripperda's life would not be worth a pistole if he was seen in public: while in France, Bourbon scarcely governs his kingdom, while Madame de Prie and Paris Duvernay completely govern him. In England, the emperor's creature, Mr. Palm, is bribing right and left to secure all the Hanoverian partisans possible. The King of Prussia has flouted the Hanover alliance, while George begins to fear lest the electorate should be endangered— an object of far more interest to him than England's safety.

Philip has been sick for the last few days, a state of body which has had its effect on his not unchangeable ideas and resolves. After he had calmly reviewed his conduct at Mr. Keene's house, his better feeling reigned triumphant. Accordingly he had written a humble, penitential letter to him, apologizing for his actions, and hoping that all would be forgotten. The following postscript he added at the bottom of the paper: " If you mean to take my challenge in earnest, of course I am still at your service." The consul's answer was mild and conciliating, and he has waived his right with many thanks for his grace's condescension.

He is alone in his room, sitting at his desk, intently perusing a letter sealed with the arms of England. It is an order under the privy seal, commanding him, on his allegiance, to return home forthwith, or he will be outlawed, and all his property and valuables sequestrated.

" Ah, ha! so he threatens me? Eh bien! I prefer his threats to his favors; that he shall know. What do I want with his pitiful favor? I would rather carry a musket in an odd-named Muscovite regiment, than wallow in riches by the help of that tallow-headed usurper. It is very curious, though, how intimately acquainted he is with my most private actions. I must have an enemy here somewhere. I'll write to Jamie. An account of this offer will amuse him, while at the same time it must bring me into high favor by showing my entire devotion to his cause. Egad! I may be appointed prime minister yet. He is a Stuart, though—new toys are his hobbies. I fear that even I might be out in the rain of royal frowns once in a while."

Drawing a sheet of paper toward him, he proceeds to give an account of the royal mandate to the Pretender, embellishing it with many little conceits and witty sparkles, one or two of which, edging slightly on the immoral, are scarcely fit for the eyes of a pious prince. Philip also announces to him his intention of openly espousing the Roman Catholic religion. Finishing his letter, he rises and exclaims: "Pedro, Pedro! you dog, come here!" Pedro enters, and the preparations for his grace's toilet begin. "Who is at the palace to-day, Pedro?"

"I know not, your grace; stories are afloat, though, that the Marquis de Villadarias will be there; also the Conde de Las Torres."

"Falstaff and Alexander—who else?—what ladies?"

"Your grace, on that point I am still more ignorant."

"Will Mlle. O'Beirne be there?"

"Oh, yes, your grace, I thought you meant ladies!"

"S'death! Pedro, never mind your thoughts; thinking is your master's privilege."

Applying a trifle of powder to Philip's chin, he replies humbly: "Yes, your grace."

"Recollect that Mlle. O'Beirne is—pah." Turning pettishly away, he pulls his lace ruffles over his hands and smooths his sleeves.

As Philip enters the royal gardens, his attention is attracted to a couple who are only a few yards distant. The lady is Mlle. O'Beirne; the cavalier is Edgely Valentin; she is leaning on his arm, apparently gently chiding him for some fault or inattention; while his eyes are filled with an admiring, loving expression which arouses an angry jealousy in Philip's bosom. He exclaims: "Again, Edgely Valentin! The threads of our lives are strangely twisted! whether is it chance or design? Be it either, by Heaven I'll cut them, if he pushes himself upon me!"

CHAPTER XLIX.

Anguis in herbâ latet.

EDGELY VALENTIN is dressed in black velvet, which sombre color is scarcely relieved by the row of purple rosettes or buttons attached to the facings of his coat. Philip instantly decides to accost them, expose the impostor Edgely Valentin, and upbraid her—for what? for inconstancy, fickleness? As yet he has scarcely spoken with her an hour at a time, and already jealousy is agitating his mind. Rapidly walking up to the unconscious pair, he lifts his hat haughtily to Mistress O'Beirne, at the same time bestowing upon her companion a long, insolent stare, and sneeringly surveying him from head to foot. Meanwhile Valentin's countenance is lowering and angry, his eyes sparkling with a look of hatred, as he undergoes the scrutiny.

"Has your grace completed your examination of my person?" handing his card to Philip, who reads out "Sir Edgely Warely!"

"You lie, sirrah! It should be Edgely Valentin, spy and traitor!" Tearing the card to pieces, he throws it on the ground.

With a quick, silent movement, Valentin draws his rapier. Mistress O'Beirne, noticing his motion, quickly places herself in front of him, and grasps the sharp blade in her gloved hand; exclaiming to Philip, with a steady reproachful glance: "For shame, your grace!—such language and behavior in my presence! in the royal precincts as well?"

Stammering an indistinct apology Philip lifts his hat and strides away.

Sheathing his rapier, while his teeth are set, and his face drawn as with pain, Valentin says: "An old feud, Nora!"

"A strange time and place to settle an old feud!" replies the offended girl.

"It was not of my seeking," he replies, in a low, pleading voice.

"I know it, Sir Edgely. I blame only his grace for the disagreeable rencontre. I thought him more of a gallant—more truly courteous in his manners."

"He is, generally; he doubtless desired your company more than the adjustment of a quarrel."

Her color heightens at his words. Turning to an orange tree close by her, she plucks a twig, at the same time replying in a careless manner, "Flatterer! what could his grace want with me?"

"What many a better man would: win you for his wife."

Dropping his arm, she says warningly: "Sir Edgely, you are again approaching that forbidden topic! Alberoni's letter of introduction commended you as a true friend to the cause, and an able counsellor. He did not specify that you were to be a lover as well as an adviser."

Hanging his head, he is silent, and his lips tremble for an instant.

Grinding his teeth with rage, Philip invokes curses on his supposed rival. "A base-born, fatherless hireling! flying at my game! 'Tis a pity I did not slit his nose while he was in London, as Cowper suggested; he would have probably found less favor in her eyes! As she likes—she prefers the crow to the eagle; she certainly has a right to a choice. I'll to Stanhope; he can, may be, tell me more than I already know about this Sir

Edgely Warely—forsooth!" Leaving the garden, he walks towards the minister's house.

Arriving at his destination, he is announced by the servant, and requested to walk up stairs and await the coming of the minister. Opening the first door he meets, a scene greets his eyes which roots him to the floor in speechless amazement. Stanhope is standing in the centre of the room, his face wearing an expression of mixed annoyance, perplexity, and contempt; while, grovelling on the floor, with his arms around the minister's feet, and his clothes in sad disorder, is the once vain-glorious Ripperda, late prime minister. He exclaims in a guttural patois: "Your kind excellency, you shall know everything, if you will only save me from the cut-throats and assassins who would murder me. I will tell you all about the Vienna affair, which means the entire uprooting of the Protestants and the universal power—"

Quickly clapping his hand on Ripperda's mouth, Stanhope turns, and looks sternly and suspiciously at Philip, saying: "It seems your grace has a new occupation—spy."

"Mr. Stanhope, appearances are against me; but I give you the word of an English gentleman, that it is an entire accident which has made me a witness of this scene."

Bowing politely, Stanhope replies: "I believe you. It is needless for me to ask your silence in regard to all you have seen or heard?"

"On my honor, it shall never be mentioned."

Hurriedly retiring, he exclaims: "Euge! Ripperda at Stanhope's feet, blabbing secrets of state! the brave Ripperda, the invincible, astute Ripperda, Spain's chiefest honor, wearing out his satin breeches at English Stanhope's feet! This is indeed a discovery! I'll not wait for his excellency's opinion of Valentin: the greater absorbs the smaller matter." Walking along absorbed in his thoughts, he brushes against a tall cavalier, with military moustaches of wonderful length. Turning to apologize, he sees his friend Count Königsegg, to whom he was introduced by Ripperda.

"Well met, Count, the man above all others whom I wish to see!"

He replies: "I am flattered, your grace."

"Not the slightest necessity, Count, I assure you. You see I have been unable to leave my room for the last week; consequently I am rather behind the rest of Madrid in regard to passing events. You are always well versed in current news and items. I beg you, share your stock with me!"

"With pleasure, your grace."

"One moment, Count, before you begin. Do you know aught about a fellow who styles himself Sir Edgely Warely? He seems to ruffle it gayly at court!"

"Nothing, except that he was—and is still, for all I know—a favorite of Alberoni, who has often trusted him on errands requiring a cool head and a strong arm."

"A good cheek, as well, by St. Jago!" adds Philip.

"I have heard that he is to be married in a short time to one of her majesty's maids—a Mlle. O'Beirne."

Philip starts, exclaiming, "Never; she would never accept him!"

"Why not? He is quite a fine-looking man, and he appears to possess plenty of money—far more than she has, at all events."

Philip vacantly replies, "Yes;" and he walks along in silence, musing over Mistress O'Beirne's wit and beauty.

CHAPTER L.

Vain human kind! fantastic race!
Thy various follies who can trace?

SWIFT.

"MLLE. O'BEIRNE, you say I am a stranger to you!—that you are unknown to me. Does not our acquaintance date years back, in your father's birthplace—Dublin? Can you repulse me when I tell you that, ever since that day in the cathedral, I have never ceased to think of you, while mourning the fate which separated us?"

Philip was kneeling at her feet, the moon shining on his upturned face as he pleaded his love, and asked her to be his wife. Looking steadfastly at him, she replied in an unsteady voice:—

"Your grace, to say that I have never thought of you since that time would be untrue; but my feelings toward you have never been greater than those of friendship." He was about to interrupt her; but, silencing him with a motion of her hand, she resumed: "You must recollect, moreover, that I am penniless! I could not bring you the dowry a duke's bride should possess!"

"Mlle. O'Beirne—Nora! I will not argue with you. If you refuse me, my death be on your hands. I could not live alone when you might be my constant companion and beloved wife."

"Your grace, this is a threat which no gentleman would make—rise, I pray you! To-morrow, when you are cooler—when you have reflected on what you have said—"

"You will allow me to renew my proposals, dear Nora?"

"No! I was about to say that you will blame yourself and me also for your rash conduct and unconsidered words, which—which—" Bursting into tears she covered her face with her hands.

Quickly rising, he threw his arms around her waist, despite her resistance, and kissed her repeatedly while holding her hand imprisoned in his.

"This is an outrage, sir! Release me, or I will alarm the palace!" she exclaimed in quick, broken accents.

"Be Duchess of Wharton—be my wife!"

Steadying her voice by a strong effort, she replied: "Release me, and I will give you my answer!"

He did so, and awaited her reply in mute expectation.

"Your grace, consider carefully all I say; consider the bold, unwomanly words that I shall utter; consider how lost to all shame I am to make so bold an avowal—"

She paused for a moment, while her breath came quick and fast; then, in the verdurous, ivy-covered balcony, she told him a tale—true or false—which set his blood on fire, and made everything about him whirl in an unsteady dance. She told him that she had never ceased to think of him since their interview in Dublin, and that, when she had seen him on the Prado, she had felt happier than ever she had been before. "But you must not ask me to be your wife until you are sure that you know your own mind. I am proud and penniless; yet a king could not have me save as his consort. My temper is quick, and not very easily controlled. These are bad qualities in a wife; but it is better you should know all before asking me to be yours for life."

Catching her in his arms, he exclaimed: "Nora, you

are a noble woman! Unfortunately for your purpose, you have only riveted the chains which bind me to you the faster. From this moment you are my wife—"

"Wait! I will not consent until you have had time to reflect on your actions. Come to me one month from to-night—you shall then receive my answer."

Dashing his hand on the edge of the balcony, he exclaimed: "Nora, I will not leave this spot until you consent!"

She looked pained and embarrassed, while her hands clasped around each other. Taking a ring from his pocket, he placed it on her passive finger and said: "Nora, Duchess of Wharton, and, better still, Philip's love." She offered no resistance, and the ring glittered bravely in the moonlight.

CHAPTER LI.

True, a new mistress now I chase.

LOVELACE.

WHEN Mlle. O'Beirne had accepted Philip as her future husband, she had forgotten that, as a maid of honor, it was her duty to ask the permission of her royal mistress ere the step was taken. She had not thought about it at the time, and when she told her majesty, requesting her permission, the answer came quick and angrily: "No! you are both mad! The alliance would be productive of the worst consequences. The Duke of Wharton is known to be the most profligate, immoral man of the age! Moreover he is such a spendthrift, all his property is sequestrated by the English government for his loyalty to James. What funds he may have with him will soon be expended; then how could you live? You have not a pistole you can call your own."

Nora had almost swooned at this unexpected refusal, and she had faintly wondered what his grace would do or say.

When Philip heard of her majesty's indignant refusal, he became well-nigh crazy, and his after excitement and anger produced a dangerous relapse, in consequence of which he was again prostrated. The court doctors who attended him pronounced him in a very critical state, declaring that unless some change for the better took place, he could not long survive. He would not eat, and would drink nothing but brandy.

When the queen heard of his forlorn condition and the dangerous symptoms of his illness, she sent him a kindly message, hinting that if he thought his conduct and morals would be more steady in future, and if he would embrace the Roman Catholic faith, she might think of recalling her former decision.

Philip received this message during the absence of the doctors. He immediately sprang from his bed, forced his frightened valet to dress him, while threatening him with his rapier point, rushed precipitately to the palace, forcing himself through the crowd of courtiers and gentlemen in waiting, and threw himself on his knees before the throne.

Behind the royal chair stands Nora O'Beirne, frightened and thunderstruck at Philip's boldness in thus forcing himself on her majesty's notice. Close beside her is Lord North, eying Philip with a wondering stare, waiting for a dénouement of the affair. On either side of her majesty stand the Conde de las Torres, and the proud Marquis de Villadarias. Count Königsegg can be seen amid the assemblage surrounding the throne.

All eyes are turned on Philip, as he cries in a weak,

unsteady voice: "Your majesty, have mercy on me—on us! I cannot live without her!"

The queen glances pityingly at him, while inclining her ear to las Torres, who whispers a few words in a low voice. Nodding her head, she says to Philip:—

"Your grace, as a daughter of the church, we cannot allow our maid to unite herself with a heretic; that is an impassable bar to the union."

Rising, Philip replies in a louder voice than before: "Your majesty, I do here most solemnly and truly abjure the Protestant belief, assuring you that I am in heart and soul as good a Catholic as yourself; and have been all my life, privately if not openly!"

The queen and las Torres exchange a significant smile. Turning again to Philip, she resumes: "In our opinion, your projected marriage is hasty and ill-advised. We greatly fear that you will—too late—repent your step." Turning to Nora, she says rather imperiously: "Mlle. O'Beirne, if you truly love and respect his grace of Wharton, go to him! Holy Mary bless and guard you both, is our sincerest wish!"

Grasping Nora's hand with a quick movement, Philip leads her through the opening lane of wondering courtiers and smiling dames toward the anteroom, where they can be alone. Passing along, he notices Edgely Valentin, at whom he glances contemptuously, although a pang of jealousy strikes his heart as he observes Nora turn pale, while her hand trembles a little. Valentin's face bears an expression of suffering hatred as he returns Philip's look, while his eyes rest with a curiously mixed expression of envy and triumph on Nora's downcast face.

They are to be married to-night, at Philip's earnest entreaties. He intends to take her with him to Rome, there to spend the honeymoon, a project to which Nora has unwillingly acceded. She wished to delay the nup-

tials for at least three months; deprecating any delay, however, his waywardness carried the day.
Le roi est mort, vive le roi!

CHAPTER LII.

Les cartes sont brouillées.

As they enter the royal presence, the Pretender welcomes them very warmly, even deigning to kiss Nora's cheek; a liberty which she does not resent, although Philip little relishes his sovereign's freedom. Turning to Philip, James says: "A running ship collects no barnacles, Wharton; but it seems you have secured a glorious prize! We almost envy you your blushing bride!"

"If it but stop at envy, your majesty, I shall be well pleased," replies Philip, sullenly.

"Out on thee for thy churlishness, man!" James laughs, with a glance at the Countess of Inverness, who replies by surveying Nora with a spiteful sneer.

The Earl of Dunbar, noticing her disdainful gesture, remarks aside: "Terribly coarse and vulgar!"

"Very!" is the low reply.

Assuming a graver demeanor, James says to Philip: "We would speak with you in private! Our friends will amuse her grace meanwhile;" motioning Philip to follow him. Entering a small, shabby, ill-furnished room, James resumes, in a conciliating, familiar manner: "Your grace, we have heard that you have openly embraced the true faith?"

"It is true, your majesty!"

"What we now intend to say to you must be taken in good part—as we say it in good meaning. We know of your grace's gallantries and escapades, and have sorrowed anent them as being of an ungodly and immoral nature. We would desire you to curb your spirit, and so conduct yourself as to merit our special approval and esteem, as well as to close the mouths of those who are envious of your great parts and genius. It would ill become us to have the world at large say that we looked kindly on a roystering, godless gallant."

Philip answers haughtily: "Your majesty entertains but an ill opinion of me! I—"

"Nay; nay! Wharton, you are mistaken! Our last words were meant rather as a prophecy of what you might become, if you did not put a check on your wit and exuberancy. It is your sprightliness and vivacity which have heretofore led you into so many misadventures."

"Forgive me, your majesty! In future, my conduct shall be based on your majesty's, and it will certainly tend to cure one of my vices to have such an example to follow!"

"Nay! not such a good example, if Lockhart of Carnwarth speaks truly! He has many times told us of our infirmities. Assoilzie him! as our father would have said!"

Philip replies: "A good man and true, though over brusque in his ways, under favor, your majesty; I think he is as true a friend to the cause as any gentleman in Rome."

Frowning slightly, James replies: "Yes! truly he is over brusque."

There is a silence, until James says: "By the rood! it is time for mass! Our confessor may wax impatient at our long delay!"

Leading the way, they re-enter the saloon.

Philip, noticing that the Earl of Dunbar is whispering

to Nora, walks quickly toward them, upon which they begin to converse on indifferent subjects. Meanwhile my Lady Inverness looks on in disdainful silence. James signifying that the audience is ended, Philip leads Nora out, and they enter the coach awaiting them at the palace door.

Philip is apparently vexed and angry. He says, rather coldly: "Your grace will make all necessary arrangements to leave immediately for Paris, or Madrid, or perchance London, I have not quite determined which; but Rome shall contain us no longer." Settling himself in the far corner, he looks stolidly out of the window.

Nora wonders at his sullen behavior, and fears that she has offended him. She replies affectionately: "Why, Philip, how abrupt you are! Of course, wherever you wish to go, it is my happiness to accompany you. But why should you be so stern? Have I offended you?"

"No, Nora, you have not, but his fictitious majesty saw fit to take up all my old offences, warning me, at the same time, that if my conduct did not change for the better, he would prefer my absence to my presence."

She replies quickly: "Philip, you must have misunderstood him! Let us remain here a few days at any rate, and you will find how gracious he is. For my sake, dear Philip, do not call him 'fictitious;' he is our true king, is he not?"

Glancing angrily at her, he replies: "You justly consider him gracious and amiable; I add a title of my own—omni-loving."

"Yes, Philip, he has a loving heart, and in it all his true subjects have a share."

"Some have too great a share, I fear me. However, loving heart or not, amiability or crabbedness, to-day will see us on our journey."

"To where?" she asks, timidly.

"By the time we have arrived at our stopping-place, you will know. Until then—peace! I pray you!"

Her eyes fill at his words, and a silence falls between them. She glances at him with a troubled look, but his eyes are closed as if in sleep.

"Alas! when Alberoni conjured me on my loyalty to obey Sir Edgely's counsels, I knew not what they would be when I gave my blind compliance! I recollect his very words: 'Mlle. O'Beirne, Wharton must be gained to our side. Sir Edgely has failed from no fault of his own, and though I know well your mutual love, yet must it be sacrificed for our common causes—the holy Catholic faith and the support of King James, both here and abroad. Let Sir Edgely be seen with you in public where his grace may observe you, his hatred and contempt of Sir Edgely is a handle by which we can work. His pride will be aroused; your own wit and beauty can do the rest. Once married, guide him with invisible reins, and make him true to church and state;' and I have done it all; been false to him, and a liar to my husband! No! not that. I did love him when he asked me to be his wife, kissed me with his fiery lips, held me in his arms, and called me his 'duchess.' That frenzy has gone, and now—Alberoni must commend my talent, however. He will praise me, for Philip is now a Catholic, a Jacobite, and my husband—all by my exertions! I must write to his eminence and inform him of Philip's anger at his majesty; it may be dangerous to the cause! Edgely can take the message, poor fellow." She shudders, while the coach draws up with a loud clatter, and they alight.

28

CHAPTER LIII.

The wondering world, where'er he moves,
With new delight looks up.
SWIFT.

IN a lofty, sombre chamber of the convent of St. Cecilia, Cardinal Alberoni and the titular Queen Clementina are conversing in low tones; while Edgely Valentin is standing behind the cardinal's chair, calm and motionless. Alberoni is short and squat, with ponderous shoulders and a bull neck; his head is unusually large, and his complexion swarthy; his jawbones are prominent; his eyes deep in their sockets, yet bold and piercing; a moustache hides his upper lip, while a small, peaked tuft adorns his chin. On his head is a tight skullcap; his person is enveloped in a cardinal's robe. He is attentively reading a short note bearing the signature: "Nora, Duchess of Wharton." Laying it down, he says: "Sir Edgely, accept my thanks for this; I will attend to it, and see that his majesty pursues a more conciliating policy toward his grace."

Bowing low, Valentin replies: "Your eminence, he is a valuable acquisition to our party; under favor, I think it was because his majesty showed a liking for Mlle.—her grace, that he was displeased; I judge so from a previous interview with her grace."

Clementina says, with a sigh: "Surely James has enough without her, to grace his reputation and divide his attentions."

Covertly smiling, Alberoni inquires: "How does my Lord Dunbar now?"

Valentin replies: "High in favor, your eminence, and likely to continue so, as is also my Lady Inverness."

Striking her hands on the table, the queen exclaims, with an angry look: "The courtesan!"

Valentin pursues: "She is as conceited and arrogant as ever!"

Alberoni adds: "Two qualities tending to shame and mortification. Is North in town?"

"No, your eminence; he has gone to the trenches at Gibraltar, to offer his services to las Torres."

"Indeed! If the Condé appreciates him at his true worth, he will send him back again—a blustering, ill-bred fellow, with scarce a spark of talent or energy!"

"He is a good Catholic!" exclaims the queen.

"Your majesty, a Catholic may do more harm to his religion as an exponent than an opponent," he dryly replies, adding: "Villadarias should have taken the command at the trenches; I distrust las Torres, he is too wordy—too wordy."

The queen replies: "Yes, he should; but he is too shrewd. He thinks there is little prospect of gaining honor there, and is willing enough to allow his colleague to reap the crop of bombs and bullets. In his opinion, the Rock is impregnable. Las Torres has declared that his majesty's flag shall wave over its ramparts in a very short time?"

Alberoni replies: "Villadarias is culpably timid in this affair. Gibraltar is feebly defended; our land forces are strong, and if necessary we could safely attack it on the water side! There will be a terrible slaughter; but the Rock must capitulate; then the desire of my life will be gratified!" Rubbing his hands together, his eyes sparkle joyously.

Glancing at him, the queen says: "Cardinal, it is long since we have seen you so happy?"

"Your majesty will see me happier if the Rock capitulates!"

"Pardon me, your eminence," interrupts Valentin in a low whisper: "Here is a communication respecting Fleury," handing him a small packet, which Alberoni conceals in his gown.

Overhearing the name, the queen inquires: "Speaking of Fleury, cardinal, how does he stand in your estimation?"

"A second Mazarin, with rather more honesty and principle." Turning to Valentin, he resumes: "How did Mlle. Nora relish the change in her name and quality?"

He replies bitterly: "Too well, I judge, your eminence."

"Too well! What mean you? Can aught be done in too willing a spirit for Holy Mother Church?"

Valentin replies confusedly: "Forgive me! I hardly knew what I said!"

Looking fixedly at him, he replies: "My son, take heed that you have no thought outside of the church, except such as I may bless and sanction."

Counting her beads, the queen mutters her prayers with eyes downcast and humble.

Alberoni continues, "You may retire, my son."

"Pardon me, your eminence! Before I go, I would like to intimate that if his grace could be induced to serve in the trenches in some superior capacity, he would be still further involved with us, less likely to return to St. James'?"

"My son, your astuteness is commendable. True—his connection with England severed, he would be with us from sheer necessity. I will have his thoughts turned in that direction, if possible!"

Touching a small bell, a young girl enters, dressed in

the robes of a novice; Alberoni says quickly: "My daughter!—Wharton—hint to him that honor and fame are to be gained at Gibraltar—send at once—anonymous."

Bowing low, she kisses his hand, retiring as silently as she had entered. Turning to Valentin, he says: "You can mention to her grace our design, so that she may work in unison with us!"

The stone floor echoes under Valentin's feet, while the door creaks harshly as he closes it after his exit. He does not leave immediately. Standing on the threshold, he places his ear to the door, through which the voices of the queen and Alberoni can be dimly heard.

"Not a word that interests me! A pest on the cardinal! one would think he knew I listened outside, he broaches such trifling subjects?—if *he* will but fight against old England, it will be one step more in the right direction; one step nearer to the consummation. Once I was Jacobite for James' sake, but when she told me the story of her life—of the violated promise, I became Jacobite for my own sake, and when for that cause. I had either to lose my revenge or Nora, I chose the latter, letting him have her as his wife!—a Delilah and a Samson! My king, my honor, and my love have I surrendered! For twenty-seven years has the finger of scorn been pointed at me; for twenty-seven years have I been gibed and taunted with a bastard origin!—Furies! Never will I forget that day when he drove me from him at Stair's, with the old taunt, the same sneer which has been my portion all my life. Act of attainder—sequestration—ignominy. They shall be my weapons, forged by deluded ministers. His nature is not like mine. He would sink under poverty and disgrace; but he shall try them, he shall try them! curse him! If I can reduce him to beggary and despair, I'll never lose sight of him; I'll close my hands around his white neck and press the life out of him. Let him die with my face close to his, my eyes looking into his, my breath on his lips—then I'll tell him who—what I am; describe to him my long life of wounded sensibilities that would *not* grow callous. Then—"

In his blind anger he runs against the iron wicket, bringing out the portress—a blear-eyed, toothless woman, who unlocks the gate, and he walks rapidly in the direction of the palace. As he arrives within sight of his destination, he notices a coach drawn by four black horses, being driven toward him. The next moment he observes a ragged fellow toss a letter through the window, Philip's face appearing at the same instant. He mutters: "Wharton! strange! The coach is loaded down with trunks and bags as if he intends to leave us; I must let his eminence know of this."

Let us glance into the coach. The letter thrown in is on the floor, rumpled and torn. Stooping and picking it up, Nora inquires: "May I read it, Philip?"

"Yes, if you choose," he replies.

Throwing it down after a hasty perusal, she exclaims: "What a field in which to gather fame! The eyes of the world are turned on this coming contest!"

He replies: "It is anonymous! A friend seldom conceals himself, an enemy almost invariably!"

"*I* think this is from a friend, who, being aware of your talents and ambition, is desirous of pointing out the way, while fearing lest you might dislike his officiousness."

"Probably. However, friend or enemy, the suggestion suits me exactly. We will stop at the next cabaret, then I will write to las Torres, offering him my services at Gibraltar. We can go by sea to Barcelona, thence to the scene of action."

Nora replies: "Would it not be better to write to his majesty that you design to take arms in his service?"

"I will do so, Nora; your advice is opportune."

"Of course, you will await his majesty's answer?"

"Not at all; we shall continue on our route. I am sure that he will gladly accede to my proposal. Las Torres is the commandant, I believe; he will doubtless carry on the siege with credit and success."

"If you help him, he could not do otherwise."

"I would that others could appreciate my talents as well as you, Nora," he replies, thinking with regret on his cool reception at Rome.

"Force them to appreciate you; show yourself to the world in your true colors as a loyal, talented commander."

He does not answer her. He is thinking of the daring deeds he will accomplish in the trenches, of the brave show he will make in his Spanish uniform, which, he has determined, shall be violet with pearl facings, and gold lace; colors harmonizing well with his complexion, which he keeps clear and fresh with an unguent used by Mlle. Paris Duvernay.

CHAPTER LIV.

"For who could be blind to so brilliant a star?"

CONDE DE LAS TORRES is commander-in-chief of the army before Gibraltar; his aide-de-camp is the Duke of Wharton, who has come hither prepared to draw his sword and fight against his mother country. Nora is also here, not liking to leave him alone for reasons of her own. Not caring to await an answer to his letter from the king, he has come at once to the camp. Fortunately or unfortunately, his majesty's letter has preceded him, appointing him to the before-mentioned position, an office of trust and danger. It is a position, moreover, in which his name is sure to be blazoned abroad.

The Marquis de Verboom and Don Lucas Spinola are part of the staff, although they are both greatly opposed to the siege, while Philip and las Torres are in favor of its continuance. General Gaspar Clayton is in command of the Rock, which is feebly defended inside, but supported by a powerful fleet standing at anchor under the precipitous walls. From the summit of the Promontory can be seen the tiny huts of the Catalonian fishermen far down on the sparkling, crested beach. To the occident, Barbary's fierce shores protrude their beetling crags, and barren Mons Abyla rises boldly against the horizon.

Las Torres has systematically proceeded in his hostile approaches. Besides throwing up formidable trenches, he has erected many outposts, and excavated numerous mines. His batteries sweep every penetrable point, also commanding, in a measure, the waters of the bay. A large detachment is, at present, stationed on the beach at Genoese Cove, while the trenches are filled with watchful troops.

Philip is at headquarters with de Montemar and the rest of the staff, who have decided that the new batteries are to open on the besieged at once. The decision has been arrived at only after great discussion, during which Philip gave many important suggestions. At his urgent solicitations his grace is given the command of one of the attacking detachments.

Orders are given to the artillerymen, the troops placed in position, guns inspected, swords loosened, weak points anxiously scanned, and strong positions approved. The besieged, seeing the preparations for an assault, hurriedly busy themselves in strengthening their defences with sand bags and butts bound with fascines.

All are in a state of great expectancy; every man is at his gun, matchlocks lighted, sponge and rammer ready. All are awaiting, yet dreading the first BOOM, telling the deadly batteries have begun their work. De Montemar says to las Torres: "Saint Jago! I am terribly anxious about the power and effect of our guns!"

"Montemar, you are nervous—excited. I will give the signal as soon as Spinola returns from his inspection of the Land Port wall?"

Verboom inquires: "Conde, how many balls and shells can we throw into the fortress a day?"

"Seven hundred per hour!" is the concise answer.

Brightening at the estimate, he turns to Philip, saying, "That gives me more hope; I begin to think it even probable that we may succeed."

Philip replies in a chiding manner: "My dear marquis, before to-morrow we will have Gaspar Clayton begging for a respite, sending us their surrender. As my countrymen, I expect las Torres will so far favor me as to allow them to march out with the honors."

"The Virgin defend us from such a fate at all events."

Spinola, galloping up at this moment, delivers a field glass to las Torres, saying, in quick, hurried accents: "The enemy have erected a strong battery at the Moorish castle, while the Jews are so helpless and cowardly, that it is impossible to make them work at the trenches! A detachment should be sent at once, for the enemy's vessels are decimating our troop in a terrible manner! They are entirely unprotected, and are rapidly losing all courage and vigor."

Las Torres, startled at the news, exclaims in a loud voice: "To your posts, gentlemen! the attack must be made at once! Your grace, much depends upon your coolness! Spinola, be wary—not too impetuous! Ribadeo, recollect we are Spaniards; the Rock must be ours. Away! in two minutes I will give the signal to open the batteries! Then, sweeping them from north to south—east to west, we will teach these heretics that Gibraltar can be taken." Turning to Spinola, who still lingers, he cries: "Away! I will attend to the trenches immediately—curse the Jews!" Calling a captain of cavalry standing a few yards away, he continues: "Señor Juan, take fifty men to the trenches, throw them up as quickly as possible, and stay there until you receive further commands."

Sinking on his knees behind a low parapet, las Torres prays: " Santa Maria, grant us victory; we fight against heretics—" Stopping short, he exclaims: " Maldito! I have neither time nor words for prayer!" walking hastily toward the officer of the batteries, he exclaims: "Señor, open all your batteries—pour in shot and shell unceasingly, until further orders. Inform Señor Perilas, so that in case you are struck there will be no confusion or stoppage."

" Yes, general."

Glancing around at the disposal of his forces, las Torres' face brightens with satisfaction at the commanding positions in which his troops are stationed.

BOOM!—ah, how terrible is the long line of lurid flame! how deafening the appalling echoes shaking earth and sky! Showers of shell and chain-shot, grape and shrapnel whizz singing through the air, while the black smoke puffs slowly up from the belching embrasures. The firing is very effective, dismounting the guns of the besieged faster than they can be replaced, while the courageous defenders are torn to pieces, endeavoring to repair the shattered, crumbling ramparts from which whole tons of earth and masonry are constantly detached by the rapid firing. Their sand-bags and butts are swept away like chaff, while their poor ordnance is almost unable to reply, being old and defective.

Philip, receiving an order to make a sortie on a strong outpost, whence the besieged are harassing Spinola's troops with deadly effect, hoarsely cheers at the welcome news. Hastily forming his men into line, he tells them what must be done. Placing himself at their head with his sword drawn, his hat off, and face aflame with joy and excitement, he boldly advances. Far outstripping his men, he pauses a moment, but unable to restrain his impetuosity he again rushes forward. At this moment there is a fresh volley from the Rock, the bullets and shells singing about him in a dangerous chorus. Still he advances, pointing with his sword to the outpost. Suddenly with a thud and a hiss a shell falls at his very feet. Starting back, he looks in alarm at the sputtering fuze rapidly being consumed; fascinated by the sight, he is rooted to the spot. A loud report—a blinding glare, a sound of missles whistling through the air, and the smoke hides him from view.

Rushing wildly to the spot, his soldiers lift and bear out his lifeless body. His face is blackened and singed, his clothes torn to fragments, while one of his legs is shattered and maimed. A loud cry bursts from the men at the sight, Philip's generosity and bravery having endeared him to their hearts. Carrying him swiftly to headquarters, they approach las Torres, who exclaims anxiously: "Is he dead?" They only point to his face. With a quivering lip the general directs them to the tent. Carrying him thither, they lay him gently on the bed. A physician is immediately summoned, and an order sent to the priest to attend the dying man.

The physician, Señor Arsenicato entering, is surprised to find his patient sitting erect in bed, rubbing his face in a bewildered manner, meanwhile muttering curses in Spanish and English. Laying his hand on his shoulder, he persuades him to lie down again.. Examining his leg, after cleansing off the blood and dirt, he finds the wound is not of a dangerous character; the shock of the explosion had stunned him, while a piece of the shell had torn open his ankle; otherwise he is uninjured. Carefully bandaging the ankle, he pats him on the back, saying encouragingly: " Bueno, bueno! your grace, we will soon cure you; but you must not attempt to leave your bed until we permit you!"

Philip replies: " Why, man, think you I could lie here all day, hearing the guns outside, and repose idly on my back? No!"

Arsenicato, shrugging his shoulders, looks incredulously at him. " Bueno! but first take this little draught; it is harmless, and will steady your nerves."

Pouring two or three drops of a white liquid from a small phial, he mixes them in a glass of wine. Philip swallows the potion at a gulp, his eyes close almost immediately, his head falls back on the pillow, and he is asleep. " Your grace is secure enough now! A good sleep is his best restorer." Throwing a mosquito net over him, the wily doctor returns to his other duties.

On awakening the next morning Philip is nearly suffocated with the strong smell of powder filling the tent with a blue, acrid vapor. Rapidly dressing himself, he almost forgets his wound, until he attempts to draw on his shoe, the consequent pain makes him wince and groan; limping outside, las Torres surveys him in surprise, congratulating him, however, on his rapid recovery.

" Where is my detachment, Conde?"

" It is at present incorporated with Spinola's, whose troop has been frightfully thinned."

" He must return them to me now, and I hope I shall

fulfil more creditably the next order I am fortunate enough to receive!"

"That would be impossible, your grace."

"Flattery, Conde, flattery; however, it could not be helped." After a pause he resumes: "I neglected to inquire, have you sent the duchess to the rear?"

"Still further away. It is possible we shall have to raise the siege, so last night I went to her grace's apartments, told her of your accident, whereat she was greatly affected—and sent her to Madrid under the protection of a strong guard of Valloons."

"Thanks; it is better she should be away. Did her grace ask to see me before she went?"

"Oh, yes; she entered headquarters, but you were asleep. Not daring to violate Arsenicato's orders by awakening you, she kissed you good-bye; she was greatly moved at the sight of your wound."

"When is it probable the siege will be raised, Conde?"

"To-morrow, unless reinforcements arrive to-night, an almost impossible event!"

Philip sighs as he thinks over the misfortune preventing him from gaining honor and glory by leading a forlorn hope against the stubborn fortress.

Ordering his staff to assemble at headquarters, las Torres enters the tent, where he is soon followed by Philip, De Montemar, Verboom, and others. No sooner, however, is the project of raising the siege broached, than Philip glides noiselessly outside, while a smile is playing on his features.

"I am of no use there! Moreover, there is little honor in advising on a surrender, so that I am better here than there! Besides, if my opinion were needed, I should undoubtedly be against retreat! Moloch is more to my taste than Belial! I want action—action, and, egad! I'll have action."

Securing his hat on his head, he cautiously lowers himself over the parapet to the ground. Drawing his rapier, he walks slowly toward the walls near one of the hostile posts, meanwhile between the opposing fires, whose various missiles whirr and sing above and about him. Proceeding until within talking distance of the outpost, he halts, and exclaims in a loud voice: "Halloo within there, cuckoldy heretics!"*

In answer to this polite greeting, a dozen muskets are levelled at him, while a stern voice replies: "Who goes there? Advance, and give the password!"

Philip drawls: "Demme, sir, your voice is as harsh as any peacock's. In reply to your excessively rude summons, allow me to introduce myself. The Duke of Wharton and Northumberland, officer in his most Catholic majesty's service."

There is a few moments' silence after this, until the same voice replies: "If your grace will promise to return immediately to camp, you will be allowed that privilege in consideration of your high rank and youthfulness, otherwise I will order your arrest as a spy and a traitor! Your grace is aware of the laws of war, I presume?"

Slowly drawing out his handkerchief, Philip says: "Well, I suppose I must return; but one moment, my dear fellow!—oblige me by reporting this affair to Clayton, so that my friends in England will know that I am alive! *Au revoir, mes cochons!* We will batter your boasted fortress to the ground to-morrow. His majesty has just sent us enough material for a dozen more batteries as heavy or heavier than those we have, *au revoir!*"

A dead silence greets this intelligence, while the rising moon illuminates the threatening barrels directed towards his breast. Retracing his steps he opens the door of the

* Fact. See various histories.

tent, inquiring: "Well, gentlemen, how goes the verdict—a raising or a continuance?"

Las Torres replies gloomily: "Suspension of hostilities."

Philip answers: "Ah! If that is the case, I will return at once to Madrid. This nitrous smoke is utterly spoiling my voice; I shall be as hoarse as Walpole if I stay here any longer!" So saying, he withdraws to his own quarters to make preparations for leaving.

CHAPTER LV.

"His passion still, to covet general praise,
His lips to forfeit it a thousand ways;
A constant bounty which no friend has made;
An angel tongue which no man can persuade;
A fool with more of wit than all mankind:
Too rash for thought, for action too refined."
POPE'S "WHARTON."

JAMES is reclining in his chair looking ill and tired; in front of him stands Edgely Valentin, bare headed and respectful.

"You say that las Torres has raised the siege, and retreated?"

"Yes, your majesty."

"Who informed you of the reckless acts of which you accuse his grace?"

"A trustworthy witness, your majesty. 'Tis a pity he was not in England instead of at the trenches."

Frowning angrily, James replies: "That is for us to say. However, this mad fool must return to England; he is doing us more harm than good with his audacity, immorality, and want of respect to his king. We would almost rather deal with him as an enemy than a friend; he would certainly do us less harm. 'Tis a great pity, too; he has both talent and ability, but it is seldom he exerts them; in such cases, it is too often to circumvent a grisette or rob a friend at piquet or ombre." After a slight pause: "Where is his duchess—the lovely Nora?"

"Her grace is with him at Madrid, your majesty."

Looking suspiciously at him, James inquires: "How is it, sirrah, that you are always so well instructed in the incomings and outgoings of his grace? For a rather cool friend you appear to take a pretty deal of interest in him!"

Edgely replies with downcast eyes: "It is for your majesty's sake that I am watchful; for, as your majesty has said, he does more harm to the cause I love—the king I adore—than many of our enemies."

Mollified by his assertions, James permits him to kiss his hand, replying, with a smile: "We did but jest. How likes our consort her residence in gloomy St. Cecilia?"

"Not over well, your majesty; Madame is often troubled with the vapors. She would willingly return, but for her aversion to several at court."

"Truly, truly! my Lady Inverness for one," he pettishly replies, twisting the rings on his fingers.

Ringing a bell, the signal is answered by a page, who stands on the threshold, bowing low.

"Curlle, say to my Lord Inverness that we desire an audience."

Resting his chin on his palm, James silently muses on an apparently vexatious and perplexing subject; Valentin remaining quiet and motionless. Inverness entering bends and kisses the royal hand, which ceremony being completed, James says: "Inverness, we need your aid in a matter nearly concerning our beloved court.

Doubtless you have heard ere this of his grace of Wharton's doings before Gibraltar? Those actions reflect on us very severely. Having formerly looked kindly on him, therefore we have resolved to send—"

A tap at the door interrupting him, Valentin opens it, and Curlle enters with a letter for James. Examining the seal, he exclaims: " By my soul, it is from the madcap himself!"

Valentin, starting forward, turns red and pale alternately.

Inverness mutters: " Speak of the deil!—" Opening the letter James reads in low, almost undistinguishable tones: " Your majesty—um—um—regret my culpable behavior in leaving Rome so suddenly and disrespectfully—um—not knowing whether your majesty approves my recent actions in the trenches—um—I write to crave permission to return to Rome—um—um—sun myself—your majesty's favor—um—your loving, devoted—"

Frowning impatiently he throws the letter down, exclaiming: " Inverness, bring me paper and a quill! The malapert asks our approval of his conduct; he shall have it, with a moral affixed, pardieu!"

A smile of gratified malice passes like a flash over Valentin's face.

Dipping into the inkstand with a vicious jerk, James splashes the drops about in close proximity to Inverness' peach-colored hose, murmuring as he writes the following reply:—

" Sir: We blame you severely for your ill-considered conduct in taking up foreign arms against our kingdom. As our court is at present full to overflowing, we do advise you most strenuously not to come hither, but rather return to England, condone your numerous offences, and act a part more useful to us and yourself.

James Rex."

"But that it were high presumption in me, I would gladly sign my name under your majesty's."

"We know that, Inverness. You were always our true friend and adviser." Valentin, lifting his eyebrows, smiles incredulously. James continues: "This must to Wharton at once, or he may forestall our refusal of his company by coming upon us unawares."

Inverness, laughing low, expresses his appreciation of the jest by divers nods and chuckles.

Sealing the letter, James hands it to Valentin, enjoining him to use the greatest despatch in its delivery; he replies: "Under favor, your majesty, none could use greater."

Giving his arm to Inverness, James replies: "Ay! we know your loyalty, Sir Edgely."

Bowing low, Valentin leaves to execute his commission; while James and Inverness retire to the queen's chamber, where a number of ladies and gentlemen are engaged in playing ombre or conversing.

* * * * * *

In a large room at Madrid are Philip and Nora; he is alternately writing and reading. Leaning back in his chair, he says: "Attention, Nora! 'To his excellency Mr. Walpole'—I will give only portions of the letter, those most interesting—' Sir: You will doubtless be surprised to receive a letter from me.——Since his present majesty's accession to the throne, I have absolutely refused to be concerned with the Pretender or any of his affairs; and during my stay here I have behaved myself in a manner that Dr. Peters, Mr. Godolphin, and Mr. Mills can declare to be consistent with my duty to the present king. I was forced to come here to get out of Rome, where, if my true design had been known, I would have been treated a little severely.——If your excellency would permit me to wait upon you for an hour, I am certain you would be convinced of my repentance for my former madness.'" Stopping here, he laughs long and loudly, while Nora appears perturbed and displeased. "Egad, how he will stare! ah-ha! But to proceed: 'If you would become an advocate with his majesty to grant me his most gracious pardon'—— ahem! 'I do not intend, in case of the king's allowing me to pass the evening of my days under his royal protection, to see England for some years, but shall remain in France or Germany, as my friends shall advise, and enjoy country sports and pastimes' (his lips curve in a smile) 'till all former stories are buried in oblivion. I beg of your excellency to let me receive your orders at Paris. The duchess, who is with me, desires leave to wait on Mrs. Walpole, if you think proper.'"

Nora exclaims indignantly: "Why, Philip, you seem very desirous of lowering your dignity, in addressing this Mr. Walpole so servilely, begging so humbly the favor of being allowed to see him. He may be an ambassador, but you are the Duke of Wharton and Northumberland, and should be above truckling to any man alive!"

"Or woman either, Nora; put a bridle on your tongue and let me alone. I have been too long in this world, *querida mia*, not to know how to talk to ambassadors, or kings either, for that matter."

She is silent. Walking up and down the room for a few minutes, he resumes in a decisive manner: "Nora, you must be ready to set out for Paris the day after to-morrow. I will give the letter time enough to reach Walpole, and then for plans to upset the Captain King!"

"And assist the English whigs!" Nora adds.

"An entire mistake. It is our mutual party which shall reap the advantages of my sojourn in Paris, as you will see. James declines my company at court, therefore I must work for him in exile. His letter was vastly curt and impolite! The Jesuits declare that the end justifies the means; on that axiom I base my conduct."

"Debase it sometimes, I fear, Philip."

Unheeding her remark, Philip inquires abstractedly: "How stands our exchequer, Nora?"

"Low, much lower than you probably think."

Shrugging his shoulders, he replies: "Low enough, no doubt! I have not received my usual remittance from London."

"That is not the chief cause of its depletion, Philip dear; it is because you spend your money so foolishly, buy everything you see, give to every one who asks, and squander it at the gaming table!"

"Hoity-toity, a lecture on economy from her Grace of Wharton! Pray proceed; I am all attention!"

Half smiling at his mock attentive attitude, she turns away and looks out of the window, while he surveys his person in the mirror.

CHAPTER LVI.

"Saw mischief by a faction brewing."
SWIFT.

ALTHOUGH an inventory of their possessions disclosed the fact that all their present effects were about two hundred pounds, their clothes, and jewelry, Philip's high ambition could not descend to trivial economies. Accordingly, he has engaged the most fashionable and expensive rooms in all Paris, decorated them anew with rich furniture, engaged a dozen or more valets, waiters, and runners, and bought a superb coach. All this he has done on credit and the influence of his representations. Nora, alarmed at his vast expenditures, dismally wondered whence would come the money to pay the bills when they were presented. His reply was a careless laugh, and an assertion that "he had such an implicit reliance in Providence, he did not trouble himself at all about the future, but obeyed the precepts of the Bible, in trusting in the Omniscient not to fail him in the hour of need."

Walpole's reply has been received, being now the subject of their conversation. Turning to Nora with a surprised look, Philip replies in answer to her previous question: "Certainly, our visit shall be in a public capacity. Why not? have you any great objections, Nora?"

"Well, you know our expenses are very great, and with no expectation of a remittance for some time, it would be as well to retrench a little. We have very little left to draw upon, while the bills for the coach, horses, and the furniture will pour in before long."

"Never mind, Nora, we must not meet trouble half way! Ah! there is the coach! Come along!" Leading her to the door, they both enter, and roll off in the direction of the ambassador's house.

Mr. Walpole, awaiting them in the hall, courteously leads the way to the drawing-room, where they seat themselves, partaking of a slight luncheon furnished by their attentive host. During the repast, Philip is guilty of many loose witticisms and licentious puns, often causing Nora to blush to her temples. The conversation is general and unimportant, until Philip carelessly inquires:—

"Your excellency, is Atterbury in town?"

"He is, your grace; unfortunately, his society is debarred us. You are aware that all communication with him is forbidden and felonious?"

Philip nods assent, and the conversation again becomes more general. Nora is cold and distant, appearing to prefer her own thoughts to Walpole's honeyed speeches and flattering words. Philip, noticing this, says: "Well, we must be going; are you ready, Nora?"

She replies in a relieved manner: "Yes, your grace, and have been for some time."

This pithy rejoinder causes Walpole to frown, while a piqued expression, clouds his face.

As they are entering the coach, Philip calls out: "Oh, Walpole, I am going to dine with the Bishop of Rochester now. What think you of my plan? Does he keep a good table?"

Smiling at such an odd, bold declaration, Walpole replies: "If your grace has a design to pay that prelate a visit, there is no occasion to tell me of it."

"By the way, I forgot to tell you how I enjoyed myself at Rome, also of my conversion to Catholicism, two subjects in which you would have been interested; however, they will be food for conversation at our next meeting; good-bye!" Kissing his hand to the astonished Walpole, he slams the carriage door, and cries: "To the Bishop of Rochester's house!"

Atterbury is both pleased and startled on seeing his unexpected guests, but withal pained at Philip's levity and profaneness, so ill suited to his own sober gravity and advanced age. With Nora, Atterbury is well pleased, greatly admiring her beauty and vivacity, which compare curiously enough with her previous sullenness at Walpole's. Although delighted with their affection and devotion, the Bishop gently blames them for incurring the government penalties by holding any communication with him, for in this land of strangers, the aged, worn-out prelate is debarred from seeing a friend or a relative, even his loved daughter dare not come to him to receive his caresses or to soothe him in his sickness and loneliness.

As they are driving homewards after the interview is over, Philip says in a settled manner: "Nora, I have just come to the conclusion that Paris is too expensive for us, Rouen will suit us better, especially as I see no chance of a remittance from home, and our creditors will not be always satisfied with smiles and promises."

Lifting her hands in dismay, Nora replies: "Leave Paris! impossible. We have made every arrangement for a permanent residence here; rented the apartments, hired servants and footmen, bought carriage and horses, and I know not what besides; the idea is absurd." Adding, with a smile: "But of course you did not mean it, for our creditors would not allow us to leave unless they were paid."

He replies: "Nora, those people are sufficiently well paid by our patronage; you appear to forget who we are."

She rejoins: "Pardon me! not at all; but even the Duke of Wharton will find that Parisian tradesmen are not well-bred enough to be satisfied with patronage instead of payment. I know them too well to believe in their forbearance."

Philip says with a frown and a pettish jerk at his ruffles: "Repique me! I care little about their politeness or charity. I am not considering them at all. They must look out for themselves and we will do the same. Economy is our aim at present."

She sighs at his obstinacy, and is about to answer him, when he adds: "Nora—your grace, no more remonstrances, I beg! I have said Rouen is to be our future home—Rouen it shall be until our circumstances guarantee a residence in Paris. Your grace has become strangely whimsical and fantastical of late. Let me hope you will be a trifle more rational and collected in your actions in future," looking askance at him, she laughs amusedly, and settles herself in the corner with a shrug of her shoulders and a mocking gesture at his stolid gravity.

CHAPTER LVII.

*"He marks the dawn of every virtuous aim,
And fans the smoking flax into a flame."*

STROLLING about Rouen accompanied by Nora, Philip observes a number of ragged, filthy vagrants who attack every passer-by for alms in the most piteous manner. Toward this motley crew he proceeds, leaving Nora to await his return. After satisfying their clamorous demands, he exclaims in a loud voice: "Brother vagabonds, I am the Duke of Wharton." A piece of information eliciting uproarious applause. He continues: "I want every one of you to call at my lodgings this evening at 8 o'clock, having prepared a supper for the poor of Rouen."

Giving his address to them, he returns to Nora amid renewed applause and cheering. She asks: "Philip, what is the meaning of all the clamor? I truly believe you have given those wretches half of all our little stock, much more than we can afford at any rate. However worthy the objects of your charity, recollect that charity begins at home!"

He rejoins with a significant laugh: "Faith, it shall begin at home, Nora!"

At this moment Nora directs his attention to a most ludicrous sight. In the street stands a gay, fashionable coach, with open door, as though its occupant had just alighted; while about twenty yards away are two gentlemen in most peculiar attitudes. One is tall and thin, but quick and graceful in his movements. Holding his drawn sword in front of him, he pricks his comrade behind with its sharp point; meanwhile his face is a study for its gravity and immobility. The assailed, who is attired in white silk stockings, peach-colored coat and small clothes, is capering about as though hot mercury were dancing in his heels, as well he may; with his tormentor prodding at him so viciously behind.

Nora cannot help but laugh at the spectacle. The street being wet and muddy, every step he takes he splashes his whole person with the thick ooze. Philip gives free vent to his noisy merriment, finally calling out "A Wharton, a Wharton to the rescue!" Turning around at this exclamation, they are both surprised to see the long, sallow face of the Earl of Peterborough. This diversion giving his victim time to escape, he flies down the street like one mad, while the earl advances to Philip and cordially salutes him, saying: "My dear Wharton, how ever have you managed to be here?"

"By the same means as yourself, I suppose, Mordanto, but—" He laughs again. "What was the meaning of your one-sided fight?"

Peterborough replies: "Really, I scarcely know myself! Happening to look out of the window, I saw yonder galliard picking his way over the stones in a vastly lackadaisical manner, as though he feared for his spotless stockings; so I sprang out and was teaching him a few capers with my Toledo when you interrupted me."

"He did not seem to relish the lesson overmuch."

"Faith, no; it did seem distasteful to him."

Introducing the earl to Nora, Philip requests him to go along with them; but he declines, excusing himself on the score of important business admitting of no delay. Philip inquires: "What business can you have requiring such immediate attention, Mordanto?"

"Quills and paper, for the construction of the memoirs which will to a certainty convulse Europe to its centre."

"Memoirs of the Duke of Wharton, for instance!"

"Charles Mordaunt rather!" adds Nora, with a smile.

Philip replies: "Join them; then not only Europe will be convulsed, but all the world, even to that abode of Pluto—Terra del Fuego."

"Yours alone would be sufficient," replies Peterborough as he sheaths his sword with a sharp click, adding: "Good-bye!" He raises his hat and re-enters his coach.

Punctually at eight o'clock arrived the invited beggars, who were met by Philip and ushered into the dining-room, where Nora awaited the arrival of the "distinguished guests" who she had been led to expect were coming. The scene that followed baffles description. Nora rushed from the room in angry haste, while Philip laughed aloud at her discomfiture, inviting his dirty, ragged guests to partake of the delicacies spread on the table. He plied them with wine until their senses were inflamed and riotous. Oaths and slang, horrible tales and anecdotes, the jingling of broken goblets and cracked dishes, combined to make a sickening tumult; while Philip presided at the head—a worthy Mecænas of the rabble herd. The only apology I can offer for Philip's freak is that "*Il a le diable au corps.*"

On awakening, Philip finds himself under the table amid bottles, glasses, fruits, preserves, and a mixture of everything that had previously been part of the repast. Rising unsteadily from his recumbent position, he retires to his room in a very disagreeable humor, intending to sleep off the effects of the night's debauch; an intention frustrated, however, by the entry of the maid with a letter for him, signed "immediate" on the cover. He opens it with a pettish air. Its contents fill him with apprehension and alarm, at the same time opening his eyes to the enormity of his offences against the laws of his country. The document is a succinct report of proceedings in Parliament, concerning both his life and property; no more nor less than a motion, strongly sustained, to outlaw him and confiscate all his possessions—to place him on the same footing as the Bishop of Rochester. At the bottom of the letter is written in a hurried, scrawling hand: "See your *errors* immediately on receipt of this—sue for pardon; it is your only chance."

Bewildered by this ominous intelligence, he calls for Nora. As she enters he hands the letter to her. After reading it, she says contemptuously: "Tut! the work of some lying Hanoverian, who wishes to frighten you into submission to the usurper. Let me tear it up." Suiting her actions to her words, she tosses the pieces into the fire.

After a short silence, Philip says: "I believe you are right, Nora; I hope so, at all events."

"Certainly, I am right! If such a measure had even been contemplated at home, you would have heard of it long before it could be broached in the house. Undoubtedly, it is a Whig scheme to induce you to turn renegade and help their schemes with your pen and tongue."

A tap at the door, and the maid re-enters—"Please, your grace, two gentlemen await your grace in the parlor, Monsieur Thurton and M. le Baron Norfolke."

Turning pale, he exclaims: "Que diable! what can these countrymen of mine want with me?" Quickly arranging his disordered garments, he walks down stairs and enters the room. "Good-morrow, gentlemen," he says pleasantly, and apologizes for keeping them waiting.

Returning his compliments, the elder of the two presents him a letter of introduction from Sir Robert Walpole. Tearing it open he peruses it for a moment, then exclaims haughtily: "Advice! Gentlemen, Mr. Walpole speaks of advice!"

Baron Norfolke replies: "Yes, your grace, advice anent recent acts in Parliament derogatory to your dignity, and prejudicial to your interests."

Philip, starting, says: "Ah! pray tell me all about it; this is indeed news!" and he draws a chair close to Norfolke, who proceeds in an apologetic, conciliating manner: "Your grace must not take it ill if our words are sometimes rather coarse, for the subject we are about to discuss is a delicate one, requiring plain speaking and truthful words. You may or may not be aware that your enemies—nay, even some of your friends—have, on account of your grace's recent actions at Gibraltar and Rome, sustained a motion that you be outlawed, and a price set on your head, besides the confiscation of all your property and revenues; but Mr. Walpole, who has a real love for your grace, prevented the awarding of the exigeant, and has sent us hither to induce you to submit yourself to the government, and return home with a full pardon and forgiveness for all your acts. A pardon you can obtain by merely writing a letter to his majesty or the ministry, with a respectful apology for your past conduct, and a promise of more loyal behavior in the future. Your grace can thus, without other trouble, re-establish yourself in favor, and also have your estates, revenues, and an enormous income free of debts or mortgages."

Looking at the speaker with an expression of sarcastic hauteur, Philip rejoins: "So! by merely turning traitor to his most Catholic majesty, and humbling myself before all the world, I can have my own, as well as incur the favor of your avaricious master George, eh? Listen to me, gentlemen! You are but the useful tools of Mr. Walpole; otherwise you should both answer for the insult you have passed upon me. Take this message back with you, and tell it as plainly as you have delivered your instructions to me. I'll see George and his whole ministry in perdition before I'll write a word to either, except a cartel to any man who chooses to want one!"

Mr. Thurton and the baron flinch under this rough language. The former, half-rising from his chair, places his hand on his sword; wisely screening his movement, however, Norfolke forces him back unobserved by Philip, replying in an injured manner: "Your grace, we deeply regret your anger, and are sorry you look on us with such ill-will. If you will even allow your secretary or valet to write an explanation, we doubt not that all can be right again."*

Half-rising, Philip replies: "Baron, if a pardon was presented to me, I might take it; but I'll never beg for one, either personally or by proxy."

Nora, entering at this moment, the *envoys* rise and bow to her, Philip, turning his head at the same time, discerns the expression of triumph beaming on her face, and he shifts uneasily in his seat. Looking spitefully at Thurton and Norfolke she whispers: "Be firm, Philip darling. King James must and shall reward you for the test you are undergoing! Let it be said that you stood where others fell. Be firm!"

He nods his head, while Norfolke continues, in a tone of mortification and astonishment: "Are we to understand that your grace's decision is fixed and final?—that you will not accept his majesty's most unprecedented kindness?"

* Fact.

"My decision is final, gentlemen."

Opening his doublet, Mr. Thurton pulls forth a sealed packet, and hands it to the baron, who delivers it to Philip, saying: " Then, your grace, we have a very painful duty to perform. We will wait until you have seen the contents of this packet; then our sad errand will be over, and we must return to England with heavier hearts than we intended!"

Opening the crackling folds with nervous fingers, Philip eagerly peruses the letter, while Nora bends over his shoulder with a pale face and glittering eyes. His eyes grow dim and his head throbs as he reads:—

"YOUR GRACE: We, the trustees of your estates, are tied up from remitting you any more money on account of your annuity, by the indictment lately found against your grace. We do therefore most strenuously advise you to use your best endeavors to have the proceedings stopped."

Turning his head to Nora, he says ruefully: "A fine prospect ahead, Nora! No remittances, edict of outlawry, and entire sequestration!"

She replies, in an eager voice: " His majesty will provide for us, Philip."

He laughs as he says: " Faith, if he does not, I shall have to take to scribbling for bread, and you to teaching for butter."

Turning to the gentlemen, who have been watching him very closely, he says, pointing to the letter: " Well, this does not interest me so vastly! Have you anything more to say on this disagreeable topic? If not, I must bid you good-morning, gentlemen. The duchess wishes me to take her to the cathedral; she is a great admirer of its peculiar architecture—the EARLY pointed. While there, we also intend to see the spot where the head of Cœur de Leon lies buried."

Dismissed with a gesture, the disappointed *envoys* retire from the room.

Nora kisses Philip again and again, meanwhile praising him for his heroism and loyalty. Responding to her caresses, his hand accidentally touches a locket fastened to her neck. Taking hold of it, he exclaims laughingly: "Whose portrait, Nora—an old beau's or your own sweet face?"

A slight flush dyes her cheeks as she carelessly answers: "Yes, it is a former lover—now my husband. I had it painted by an Italian artist while we were at Rome. He painted it from memory. It is not very good; however, it suits my purpose."

Pressing the clasp, she shows him his averred semblance. At first he casts a careless glance at it; then scans it more closely, muttering: "Curse me! 'tis a better portrait of Edgely Valentin than of me! Who painted it, did you say, Nora?" he abruptly inquires, while looking keenly at her.

Half turning her face, she replies: "Really, Philip, I forget his name."

"How long did it take him to paint it?"

"How vastly inquisitive you are, Philip! I forget the precise minute, or you should know with pleasure."

"If this was painted during the short time we resided in Rome, it should be placed among the wonders of the world; it is extremely delicate and highly finished; he must be a very giant in his art."

Not vouchsafing any answer, he returns it to her, and begins to consult with himself on the future, wearily wondering whether James will prove a friend in the hour of need.

CHAPTER LVIII.

"And what may be the consequences of a neglect of such opportunities? The succession of the crown has but a dark prospect, another Dutch turn may make the hopes of it ridiculous."

DEFOE.

AFTER the occurrence described in the preceding chapter, Philip had applied to James for assistance and been refused, since when he has been wandering hither and thither in search of money, borrowing from all his friends, and victimizing easy, credulous shopkeepers with boasts and promises.

Nora is living at St. Germains, where a kind relative provides her with food and clothing. Hither has Philip just arrived from Paris, almost broken down with nervous debility and sickness, penniless and almost hopeless.

Entering Nora's room, he embraces her affectionately, and, after inquiring the state of her health, borrows what money she possesses at present, and turns his attention to her several companions; a bevy of laughing, vivacious court dames, who receive his attentive regards with demure gravity or easy freedom, according as they are inclined. In the middle of the ensuing conversation, while merriment or jocund wit pervade every word or look, Philip exclaims abruptly: "Nora—mesdemoiselles—I am going to enter the convent! I have suddenly discovered that life is a void, a nonentity, and—"

Peals of laughter drown his words, while all are amused beyond measure at his antithetical words. However, keeping a calm countenance until quiet is restored, he resumes, in a steady voice:—

"I am in earnest, as you will see. Life is only for the gay, the wealthy, the happy. I am miserable, poverty-stricken, and afflicted. I feel that my years are few and numbered; and it would be far better if those few years were dedicated to my Maker, than to the trifles which have heretofore depraved and demoralized me." Slowly rising, he leaves the room without another word, while his companions wonder whether he is drunk or crazy.

Walking down the stairs with measured step, he opens the door, and stands irresolutely on the stone steps. Raising his hands he exclaims in a passionate voice: "Holy Mary, look down on me! Blot out my whole life, with its schemes and villanies! They are ever before my eyes, ever festering in my breast!" He pauses to cast a glance about him, while his hands are tightly clenched and trembling. "What a life it has been! scarce a commandment I have not broken from the first to the last. Would the remnant of my years passed in prayer and meditation be a fit condonation? I fear not! Mother of Christ, have pity on me!"

Sinking on his knees with a stifled sob, he covers his face with his hands, while he murmurs a broken prayer to the God he has so often offended. In a short time he rises and walks toward the Convent de Notre Dame. Arriving at his destination, he sounds the heavy knocker, and requests admittance. "I am Philip Wharton."

Silently ushering him in, the brother signs him to wait, while he informs the father superior of the arrival. The superior is a tall, bony man, whose pale, ascetic face tells how faithfully he practises the penances and severities of one of the most celebrated monkish orders.

With lowered face and beating heart, Philip awaits his welcome. The superior enunciates in clear, stern words, that have no ring of kindliness or encouragement in them: " My son, what seekest thou?"

"Most holy father, I would leave the world and retire into a seclusion where I could direct my thoughts, my life solely to Him."

"It is well. Knowest thou the rules of our order?" Drawing a roll of parchment from his bosom, he pushes it into his hands.

Opening it with nervous fingers, Philip casts a glance at its contents. To a man of his sybaritic temperament and luxurious disposition, the maxims and rules are terrible. Returning them after a careful perusal, he says, in a humble voice: " Father, I have read them, and am willing to submit to everything, if you will accept me!"

"Follow me!" replies the monk.

Obeying the laconic order, he finally enters a small, stone cell, dimly illumined by a tiny taper, which throws a yellow light on an ebony crucifix and a vellum-covered missal.

The cold, damp air strikes through his feverish frame, and he shudders in spite of himself, which his companion noticing, he exclaims: " Go, Philip Wharton; you are not fit for our society; the world and its fascinations hold you in their toils." He does not reply, for he feels the keen, cold eyes of his leader riveted on his face. The father resumes in a kindlier manner: " My son, your resolutions are as water, you are a sybarite. A Spartan or a stoic alone could stand our discipline. I know you, Philip Wharton; and believe a man who has seen the world and knows its pleasures—you could never reconcile yourself to our lot."

Philip answers in a desponding manner: "I fear not; my heart already fails me—forgive me for trespassing on your time!"

" My son, pursue a better course in the outside world,

and God will reward you. All are not capable of giving their whole being to religion and seclusion."

Hastily retracing his steps, Philip again breathes the fresh, sweet air of the open sky, slowly purpling under the rising sun.

"S'faith, a narrow escape!" he exclaims with a half sigh.

Suddenly an arm is thrust into his, and Peterborough's familiar voice sounds cheerily on his ear: "Halloo, Wharton! propping the convent with your peccadilloes?"

"No, Mordanto; I was nearer razing it with a conversion of my precious self."

"Ah-ha-ha!" laughs the carl. "What a superb joke! I wonder what the Delamour would say to it, eh?"

Joining in the laugh, Philip inquires: "I understood you were at Lisbon; how is it that you are here?"

"I was at Lisbon; but, hearing that Saint Germains boasts a new beauty, I have come to see her. Saint Jago, the Lisbonians fall conquered at the first attack, and I am tired of such easy victories, so I have visited you to discover whether this new star will not be cold enough to spur me up to real exertion."

Philip sympathizingly replies: "Poor fellow, I hope so, from the bottom of my heart."

"Jesting aside, Wharton, I have some news for you."

"News, eh? From my trustees, probably?"

"No—from England generally, and London in particular. You are being wofully used both by type and tongue. Every broadside in the kingdom vilifies you, while all desiring promotion slander you and tell marvellous lies about you and your doings."

Twirling his moustaches, he replies: "My lord, can you mention a few names of either public writers, private friends, or enemies who have done these things in my behalf?"

"That can I. In particular are the 'Evening Post'

and ' London Journal,' vastly minute in their comments on your past and present actions, and defile you with a venom that ought to be let out of them with a few rapier thrusts."

He says with a savage curse: "If ever I beg George for pardon, it shall be for the pleasure of treating these backbiters to a Mohock 'sweat' and a sound drubbing."

"Well they deserve it. When I return, I shall make it a special point to hunt out these cowardly defamers, and treat them as you would yourself. A few brawls would be quite a Godsend to me."

Philip answers in a thick voice: " Thank you, dear Mordanto, I know that my honor is safe in your hands. When I am a little calmer, I intend to write a short fable for English ears, which will, if properly appreciated, interest them exceedingly."

The earl resumes: " I have also received news from one at court, who is well versed in back-stairs intrigues, that George is continually receiving anonymous letters from abroad in regard to yourself, which, while deploring your *sad indiscretions*, convey full information of your slightest actions to him, inflaming his majesty's anger against you by subtle insinuations and crafty remarks."

Philip exclaims with a start: "Sainte Vierge! it seems I am an object of greater interest at home than I thought for. S'blood! what more can they do to me than they have done? Mordanto, I stand here an attainted, outlawed, beggared traitor, according to their laws, while you are guilty of felony for speaking to me."

Peterborough replies: " A fico for them; you are my dearest friend, and my whole wealth is at your disposal."

Philip's face assumes an amused expression as he says: " Then, Mordanto, I'll borrow a hundred Louis d'or, if you have them on hand."

"With pleasure; let us step into this gaping goldsmith's, who is just opening his shutters. I shall be overjoyed to draw you a draft for two hundred; one hundred is such a beggarly sum."

Securing the draft in his bosom, Philip says: "I have still another favor to ask of you. Will you prosecute all the editors who have vilified me, or defiled my name?"

Peterborough quickly answers: "'Tis as good as done, and if they escape from justice by a legal quibble, I'll trounce 'em with the flat of my sword, up and down Grub Street."

"Thank you, Mordanto; I must leave you now; her grace will be uneasy at my long absence."

"Ay, and checkmate your monkish move by turning nun."

"Little fear," replies Philip, as he turns his steps to the palace.

Taking the opposite direction, the earl saunters down the street, humming "Which way shall I gae me," occasionally striking the shutters of the still sleeping bourgeoisie. Entering Nora's room, Philip awakes her with his tread, and she sleepily exclaims: "How now, sir monk! back again?"

"Yes, Nora; I abjure Notre Dame's hair shirts, iron beds, and damp cells, for a time, at all events; although I sometimes feel as if—"

"Do let me sleep, Philip, and cease your homilies; clear water cannot run from an impure source."

"But the diamond can trace its origin to the coal bed."

"*Tres bien*," she replies with a yawn, and apparently falls asleep.

Drawing his chair to the table, he begins to scribble some figures on a piece of paper, meanwhile muttering: "Mordanto 200 louis, Wharton 3 livres, amount in hand 200 louis, 3 livres; hum!—Voiture to Paris—nothing.

Supper say 5 louis; fees say 20 louis. Debts in Paris say 3000 louis. Debtor and creditor scarcely balance! Now for my wardrobe—Egad, I am my own valet! one black velvet suit with point lace, one shabby suit of Spanish regimentals, one blue satin with black facings, slightly soiled. Ah, well, *sic transit gloria!*"

Impatiently throwing down his quill, his lips contract as though he is under the influence of strong emotion. The sun, slowly rising above the horizon, streams in through the half-drawn curtains, and gives his haggard countenance a pale, waxen tinge. Gazing at the rays piercing the room in dusty lines, he murmurs: "Ay, ye are a trifle like the radii of my own life, lustrous enough, but your lustre dimmed by the motes and dust in which ye choose to shine. All my life I have spent in pursuing a myth, and like the rest of the *genus homo* find it out just too late. What have I been? A patriot, a Christian, a husband, an obedient son, anything that is creditable? No! Catiline, Caligula, Bluff Hal, Villiers—all are synonymes for Phil. Wharton, the merriest undone man in Europe as they choose to call me. If Tarpeia's Rock were—but hold!—ere I cross the Styx, I would vastly like to know who my dear friend is who kindly forwards my words and actions to King George. I would put another sin in my chapter if I could find him out or her. 'Tis more like a woman than a man. Anonymous letters smack of femininity; if it was a woman, I would—"

"What, Philip?" breaks in with a strange effect, and Nora half turns her head.

Casting a quick apprehensive glance at her, he replies: "Let her live as the worst punishment I could devise. If she were a soulless, heartless brute, I would have her attended to by Pierre Canif, the Parisian bravo, who can slice as many ribbons off a pretty face as there are laws in England."

She replies, with a shudder, "How brutal! you have been drinking more brandy, Philip?"

"'Tis my only solace."

She says in a pleading voice: "What am I, Phil?"

"*You*—part of the necessary appendage of a duke's household."

Her eyes blaze and her cheeks grow fiery red at this wanton insult, and, covering her face with her hands, she buries her head in the pillow. Apparently heedless of her anger, he remains absorbed in thought for a time, then says abruptly: "Nora, we must return to Paris to-morrow; I will order the voiture to be ready."

"Have you any money?" she inquires, in a dubious manner.

"Golconda's wealth, or rather 200 louis."

"What will the voiture cost?"

"Nothing; it is put at my service by a friend of mine at Paris, Mlle. Delam—but the name is of no consequence."

She replies: "I know whom you mean, Mlle. Delamour—quite a creditable friend!"

"Scarcely, Nora, but she is a lovely woman, and the manner in which she insists on loaning me any amount of money is vastly charming."

CHAPTER LIX.

"Coming events cast their shadows before."

In the fourth story of a miserable house in the Rue Aubry-le-Boucher, Philip and Nora gloomily survey the aspect of their affairs. Outside a chilling rain is falling which splashes drearily on the window-sill and filters through the broken windows and the decaying framework.

Philip is dressed in a tawdry suit of Spanish regimentals, which is worn and shabby, while his hat is pushed over his eyes. He taps his foot in a manner denoting a ruffled temper, while Nora sits on a rickety, three-legged stool in a state of weariness and lassitude; her eyes roam around the room, and she vacantly notes the prominent absence of all comforts which their new quarters can boast.

Philip has not a sou left of the money he borrowed from Peterborough. He has sold his black velvet suit, and also all of Nora's dresses, except the one she is wearing, and their whole wardrobe now consists of one shirt; a periwig; a Spanish veil, torn at the side; a pair of red silk brodequins; and several pairs of tasselled kid gloves. Everything else has gone to pay for their board and lodging. Philip breaks the silence by saying: "Nora, how are we to procure the next meal? My rapier furnished the last. Shall I write to his majesty?"

"No, Philip; you would only make him angry, and—"

"S'blood, angry? Why, woman, what have I given up for his sake? A vast revenue and the finest estate in England." Angrily rising, he walks about the room with hasty steps.

"I know it, Philip; and God will reward you for your loyalty, even if King James cannot. He is very poor himself, or else I would at once advise you to request a loan; but the cause needs every penny we can procure."

"Umph! am I not part of the cause?"

"You are, darling, and one of the best parts; for that reason you will bear this trial; *I* will, and I am but a woman."

After this, there is a dull silence, until Philip resumes

more hopefully: "*Vive les lettres!* I'll translate Télémaque, and sell it for what it will bring!"

She answers, rather doubtfully: "You have the ability, but I fear that such work will be too dry and uninteresting for you to continue at it very long."

"A great mistake, Nora. I will begin it at once, and it shall not be laid aside until it is finished. I intend to write a tragedy on Mary, Queen of Scots, also, ere long; Lady Montague once wrote me an epilogue which will suit it admirably; or else I'll turn poet and indite an ode to Atterbury, the most saintly sinner I have ever known. Quick! quill and ink! Topple your empty trunk upside down: 'twill do for a table; then find my Télémaque and MSS., they are at the bottom of my holster bags, yonder in the corner!"

* * * * * *

He did finish the first book of Télémaque; then gave it up in disgust. The tragedy he almost completed, while the poem on Atterbury he did actually finish. The latter was published in Paris, but its impiety and scurrility damned it at its outset, and it brought him in no money. He became shy and morose, refused to see any of his friends, and secluded himself entirely from the world.

Nora was too proud to write to the queen for assistance, and her relatives, though poor themselves, were forced to send her money to keep Philip and herself from starving.

Says Philip, after a long silence: "Nora, I am going to put an end to this state of affairs. You must write to the queen at once, and ask her for a sufficient remittance to enable you to get to Madrid! Once there, you will be well cared for. I shall enter Notre Dame. The conviction becomes stronger in me, every day of my life, that my hours are numbered; and it is sheer selfishness in me to doom you to this miserable life. I will take no remonstrances."

With an exclamation of affright, Nora runs toward him; but her design is foiled by a masked ruffian who places his hand over her mouth, while threatening her with his poniard. At the same instant, Philip is grasped from behind, and thrown headlong to the floor, where he is gagged and bound hand and foot ere he has recovered from the bewildering effects of his fall.

Casting a glance at the two men kneeling beside him, he then looks towards Nora, who is almost swooning. The two intruders guarding Philip are poorly attired, and apparently belong to the class of common bravoes which infest the purlieus of Paris. Nora's assailant is, however, richly attired in a velvet suit, slashed with violet satin; he, like the rest, is masked from chin to forehead. Motioning to the smaller of the two, he gives Nora into his charge, and steps toward Philip. Kneeling down beside him, he draws a knife from his bosom, somewhat resembling those used by the vine-growers in Oporto; the blade is about four inches long, and slightly hooked. Passing it carefully over his palm, he says to Philip, in an evidently disguised voice: "Your grace, a handsome face like yours needs little adornment; but in my humble opinion the removal of its present covering would benefit it mightily; in other words, I intend to use you in the same manner as you would others. In so doing, moreover, I consider myself as acting in the light of an instrument of divine justice."

Twisting his fingers in Philip's hair, he lowers the knife with a firm, quick motion, when Nora, freeing herself by a violent effort, cries in an imploring voice:—

"Edgely, spare him! it is too cruel. For my sake!"

Abruptly ceasing, she clasps her hands in mute entreaty,

while Philip looks at her with a strange light burning in his eyes.

Dropping the knife, the leader quickly rises to his feet, and motions his companions to follow him. They are gone in an instant, and their cautious tread echoes softly down the stairs. Picking up the knife, Nora cuts the stout cords pinioning Philip's arms, and removes the gag from his aching mouth. Springing erect, he pushes her aside, and darts out of the door in pursuit of his assailants.

Running to the window, Nora sees him standing on the pavement, uncertain which direction to take. Holding her head with both hands, she murmurs: "I knew his voice. Poor fellow! His love must indeed be great when it can tempt him to such a crime!—I cannot help it—my religion, my country, Alberoni, all—all."

Leaning her head against the mouldy wall, she thinks with a shudder of the scene just enacted.

Entering with hasty footsteps and haggard face, Philip exclaims: "Nora, who were those men? I swear I heard you call their leader by name—Edward, or Egerton, or one similar in sound." Grasping her white arm, he sinks his fingers deep in the soft flesh as he gazes at her.

She replies, in an unsteady voice: "Philip, on my honor, I do not know them; they must be robbers who came in for booty!"

"You lie, woman! What do robbers want in a fourth story garret? Such men do not gag one, then rant about vengeance and divine justice, threatening to peel one's face *à la* Mohock! No, there is some underhand work here which I shall find out ere long; and if you are implicated in it, I'll do to you as my ancestor of old did to a faithless wife—strangle you with my own hands."

She becomes very white, and her lips move unsteadily, but her throat is too parched and dry to speak.

He resumes in a sneering, sarcastic manner: "Your grace is inclined to be melo-dramatic on this occasion—a useless proceeding, I assure you!" Receiving no answer, he proceeds: "Nora, I leave with you all my manuscripts; sell them or burn them, as you choose; I am going at once to St. Germains; you shall never see me again in this world. I could not bear to look upon you, with my present suspicions of you; I might harm you." Forcing her to look him in the face, he says, in an unsteady voice: "Nora, I think you loved me once. By that past love, I entreat you to tell me truly whether you know aught concerning this cowardly attack."

Her answer is low and indistinct. "No, Philip, I do not."

"Thank God! I could not entirely believe you guilty of complicity in such an affair. Nora, sweetheart, this day we part forever in this world. Kiss me just once! Its fragrance shall never be sullied by another's lips."

Placing her arms around his neck, in a half-unconscious manner, she presses her lips on his.

"Good-bye, Nora; on to Madrid, and God bless you! will send you enough money to-morrow to keep you from starving, at all events. Good-bye!"

Speechless and motionless, she mechanically counts his steps until they die away in the distance. Catching a last glimpse of him as he passes up the narrow street, she exclaims, with a sob, "Holy Mary, help me in this, my hour of need! Oh! I feel like a vile, guilty thing, full of bad thoughts and evil intents."

Laying her head on the wet sill, she lets her hands dabble in the cold rain water, while bitter tears run down her hot cheeks, and her breath comes in sighs and sobs.

CHAPTER LX.

"The George and Garter dangling from that bed,
Where tawdry yellow strove with dirty red,
Great Villiers lies : alas! how changed from him,
That life of pleasure and that soul of whim!
Gallant and gay, in Claverdon's proud alcove,
The bower of wanton Shrewsbury and love;
Or, just as gay, at council in a ring
Of mimic'd statesmen and their merry king.
No wit to flatter left of all his store,
No fool to laugh at, which he valued more.
Then victor of his health, of fortune, friends,
And fame, this lord of useless thousands ends."
POPE.

TRUE to his word, Philip entered Notre Dame, and remained there for three months, during which time he was a very miracle of piety and devotion, until, on one unfortunate morning, he was severely reprimanded by the father superior. He answered him with a blow which levelled him to the floor. After this occurrence he stealthily left Saint Germains, and shipped for Bilboa, where his regiment lay under orders, commanded by the Marquis de Castelars. There he was attacked by paralysis, which prevented him from entering on the campaign intended to settle Don Carlos in Italy. Thence he set out for the mountains of Catalonia to try what effect its fresh scenes and mineral springs would have on his enfeebled constitution.

Nora travelled to Madrid, where she was kindly received by the queen, who appointed her to an office of trust and responsibility.

To our left is a stupendous structure built in the Gothic style, which seems lonely and deserted. It is the Bernardine convent, whose brethren are world famous for their piety, charity, and poverty.

Standing on a neighboring crag, Philip surveys it with a feeling of intense longing for its quiet shelter and sombre stillness. His heart beats with an hitherto unknown emotion, while his soul thrills with an aching, devotional pathos.

He is weak and hopeless, sick in mind and body, and is only desirous of leaving a world which has no longer any attractions for him. His former friends have all forsaken him; while his name is coupled at home and abroad with obloquy and sneering scorn.

See! his arms contract with a spasmodic motion, while his face becomes blanched and pallid! Falling with a heavy thud on the jagged rock, he cuts his forehead in a piteous manner. Heaven help him! He is writhing in the tortures of epilepsy, while none come to his relief to assuage his agony or to wet his burning lips.

For two hours he lay there, while the sun was scorching his feverish body, until the inmates of the convent, discovering the poor sufferer, sent three of the brethren to carry him inside. As they lay him gently down on the hard beds peculiar to their order, he opens his eyes, and looks around with a sad, weary smile, while a great light is glowing in them.

The clustering monks are hooded and cowled, while the superior is addressing the dying man. "Stranger, death is fast overtaking thee; art thou a believer in the true faith?"

Philip nods assent.

"Thou shalt be shrived by one of our brethren." Turning to the nearest monk, he says, in calm, measured accents: "François, I leave the stranger in thy care; thou knowest thy duty."

Motioning to the rest, the superior leads them out, François alone remaining with Philip.

Philip speaks in a slow, faltering voice: "Holy father, I am dying! I pray you, shrive me quickly, I have many sins loading me down!" Closing his eyes, he clenches his teeth to prevent a cry from bursting from him.

Brother François's actions are rather peculiar. Closing the door in a noiseless manner, he slides the bolt fast in its socket; then carefully secures the small grated casement over the narrow window. Throwing off his cowl, he advances to the side of the bed, and exclaims, in a low voice, in which triumph and malignity seem struggling for supremacy: "At last! curse you, Philip Wharton!"

Quickly rising to an upright position, Philip exclaims: "Edgely Valentin!"

"Or Sir Edgely Warely, whichever you like. Listen to me! You have about an hour more to live. That is time enough for me to tell you the story which I swore by my mother's death-bed I would ring in your ears in your dying moments."

Falling heavily back on the pillow, Philp closes his eyes to hide Valentin's glittering scrutiny from his gaze.

"In a little country village in England there once lived a pure, lovely girl, who was loved and respected by all who knew her. She was still in her teens when a ruffling gallant from London chanced to stop at this same village; he saw her; suffice it to say that his handsome face and oily tongue were her ruin. He took her to London with him, plunged her into a wild course of rioting and debauchery; then threw her on the mercy of tender London to earn her bread as best she could.

"There was but one road open to her; she took it. A little babe was born to her; this babe—a boy—she sent to her old home, with a piteous entreaty to her father to forgive her and support the child. He did so willingly, and also desired her to return; but she could not face him nor brook the shame of becoming the cynosure of the village gossips.

"On arriving at a proper age, this lad was sent to France as a soldier. There he acquired, through industry, cunning, and perseverance—family traits—a responsible position under Cardinal Alberoni; travelled over the whole of Europe on secret embassies. But lest you die ere I have finished, I'll shorten my recital."

A low groan issues from Philip's lips.

"Finding out the secret of his mother's shame, he vowed to have revenge upon her destroyer. Unfortunately he died to soon. However, he left a son to inherit his greatness. This son, the bastard swore, should reap the consequences of his father's acts.

"The girl whom he had ruined survived him but a short time; then, by her bedside, the bastard again swore that his religion, his country, and his love should all be subservient to one great end—the ruin and early death of his son.

"Well, he has kept his word. The destroyer's son is now an attainted, beggared, dying outcast! His wife is the creature of his illegitimate brother, who for years has poisoned the ears of King James and King George against him, has proved him a traitor to all parties, and made all distrust and despise him.

"Poverty and disease coming hand in hand, he travels to Catalonia, falls dying near the convent, and is carried into the hall by the monks, where the bastard brother is appointed to shrive him. Ah-ha!" Adding, in slow, sneering accents: "Do you recognize the story?"

"Spare me!" moans Philip.

Drawing a locket from his bosom, Valentin tosses it towards him. Philip recognizes his father, and he places it to his lips.

Valentin says, with a laugh: "Kiss it, brother mine; my mother did so once; then she would cry for hours after." His face grows harder and sterner, while his fingers contract, and his breast rises ominously.

Philip feebly extends his trembling hand to Valentin, who looks at it for an instant, then smites it with his open palm with such force as to leave a deep red mark on the white skin.

"What do I want with your hand? I entered this monkery, when you came to Catalonia, knowing that you would come to the springs every day; therefore I could see you and observe your gradual decay, intending, when you became very sick, to haul you in here by main force, and swear that you were a madman who had attempted your own life. You would have been here at least three days, and if you had not died within that time, I purposed to ease you of life myself. However, fate has given me even a sweeter revenge than I counted upon. Can you guess what it is?" He inquires, bending over his victim, until his hot breath fans his cheeks.

Suddenly catching him by the throat, Philip half chokes him, but he is too weak for such an adversary, for Valentin, placing his knee on his breast, soon overpowers him.

"So, your noble grace would choke me! I shall be more merciful, I will remain with you until you die; and you shall neither receive the last rites of the church, nor shall you pray; but you shall go to your Maker with a curse upon your lips."

The smile of a dying man crosses Philip's face, while Valentin pursues, in clear, distinct accents: "Brother, your wife *did* know about the attack made on you in Paris. It was her paramour who headed the gang. Your grace, I am that paramour!"

Opening his glazing eyes, Philip exclaims, in a passionate voice: "Devil! leave me! You have had your revenge; let me die in peace!"

"'Twas I who sent George those kindly accounts of your loyal conduct. It was I who. attempted to poison your first wife's mind with tales to inflame her jealousy and rouse her anger against you to assist me in my project! But it was you who killed her—a remembrance which may tend to render you calmer. It was you who sent your parents to their graves, heart-broken and tearful! Now die! as great a libertine, liar, and villain as the earth ever held!"

Philip begins to utter a Pater Noster, which Valentin perceiving, he lays his hand on his mouth, and prevents him from speaking.

Opening his eyes with one reproachful glance, he falls back dead!

Replacing the locket in his bosom, Valentin exclaims, with a low chuckle, "Now for Nora, Alberoni, and the Stuarts—my mistress, my tool, and my love!"

So ends "The scorn and wonder of our age."

FINIS.

www.ingramcontent.com/pod-product-compliance
Lightning Source LLC
Chambersburg PA
CBHW032042220426
43664CB00008B/822